FROMMER'S

BARCELONA

PLUS MAJORCA, IBIZA, AND MINORCA

F. LISA BEEBE

1ST EDITION

GW00724892

PRENTICE HALL

New York □ London □ Toronto □ Sydney □ Tokyo □ Singapore

Published by Prentice Hall Trade Division
A Division of Simon & Schuster Inc.
15 Columbus Circle
New York, NY 10023

ISBN 0-13-332966-6
ISSN 1045-9324

CONTENTS

Part Two

MAJORCA, IBIZA, AND MINORCA

MAPS

To Stuart, for his support

ACKNOWLEDGMENTS

To the many people who contributed their time, expertise, and hospitality to make this guidebook possible, I express my appreciation. Special thanks to the Spanish Tourist Office, the Barcelona Tourism Board, the Barcelona Convention Bureau, the Consorci Promoció Turistica de Catalunya, the Conselleria de Turisme del Govern Balear, the Majorcan Tourism Board, and to Don Ramón Ernesto Fajarnés.

A Disclaimer

Although every effort was made to ensure the accuracy of the prices and travel information appearing in this book, readers are advised that prices fluctuate in the course of time and travel information changes under the impact of the varied and volatile factors that affect the travel industry. The author and publisher cannot be held responsible for the experiences of the reader while traveling. Readers are invited to write the publisher with ideas, comments, and suggestions for future editions.

PART ONE

BARCELONA

INTRODUCING BARCELONA

Spain's noble city on the Mediterranean, Barcelona is all grace and good looks on the outside and driving ambition within. In fact, the dynamism in the air makes the city's languid palm trees seem somehow out of place. Usually the pace is slower wherever the palm trees grow, but Barcelona aspires to play a vital economic role both within Spain and beyond, and there is no time to waste.

Between now and 1992, much of the city will be in a state of flux as it gears up for the Summer Olympic Games. A new airport, several new hotels, numerous Olympic facilities, and a general overhaul of the city's architectural heirlooms, plazas, parks, and gardens will enhance an already-pleasing urban landscape. Though the Olympics are ostensibly the driving force behind the city's robust revival, other economic motors should ensure that the revival continues long after the last athlete has packed his or her bag.

For the past four years, Catalonia's economy, the most diversified and prosperous of any region in Spain, has been growing even faster than the booming national economy. A surge in foreign investment has contributed greatly to the commercial vigor. In 1988, almost one-quarter of all foreign investment in Spain came Catalonia's way, and virtually all Japanese investment in the country is focused here.

Nicknamed "La Ciudad Condal" for the counts who negotiated its independence in A.D. 874, Barcelona is the Mediterranean's third-largest port and has long been deemed Spain's most "European" city. Until the return of democracy to Spain in the late 1970s, Barcelona had always been the nation's indisputable cultural capital, the place where art, architecture, design, fashion, and personal style consistently overreached the limits of the imagination. But in the highly competitive post-Franco environment, Madrid, the national capital, took the initiative in many of these areas, quickly relegating Barcelona to an unwelcome second-city status. The traditional rivalry between the two cities thus heightened, Barcelona regrouped, and, true to form, sat down at the drawing board to make daring designs on the future. It set its sights on the Olympic Games and on playing a key role in a united Europe.

Barcelona has a history of successfully capitalizing on large-scale collective endeavors similar to the Olympic Games. It did so with the World Exhibition of 1888 and the World's Fair of 1929, and there is no reason why 1992 should be any different (though there are periodic rumblings as to whether all will be finished on time). For one thing, the city has secured an unprecedented $400 million from NBC for television rights to the games. It has also enlisted the services of some of the world's leading architects to attain its numerous architectural ambitions. Among them are Arata Isozaki, Richard Meier, Gae Aulenti, Norman Foster, Victorio Gregotti, I. M. Pei, and native son Ricardo Bofill. Notes Meier in the August 1989 issue of *Mirabella:* "In no other place in the world is such important work being done to transform a city as in Barcelona. Still, the city has not destroyed its identity."

"Barcelona Més Que Mai" ("Barcelona More Than Ever") is the slogan of the day. But, of course, there is also more street crime, a burgeoning drug problem, and growing indigence as Barcelona's gold-rush atmosphere attracts all comers with a dream. Already the city's population of over three million is concentrated in one of the most densely inhabited urban areas in Europe. But Mayor Pasqual Maragall is optimistic, and he, too, has a dream, which he calls "Barcelona Gran."

In many ways, Antoni Gaudí's Sagrada Familia is a fitting symbol for this expanding city, suffused with the kind of creative gumption that spurred Gaudí to conceive a 20th-century cathedral of medieval proportions. When Norman Foster Associates' radical design for the Olympic telecommunications tower got the affirmative nod, architect Kenneth Shuttleworth remarked in *Mirabella* (August 1989), "Actually, we didn't expect to win the competition, but Barcelona, we've discovered, is not afraid of progressive ideas."

Convenient to the beaches of the coast, the Penedés wine country, skiing in the Pyrenees, and the Balearic Islands in the Mediterranean, Barcelona is a stepping-stone to a variety of holiday experiences as well as being a rich tourist experience in its own right. Nearly 40% of visitors to Spain go to Catalonia. The fact that about 90% of those visitors have been to Catalonia at least twice before speaks well of the region's depth and variety. Barcelona itself is also popular with corporate planners charged with arranging meetings, conventions, and incentive trips.

Meanwhile, *La Vanguardia,* the leading Barcelona daily, publishes a running countdown of the number of days remaining until July 25, 1992—the opening ceremonies of the Olympic Games.

HISTORY AND PEOPLE

Barcelona's history goes back at least 2,000 years. Just over 1,000 years ago it became the capital of Catalonia, the region that took shape when the Condes de Barcelona (Counts of Barcelona) declared their independence in the Middle Ages and set up one of Europe's first parliamentary governments.

Although we know that the city first began to crystallize under the Romans, some historic accounts speak of a Phoenician founding and a subsequent Carthaginian identity as "Barcino." Still others allude to the earlier presence of the Laietani, an Iberian

Bronze Age tribe. But the port that was to make the city's fortunes began to develop in 201 B.C. under the Romans. After them came the Visigoths, then the Moors and the Franks.

In the 13th and 14th centuries Barcelona, as the capital of the Kingdom of Catalonia and Aragón, peaked as an Iberian and Mediterranean power. In 1259 it promulgated the first code of European maritime law, which other Mediterranean states used as a model for their own.

With the marriage of Queen Isabella of Castile to King Ferdinand of Aragón in 1474, Catalan independence was quelled for the greater glory of a united Spain. For several centuries after, Barcelona was mired in mediocrity. Not until the 18th century did its stock begin to rise again, and by the end of that century Barcelona was the textile capital of the Mediterranean.

Home to Spain's first industrial-age bourgeoisie, Barcelona embarked on a plan of modernization in 1859, tearing down the old city walls and expanding into the Eixample, whose grid plan was the pragmatic vision of Catalan engineer Ildefons Cerdà.

Imbued early on with the capitalist spirit, Barcelona was always a staunch defender of democracy, and no doubt its economic fortitude underscored the political audacity that gave rise to countless anarchist, republican, and separatist uprisings in the early 20th century. Seat of the Republican government during the Civil War, Barcelona's virulent opposition to the Nationalist forces of Franco came home to roost in a heavy-handed post–Civil War repression. Use of the Catalan language and the observance of Catalan traditions was rigorously punished. No wonder that with the return of democracy after Franco's death, Catalonia swelled with supercharged patriotic pride, promptly reinstating Catalan as an official language and reviving most of its long-suppressed customs.

A longtime rival of Madrid, Barcelona still chafes under the Castilian yoke. But as Spain's principal port and second-largest city, it is now carving a new niche for itself not only as an autonomous regional capital but as a key player in both the national and international scheme of things. Capitalizing on its long-standing fame as a fashion and design center and a hotbed of commercial activity, the city is bracing for 1992—not only for the Olympic Games but for the challenge of a Europe without economic borders.

Even though Barcelona is a city of great cultural, political, and intellectual depth, it has always evinced a brazenly mercantile spirit whose emphasis, long before it was fashionable, was on the bottom line. Not surprisingly, the Catalans are considered among the most savvy of Spanish businesspeople. And although the use of the Catalan language continues to spread, it no longer seems quite the passionate cause célèbre it was several years ago, largely, I suspect, because the pragmatic Catalans realized that their language is not the language of national and international business—and in Barcelona, business is what counts.

The Catalans (along with most other Spaniards, for that matter) have always considered themselves a breed apart. Living close to France and exposed to a diversity of foreign elements through their busy port, the citizens of Barcelona were for centuries more cosmopolitan than their counterparts in other Spanish cities. While Franco was calling all the political, religious, and cultural shots in the country, Barcelona shined the licentious light in the east. In some ways it played Hong Kong to the rest of the nation's China. When avant-garde art was denounced and actively discouraged in Madrid, Barcelona staged exhibitions that stunned the national sensibility. In effect, it was the national escape valve, both envied and disdained by the more straitlaced cities of the rest of Spain.

Proud of its strong streak of individualism, Barcelona's citizenry considers itself more "European" than Spanish. Those familiar with other parts of Spain will detect in the city's inhabitants a reserve and measure of arrogance more akin to the French temperament. A further indication of the Catalans' sense of separateness are the linguistic politics of the two Catalan TV channels that always refer to Spain as "the Spanish State," never as "the country," implying that Catalonia, in a sense, is a country too.

The resurgence of the Catalan language is, of course, a highly visible manifestation of regional jingoistic sentiments. A Romance language related to Langue d'Oc and Provençal, it has been spoken since the collapse of the Roman Empire, except during periods of political repression. Of course, it also shares many words with Spanish, and those who are fluent in Spanish or both Italian and French can often readily read and comprehend Catalan. Today, an estimated 6 to 6½ million people actually speak it, making it the largest nonnational language of the European Community. Its linguistic currency extends beyond Catalonia to Valencia, where an estimated 50% of the population speaks it, and to the Balearic Islands, where 71% of the population speaks its own version of the vernacular. At the 1992 Summer Olympic Games, Catalan will be one of the four official languages, along with Spanish, English, and French.

Unfortunately, among Catalonia's staunch separatists things have recently taken a turn for the radical. An extremist group called Tierra Lliure (Free Land) has been formed that carries out sporadic terrorist attacks in conjunction with ETA, the organization of Basque extremists.

But overall, the pendulum of regional patriotism seems to be on the downswing as Barcelona (and Catalonia) focuses on new economic frontiers. Dynamic in its drive and bold in its vision, Barcelona has the momentum—enough to carry it well beyond the watershed summer of 1992.

Time Chart

3rd century B.C.: The Carthaginians establish the town of Barcino on the site of a former Phoenician settlement.

201 B.C.: The Romans begin to develop the city's port.

874 A.D.: The Counts of Barcelona win local independence.

1137: Catalonia merges with the Kingdom of Aragón.

1259: The city promulgates the first code of European maritime law.

1283: The Catalan parliamentary courts are consolidated.

1359: The Generalitat (regional government) is established.

13th to 15th century: Barcelona dominates the Mediterranean and builds its Gothic Quarter.

1474: Catalan independence comes to an end with the marriage of Queen Isabella of Castile and King Ferdinand of Aragon and the subsequent unification of Spain.

1493: Upon his triumphant return from the New World, Columbus is received in Barcelona by the Catholic Kings.

1808–13: The French occupy the city.

18th to 20th century: Industrialization leads to the expansion of the city and, eventually, the evolution of the modernist architectural tradition.

1859: The Plan Cerdà for municipal expansion is adopted.

1888: The World Exhibition is held in Barcelona.

1929: The World's Fair is held in Barcelona.

1931: The Generalitat is revived under the Second Spanish Republic.

1936–39: The Spanish Civil War

1977: Regional autonomy is reinstated under the new Spanish democracy.

1979: The Generalitat is again revived.

July 25, 1992: The start of Barcelona's Summer Olympic Games.

ART, ARCHITECTURE, AND CULTURAL LIFE

The architectural cornerstones of Barcelona are the Gothic Quarter and the Eixample, both the result of periods of urban prosperity. The Gothic Quarter rose from the 13th to the 15th century, when Barcelona was the center of commercial activity in Europe thanks to its Mediterranean port. The Eixample was fueled by the profits of industrialization in the late 19th and early 20th centuries and became a showcase of Catalan modernism. Though part of the worldwide art nouveau movement, modernism in the hands of such masters as Gaudí, Domenech i Montaner, and Puig i Cadafalch demonstrated a distinctively Catalan flair, reflecting in part Spain's strong religious traditions and in part Barcelona's own dare-to-be-different boldness.

Though little known beyond the region, Catalonia boasts a strong artistic tradition stretching from the Romanesque marvels found in its rural churches (and to a growing extent, in Barcelona's Museu d'Art de Catalunya) to the contemporary works in the city's Museu d'Art Modern. But art in Barcelona has always been more than a mere spectator sport. Chanelled into the annals of design, the city's artistic sensibilities have continually focused on the aesthetics of daily life. Whether it's parks and plazas or trendy nightclubs, the Barcelonans devote much thought and energy to the creation of complete environments for living. Aesthetics are important here, and as a result the city is very attractive.

Although Barcelona is and always has been a business-minded city, it has earned a reputation as a center for fashion, design, culture, and the arts, especially in their more avant-garde forms. Picasso, Miró, Pau Casals, Gaudí, Montserrat Caballé, and José

Carreras are just some of the personalities weaned at the breast of Barcelona's pulsing creativity.

FOOD AND WINE

The cuisine of Barcelona is widely varied, with menus all over town based on what's freshest that day at La Boquería, the famous market in Las Ramblas. The variety of climates within Catalonia, ranging from the alpine of the upper Pyrenees to the Mediterranean of the coast, provides a wealth of raw ingredients with which to construct a hearty, well-rounded cuisine. Naturally, Barcelona offers a compendium of dishes from throughout the region, many of which have been modified by the local influence of Italian food (particularly in the 18th and 19th centuries) and French food (in the 19th and 20th centuries).

Primarily Mediterranean in their basic ingredients—such as the greenest of first-press olive oil, lard, almonds, garlic, aromatic herbs, and more recently, tomatoes—most traditional Catalan dishes combine these with what's fresh and closest at hand. Fish, beef, pork, game, poultry, vegetables, and wild mushrooms immediately come to mind. Through Barcelona's open door on the Mediterranean, many other culinary influences have filtered into the regional diet. Both Roman and Moorish presences left their mark, as did the novelties brought by Columbus from the New World—potatoes, tomatoes, peppers, corn, and pineapple. But traditional sausages like the *butifarra,* succulent roasts, robust game, delicate seafood, toothsome rice dishes, and savory stews have steadfastly remained the mainstays of Catalan cuisine. Pastas were added to the Catalan pot in the 18th century when Barcelona restaurants began adapting Italian recipes, and in the 19th century French food was also stirred into the mix.

Like the French, the Catalans have always taken their food quite seriously. The first gastronomic manuscript in the Catalan language was written back in 1324, and the first cookbook ever printed in Spain—the *Libre del Coc*—was published in Catalan, in 1520.

Given Barcelona's penchant for innovation, it's not surprising that the culinary boundaries of Catalan cuisine are quite elastic. Keeping one eye on tradition, the city's chefs constantly invent new variations on standard Catalan themes, making it difficult to affix labels to Barcelona's highly imaginative and ever-shifting culinary currents.

Like Catalan cuisine, Catalan wines vary from one area to another. The *Denominación de Origen* (D.O.), Spain's appellation system, regulates their origin and quality.

Since at least 600 B.C. Catalonia's combination of limestone soil, temperate climate, and moderate rainfall have proved ideal for wine production. Protected by two mountain ranges, the Cordillera Litoral Catalana and Montes de Garraf, most of the wine-producing region lies in a central depression, which is flat in some places and gently sloping in others. Roughly rectangular in shape, with Barcelona tucked away in the northeastern corner, the Penedés is the principal wine region of Catalonia and is divided into three subregions —the Bajo Penedés, Medio Penedés, and Alto Penedés.

The Bajo Penedés, which hugs the Mediterranean coast, is the hottest of the three zones, with a climate comparable to California's Central Valley. It cultivates mostly Monastrell, Malvasia, Cariñena, Garnacha, and Tempranillo grapes to produce traditional, full-bodied reds and some dessert wines.

The Medio Penedés is the source of traditional white wines and classic *cavas*—sparkling wines produced in the manner of champagne but known here as "cava"—made from the Xarel-lo and Macabeo grapes. However, the limestone and clay soil also permits cultivation of the French varietals, Cabernet Sauvignon, Pinot Noir, Merlot, Chardonnay, and Sauvignon Blanc. The climate here is comparable to that of Tuscany and the northern part of California's Napa Valley.

The Alto Penedés, in the foothills of the mountains, is cooler and gets more rain, like the regions of Champagne, the Rhine Valley, and the cooler parts of the Napa Valley. This, too, is white wine country, the main grapes being Parellada, Riesling, Gewürztraminer, and Alsace Muscat.

In general, Catalan wine production centers on the whites, which tend to be light and fruity. The reds, produced in smaller quantities, tend to be strong, full-bodied, and of alcohol contents sometimes reaching more than 15%.

Recently, Catalan wines have been gaining increasing cachet abroad. The wines of Miguel Torres, a fifth-generation vintner, are found all over the world and have been available in the United States for more than 50 years. The family's California vineyards are managed by his daughter, Marimar. Freixenet, the world's leading seller of cava, has also established wineries in California and has purchased the French Henri Abele champagne vineyards in Reims. Codorníu, the other leading cava producer, leads in the high-priced market both in Europe and the United States, and has become very aggressive in penetrating the French market.

TRAVEL DOCUMENTS

Americans require only a valid passport for travel to Spain, and citizens of most Western European countries need only their national identity cards.

CLIMATE

Barcelona's climate is very mild most of the year, with temperatures rarely reaching freezing in the winter. The high humidity can make the dog days (and nights) of July and August rather oppressive, but just do as the Barcelonans do and buy yourself a fan. Rain is infrequent, most likely to fall in the spring and autumn. The following table shows some monthly averages.

Barcelona's Average Daytime Temperatures and Days of Sunshine

	Jan	Feb	Mar	Apr	May	June	July	Aug	Sept	Oct	Nov	Dec
Temp. (°F)	49	51	54	59	64	72	76	76	72	64	57	51
Temp. (°C)	10	11	13	15	18	22	25	25	22	18	14	11
Days of Sun	26	23	22	21	23	24	27	25	23	22	24	25

SUGGESTED READING

Here is a list of books that may help to prepare you for your trip to Barcelona and Catalunya.

Background/Impressions

Boyd, Alistair. *The Essence of Catalonia: Barcelona and Its Regions.*
Hooper, John. *The Spaniards.*
Lewis, Norman. *Voices of the Old Sea.*
Michener, James. *Iberia: Spanish Travels and Reflections.*
Morris, Jan. *Spain.*
Plante, David. *The Foreigner.*

Spanish Civil War

Kazantzakis, Nikos. *Spain.*
Orwell, George. *Homage to Catalonia.*

Art

Martinell, Cesar. *Gaudí Designer: His Life, His Theories, His Work.*
Nonell, Joan Bassegoda. *The Guide to Gaudí.*
Penrose, Roland. *Miró.*
Sterner, Gabriele. *Antoni Gaudí.*

Food

Casas, Penelope. *The Foods & Wines of Spain.*
Read, Jan, Maite Manjon, and Hugh Johnson. *The Wine & Food of Spain.*

WHAT TO PACK

For most of the year, pack clothing that can be layered in case the weather turns cold at night. In the winter, a lined raincoat and a heavy sweater should keep you sufficiently warm. Since a large part of the old town retains its cobblestone streets, sensible walking shoes are recommended for sightseeing. Most hotels have 220V electrical current, so bring along dual-voltage appliances or a converter as well as the European round-prong adaptor plugs.

ADVANCE TOURIST INFORMATION

For information to help you plan your trip, contact the **Spanish National Tourist Office** nearest you:

New York: 665 Fifth Ave., New York, NY 10022 (tel. 212/759-8822).

Miami: 1221 Brickell Ave., Miami, FL 33131 (tel. 305/536-1222).

Chicago: Water Tower Place, Suite 915 East, 845 N. Michigan

Ave., Chicago, IL 60611 (tel. 312/944-0215, 944-0216, 944-0225, or 944-0226).

Los Angeles: 8383 Wilshire Blvd., Suite 960, Beverly Hills, CA 90211 (tel. 213/658-7188 or 658-7193).

Toronto: 60 Bloor St. West, Suite 201, Toronto, Ontario M4W 3B8, Canada (tel. 416/961-3131 or 461-4079).

London: 57-58 St. James' St., London SW1A 1LD, England (tel. 01/499-1169 or 491-1274).

Sydney: International House, Suite 44, 104 Bathurst St. (P.O. Box A-675), Sydney South, NSW, 2000 Australia (tel. 612/264-7966).

II

GETTING TO KNOW BARCELONA

1. GETTING THERE
2. ORIENTATION
3. GETTING AROUND
4. FAST FACTS

With business and tourist traffic to Barcelona on the increase, flights from the United States and Europe have increased. Nonstop and direct service is available from New York, with easy connections from other major American cities. Once there, you'll find that the city compresses its sightseeing riches into an easy-to-get-to-know ensemble of old-world alleys and broad, modern boulevards all serviced by an efficient public transportation network.

1. Getting There

BY AIR
Because airfares change constantly and special fares can materialize overnight, be persistent. Keep calling the airlines or your travel agent to secure the best possible fare—sometimes you can purchase a discounted ticket at the last minute if a flight is not completely booked. Those averse to such last-minute arrangements should know that fares vary with the season and that special excursion fares are often available. Summer, Christmas, and Easter are the peak, and thus priciest, times to travel to Barcelona. The lowest fares are offered in winter (November through March, excluding Christmas).

Airlines and Fares
Most airlines offer a variety of fares from first class (the most expensive) through business class to economy or coach—the lowest no-strings-attached full fare. In addition, promotional fares are often offered, which are restricted by advance-purchase requirements, minimum and maximum stays, and cancellation penalties. The most common of these is the APEX (Advance Purchase Excursion) fare.

Iberia Airlines (tel. toll free 800/SPAIN-IB), the national carrier of Spain, offers the largest number of flights to Barcelona from Chicago, Los Angeles, Miami, and New York. From New York there is nonstop service from April through October six days a week (Sunday is the exception) and from November through March on Tuesday, Thursday, Saturday, and Sunday. Iberia also links Barcelona with many European cities, including Amsterdam, Athens, Brussels, Frankfurt, Geneva, Istanbul, Lisbon, London, Marseilles, Milan, Paris, Stockholm, Vienna, and Zurich.

As of this writing, Iberia's full, one-way economy fare is $727; business, $1,246; and first class, $2,039. A special excursion fare that requires no advance purchase but a minimum 7-day and maximum 180-day stay runs $777 to $983 round-trip, depending on the time of year. A 14-day APEX fare requiring a minimum 7-day and maximum 60-day stay runs $577 to $833 round-trip, depending on the season and the day of the week that you fly. Special youth fares (you must be under 25 to qualify) of $480 round-trip in winter and $536 in summer are available; the maximum stay is one year, and reservations may be made no earlier than 72 hours before departure.

Two special Iberia packages are "Barcelona Stop," offering a free 24-hour stopover en route to any other city in Europe, Africa, or the Middle East; and "High Class Weekend," offering business-and first-class travelers a free weekend in Barcelona. Both packages include accommodations, some meals, and entertainment.

Iberia's 60-day "Visit Spain Airpass" is available throughout the year. Purchased in conjunction with a transatlantic ticket, it permits travel to over 25 destinations within the country, including the Balearic Islands, for $249. For an additional $50 you can choose among the Canary Islands as well.

Iberia has ticket offices on the Plaça de Espanya (Plaza de España) (tel. 325-73-58); at Carrer de Mallorca 277 (tel. 215-70-34); in the Hotel Princesa Sofía, Plaça Pius XII 4 (tel. 411-10-85); and at El Prat Airport (tel. 370-10-11). For general flight information, call 301-39-93; for domestic reservations, call 301-68-00; for international reservations, call 302-76-56.

TWA (tel. toll free 800/221-2000) has direct service to Barcelona via Madrid at comparable full and excursion fares.

Pan Am (tel. toll free 800/221-1111) flies nonstop from New York to Madrid several times a week, and **American Airlines** (tel. toll free 800/433-7300) offers daily nonstop service from Dallas to Madrid, Miami to Madrid, and Dallas to Barcelona.

Air Europa runs charter flights to Madrid out of New York. For information and reservations, contact their representative, Club de Vacaciones, 775 Park Ave., Huntington, NY 11743 (tel. 516/424-9600).

From Madrid, Iberia offers frequent, daily shuttle service to Barcelona via the **Puente Aéreo** (literally, "air bridge") as well as frequent nonshuttle flights.

On Arrival

El Prat Airport (tel. 370-10-11 for general airport information) is 7.5 miles (12km) from the city. A **train** runs between the airport and the Barcelona Estació Central-Sants every 30 minutes between 6am and 11pm (6:30am is the first airport departure; 10:30pm is the last city departure). The trip takes about 15 minutes and costs 150 ptas. ($1.25).

Bus EA runs between Plaça d'Espanya and the airport every 40 minutes from 7:15am to 7:15pm and takes about 30 minutes. The fare is 80 ptas. (65¢) Monday through Saturday and 95 ptas. (80¢) on Sunday and holidays.

Approximate **taxi** fares to various in-town destinations are posted at the baggage-claim area of the airport. With the 150-pta. ($1.25) airport supplement and 40-pta. (35¢) supplement per bag, the cab ride into town should run between 1,500 and 2,000 ptas. ($12.50 and $16.75).

The **bank** in the baggage-claim area is open daily from 7:15am to 10:45pm. The bank in the arrivals hall is open from 9am to 2pm Monday through Friday and 9am to 12:30pm on Saturday.

Note: You may encounter some chaos and inconvenience due to the current expansion that will double the airport's capacity to 12 million passengers annually. Projected completion is the end of 1991.

BY TRAIN

Direct trains from Paris, Geneva, and several major Spanish cities arrive at the **Barcelona Estació Central-Sants,** at the western edge of the Eixample, while other international and national trains arrive at the **Passeig de Gràcia station,** in the heart of the Eixample. Both are centrally located.

For information on national and international train service, call the **Red Nacional de Ferrocarriles Españoles (R.E.N.F.E.)** (tel. 322-41-42).

BY BOAT

For general information on ferries and cruises from/to Barcelona, contact **Trasmediterránea,** Via Laietana 2 (tel. 319-85-04).

2. Orientation

Though at first glance Barcelona seems every bit the immense metropolis, it soon becomes a very manageable city easily negotiated on foot and via public transportation. Given the city's traffic congestion and paucity of parking space, a car can be an encumbrance. A good map of Barcelona that you may want to purchase before you leave home is "Walks Through Barcelona," available from VLE Limited, P.O. Box 547, Tenafly, NJ 07670 (tel. 201/567-5536), or at selected bookstores and travel agencies.

CITY LAYOUT

Barcelona grew around a medieval core, and the constant juxta-position of its well-preserved past and highly progressive present gives the city a distinctive character at once provincial of aspect and cosmopolitan of manner. Between the **harbor** and the ordered grid of the 19th-century Eixample (Ensanche) lies the *casco antiguo* (old town). Bordered by the **Parc de la Ciutadella (Parque de la Ciudadela)** to the northeast and the fortress-topped hill of **Montjuïc** to the southwest, its focal point is the **Barri Gòtic (Barrio Gótico),** the majestic heirloom bequeathed to the city by its medieval prominence.

Catalan Addresses

In Spain, street numbers *follow* street names and the ° sign indicates the floor. *Dcha.* or *izqda.* following the floor means "right" or "left." *Baja* refers to the ground floor, and the Span-iard's first floor (1°) is the American's second.

Some Catalan words for street names are different from those in Spanish. Thus you may find a knowledge of the following terms useful in reading maps and street signs in Barcelona (the Spanish word, if different, is in parenthesis).

avinguda *(avenida)*	avenue
carrer *(calle)*	street
carretera	road, route
passatge *(pasaje)*	passage, alley
passeig *(paseo)*	boulevard, promenade
plaça *(plaza)*	plaza, square
ronda	outer road, ring road
travessera *(travesía)*	short cross street
via *(vía)*	road, route

At the edge of the Barri Gòtic, **La Rambla (Las Ramblas)** bi-sects the old town. Though five street names designate the different sections that stretch from the Columbus Monument to the Plaça Catalunya (Plaza Cataluña), it is really a single, tree-lined boulevard that is one of the city's best-known attractions.

At the port end of Las Ramblas is the notorious **Barri Xines (Barrio Chino),** Barcelona's seedy, seaport version of New York's 42nd Street. Though the term technically refers to the dowdy, nar-row streets west of Las Ramblas between the harbor and Carrer de l'Hospital, the hookers, sex shows, and drug deals that won it notoriety also abound on the other side of Las Ramblas. During the day the seediness can be atmospheric, but it's best avoided at night.

Below the Parc de la Ciutadella and east of the harbor is

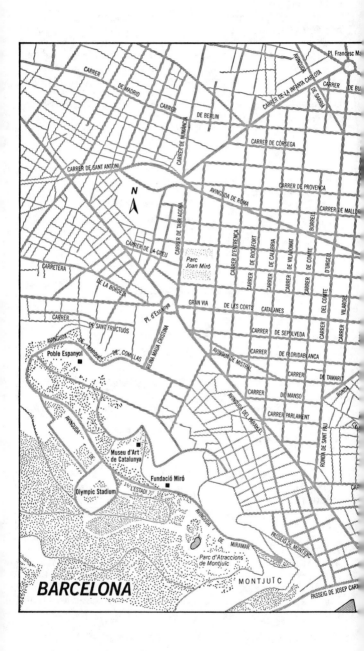

TRAVESSERA
DE GRÀCIA
TIBIDABO
CARRER DE PARIS
AVINGUDA DIAGONAL
CARRER DE CÓRSEGA
"Les Punxes"
CATALUNYA
CARRER DE ROSSELLÓ
CARRER DE ROGER DE FLOR
CARRER DE NÀPOLS
La Pedrera
CARRER DE PROVENÇA
CARRER DE BALMES
RAMBLA DE
CARRER DE MALLORCA
Sagrada Família
CARRER DE VALÈNCIA
DE GRÀCIA
CARRER DE PAU CLARIS
Pl. de la Sagrada Família
PASSEIG DE GRÀCIA
CARRER MUTANER
AVINGUDA DIAGONAL
Pl. del
Pl. de Gaudí
Pl. Doctor Letamendi
CARRER D'ARAGÓ
Casa Battló
Casa Lleó-Morera ■ Casa Amatller
CARRER DE CONSELL
EIXAMPLE
PASSEIG DE SANT JOAN
DE CENT
DE SICILIA
CARRER D'ARIBAU
CARRER DE LA DIPUTACIÓ
GRAN VIA
DE SARDENYA
Pl. de la Universitat
DE LES CORTS CATALANES
CARRER
CARRER
DE SANT ANTONI
RONDA UNIVERSITAT
DE CASP
CARRER DE PELAI
Pl. Catalunya
D'AUSIÀS MARC
CARRER
CARRER
AVINGUDA PORTAL DE L'ANGEL
Pl. Urquinaona
CARRER FONTANELLA
CARRER DE RIBES
VIA LAIETANA
RONDA DE SANT PERE
DE HOSPITAL
LA RAMBLA
VILANOVA
PASSEIG DE LLUÍS COMPANYS
AVINGUDA CATEDRAL
DE SANT PAU
Catedral
Pl. del Rei
BARRI GÒTIC
CARRER DE PRINCESA
PASSEIG DE PUJADES
CARRER DE FERRAN
Museu Picasso
Parc de la Ciutadella
LA RIBERA
CARRER MONTCADA
CARRER
DE WELLINGTON
PASSEIG
LES RAMBLES
CARRER AMPLE
Museu d'Art Modern
Portal
la Pau
Columbus
Monument
PASSEIG DE COLOM
MOLL DE LA FUSTA
Zoològic
CARRER
Santa Maria
BARCELONETA
DE CHARLES I

Barceloneta, home to the city's fishermen and a proliferation of mediocre seafood restaurants.

To the north of Plaça Catalunya is the **Eixample,** a grid of wide streets that provide contrast with the density of the old town. Bordered by two arteries that lead out of the city—**Gran Via de les Corts Catalanes** and **Avinguda (Avenida) Diagonal**—it is the product of Barcelona's 19th-century industrialization and concomitant prosperity. Each block of the Eixample was slated to have a central courtyard with trees, benches, and more, but many were ultimately converted into parking lots. Now, as part of the city's overall rehabilitation program, a number of them are reverting back to their original roles as public oases.

North of the Eixample is **Gràcia,** an area of small squares and lively bars that was once a separate village but has now bonded onto Barcelona proper.

THE NEIGHBORHOODS

From the foot of Las Ramblas to the tip of Tibidabo, Barcelona is a pastiche of distinctive neighborhoods, each with its own unique place in history and prevailing architectural vernacular.

Las Ramblas

The Brechtian parade of humanity that regularly courses Las Ramblas is Spain's *paseo* tradition carried to seedy and sublime extremes. Weaving among the kiosks packed with flowers, newspapers, and parakeets and the series of banks, hotels, cinemas, theaters, cafés, bars, and restaurants is a constant stream of passersby that draws the usual contingent of buskers as well as scores of nimble-fingered pickpockets, purse- and chain-snatchers, and other assorted criminal elements. From time to time impromptu markets blossom at the harbor end, which tends to be the diciest section of the street.

When viewed from the cable car that crosses the port, Las Ramblas cuts a green swath through what appears to be a dense, urban jungle. At ground level, it cuts across every layer of society. But this was not always so—the lavish mansions of its surrounding streets confirm that this was once the city's poshest address. Now the presence of first-rate hotels as well as the restoration of some fine art nouveau buildings suggest a more polished future for this most entertaining of street spectacles.

Barri Gòtic (Barrio Gótico)

Bordered by Las Ramblas to the west, Passeig de Colom (Paseo de Colón) to the south, Via Laietana to the east, and the Ronda de Sant Pere to the north, this quarter is the repository of Barcelona's Roman past and its medieval glory days when the city dominated the Mediterranean waters. For some 500 years the Catalan monarchy ruled from this quarter. Its historic epicenter is the **Plaça del Rei (Plaza del Rey).** Among its other noted landmarks are the **Catedral** and the adjacent Romanesque **Iglesia de Santa Llúcia.** Cobblestone streets, fountains that once served a purpose beyond mere adornment, and buildings so solid that they survived even the devastating blows of the Civil War complete this slice of history. As the seat of Catalonia's regional and Barcelona's municipal government, the quarter is as lively as ever. In the summer, music students often fill its narrow streets with the strains of Bach and Mozart. And as you sample the barrio's numerous antiques shops, bookstores, eccentric museums, and vest-pocket restaurants, you can easily imagine Columbus coming around the corner full of tales of his recent New World travels; for it was here, in the Salón del Tinell, that he delivered his first reports to Queen Isabella.

Barri de la Ribera

Adjacent to the Barri Gòtic and stretching east to the Passeig de Piccaso, La Ribera was the urban focal point of the great maritime and commercial expansion of the 13th and 14th centuries. After its founding and through the Renaissance years, numerous mansions sprang up along its Carrer Montcada. Two of them—Palau Aguilar and Palau Castellet—now house Barcelona's most visited museum, the **Museu Picasso.** A new crop of restaurants, bars, and trendy hangouts points to the growing popularity of this long-ignored barrio.

Puerto and Barceloneta

Although Barcelona owes its very existence to its port, for centuries the city turned its back on the sea and the eyesore structures of the waterfront. Now, in the same spirit of rehabilitation that spawned New York's South Street Seaport and San Francisco's Ghirardelli Square, the waterfront is being reclaimed for human consumption with seaside promenades gradually replacing the largely passé cargo piers. A sign of the reborn times is the Moll de la Fusta, a pier with bars, restaurants, and outdoor terraces that offer passersby assorted refreshment with a sea view.

La Barceloneta, born in the 18th century, is a V-shaped area wedged between the port and the sea, with a long stretch of beach along its eastern end. Originally the enclave of sailors and fishermen, its waterfront now largely caters to hungry and thirsty tourists. If you walk in a few blocks, though, you'll still find Barcelona's seafaring class going about business as usual.

The Eixample (Ensanche)

This area straddles the Passeig de Gràcia north of the Plaça Catalunya and takes its name from the urban expansion plan carried out after the old, binding city walls were torn down in 1860. Comprising a practical grid of perpendicular streets, it was conceived as a bourgeois barrio, its growth coinciding with the evolution of art nouveau (known locally as *Modernisme*). Home to Gaudí's **Sagrada Familia** and **Casa Batlló y Mila,** Domenech i Montaner's **Casa Lleó Morera** and **Hospital de Sant Pau,** and Puig i Cadafalch's **Casa Amatller** and **"Les Punxes,"** it is a veritable essay in the Catalan interpretation of that artistic and architectural movement. You'll spot its highly decorative flourishes executed in glass, wood, wrought iron, and ceramics everywhere.

Running through the heart of the Eixample are the parallel

thoroughfares **Passeig de Gràcia** and **Rambla de Catalunya,** both teeming with shops, bars, cinemas, art galleries, hotels, restaurants, and bookstores. Perhaps more so than other areas of the city, the Eixample divides its time between business (many offices and corporate headquarters are located here) and pleasure.

Montjuïc

First developed for the 1929 World's Fair and currently being remodeled for the 1992 Olympic Games, this sizable hill overlooking the harbor area is one of Barcelona's favorite urban R&R areas. Dedicated to both commercial and leisure activities, it houses convention halls, sports complexes, parks, gardens, an amusement park, museums, and the Poble Espanyol, a village with a variety of the arts, crafts, and architectural styles found throughout Spain.

Tibidabo

This mountain peak to the north of the city is the culmination of the Sierra de Collcerola. Below its 1,600-foot (500-m) zenith unfolds an urban panorama. Getting there on public transportation is half the fun; a fine restaurant and an amusement park complete the experience.

---

3. Getting Around

For **general information on public transportation,** call 336-00-00 Monday through Friday from 7:30am to 8:30pm and on Saturday from 8am to 2pm (assistance is in Spanish only).

BY METRO

The four metro lines and two commuter train lines (FF. CC. Generalitat) operate Monday through Friday from 5am to 11pm, on Saturday from 5am to 1am, and on Sunday and holidays from 6am to 1am. The one-way fare is 60 ptas. (50¢) Monday through Friday, and 65 ptas. (55¢) on Saturday, Sunday, and holidays.

Two ten-trip cards will save you money. The **Tarjeta T-1,** costing 390 ptas. ($3.25), is valid for the bus, metro, *tranvía blau* (*tranvía azul*), Montjuïc funicular, and intra-city portion of the train line. The **Tarjeta T-2,** costing 325 ptas. ($2.75), is valid for all the above except the bus. In the summer, nontransferable one-, three-, and five-day passes (*abonos temporales*), costing 275, 775, and 1,100 ptas. ($2.35, $6.50, and $9.25) respectively, permit unlimited use of the metro and buses. These are sold at the following **TMB (Transports Metropolita de Barcelona)** information offices: Ronda Sant Pau 43; Plaça Catalunya (center of the square); Plaça Catalunya (Rivadeneyra), Avinguda Borbó 12; Plaça Universitat (vestibule of the metro station); Sants-Estació (vestibule of metro Line 5); and at the Liceu, Catalunya, Jaume I, and Drassanes metro stations. Maps of the system are available at these information offices as well.

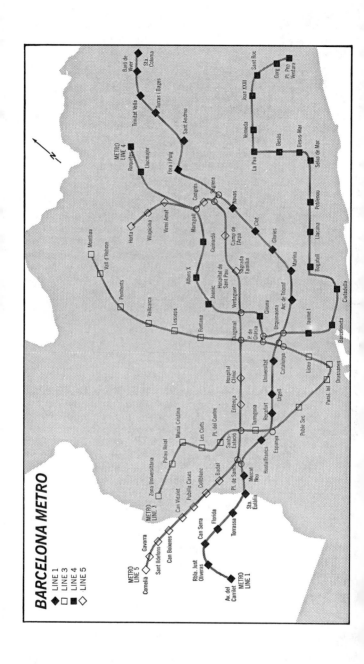

BARCELONA METRO

- ◆ LINE 1
- ☐ LINE 3
- ■ LINE 4
- ◇ LINE 5

BY BUS

Buses generally run from 6:30am to 10pm, with night buses running along the main thoroughfares between 10pm and 4am. The buses are color coded, making it easy for even the first-time visitor to negotiate the network: red buses originate or pass through the heart of the city; yellow buses cut across the city beyond the central districts; green buses serve the city periphery; and blue buses ply the night routes and originate or pass through the city center. The **fare** is 60 ptas. (50¢) Monday through Friday and 65 ptas. (55¢) on Saturday, Sunday, and holidays. Buses with more than two numbers or letters are intercity.

From the last week in June to the middle of September you can take advantage of the **Discover Barcelona** bargain, a single ticket permitting unlimited travel on Bus 100, the tramvía blau (blue tram), the Montjuïc funicular and cable car, and the Tibidabo funicular. Originating at Pla de Palau, Bus 100 makes a sweep of the entire city, passing through the Barri Gòtic, along the Ramblas and Passeig de Gràcia, by the Sagrada Familia, along the Avinguda del Tibidabo and Avinguda Diagonal, by the Estació Central-Sants, through the Parc de Montjuïc, along the Passeig de Colom, and back to Pla de Palau. It makes 15 stops along its two-hour route, and you can get on and off as you please and go around as many times as you like. Service is every 40 minutes between 10am and 7pm. An all-day ticket costs 600 ptas. ($5), and a half-day ticket, valid after 2pm, costs 400 ptas. ($3.35); both are also valid on the tramvía blau and the Montjuïc cable cars. Purchase tickets on the bus or, between 8am and 7pm, at the same TMB offices that sell the one-, three-, and five-day passes.

BY TELEFÉRICO, TRAMVÍA BLAU, AND FUNICULAR

The **Transbordador Aéreo del Puerto,** also known as the **Montjuïc Teleferic** (tel. 310-13-44 or 241-48-20), runs between Barceloneta and Montjuïc with an intermediate stop on the Moll de Barcelona near the Columbus Monument. Hours of operation are: October to June, Monday through Saturday from 11:30am to 6pm and on Sunday and holidays from 11am to 6:45pm; June to September, daily from 11am to 9pm. One-way fare is 400 ptas. ($3.35); a round-trip is 500 ptas. ($4.15). Since the Montjuïc stop is far from any sights, you would take this primarily for the splendid view of the city or perhaps to picnic in the park near the Montjuïc terminus.

The **Montjuïc funicular,** which connects with metro Line 3 at Paral.lel, operates in winter on Saturday, Sunday, and holidays from 11am to 8:15pm, and in summer daily from 11am to 10pm. The weekday fare is 70 ptas. (60¢); 75 ptas. (65¢) on weekends and holidays. The cable car linking the upper end of the Montjuïc funicular with the hilltop castle operates September to June on Saturday, Sunday, and holidays from 11am to 2:45pm and 4 to 7:30pm. Over the Christmas season it runs daily those same hours. From June to September it runs daily from noon to 3pm and 4 to 8:30pm. The one-way fare is 150 ptas. ($1.25).

The **tramvía blau** runs from Passeig de St. Gervais/Avinguda

Tibidabo to the lower end of the Tibidabo funicular. It operates Monday through Saturday every 30 minutes between 7:05am and 9:55pm, and on Sunday and holidays every 15 minutes between 7:05am and 10:25pm. The fare is 55 ptas. (45¢) Monday through Saturday, 60 ptas. (50¢) on Sunday and holidays.

Continuing where the tramvía blau ends, the **Tibidabo funicular** runs to the top of Tibidabo, 1,600 feet (500 m) above sea level. Hours of operation are every 30 minutes Monday through Friday from 7:45am to 9:45pm, on Saturday from 7:15am to 9:45pm, and on Sunday and holidays from 7:15 to 10:15am and 8:45 to 9:45pm (between 10:15am and 8:45pm it runs every 15 minutes). The one-way fare is 140 ptas. ($1.15); round-trip, 250 ptas. ($2.05).

BY TAXI

The standard Barcelona taxi is black and yellow. When available, it displays the "Libre" sign in its window and/or illuminates a green light on its roof. The initial charge is 210 ptas. ($1.75); each additional kilometer is 52 ptas. (45¢). Supplemental charges include 150 ptas. ($1.25) to and from the airport, 55 ptas. (45¢) when departing from a train station, and 40 ptas. (35¢) for each large bag. The ride in from the airport should run between 1,500 and 2,000 ptas. ($12.50 and $16.75).

You can call for a cab by dialing any of the following numbers: 386-50-00, 330-08-04, 321-88-33, or 300-38-11.

BY CAR

Considering the traffic congestion and the scarcity of parking in Barcelona, I don't recommend driving in the city. Those wanting to travel into the environs, however, might wish to rent a car for an excursion.

Car Rental

The following car-rental agencies have in-town and airport offices:

Atesa, Carrer de Balmes 141 (tel. 237-81-40), open Monday through Friday from 9am to 1:30pm and 4 to 7:30pm, and on Saturday from 9am to 12:30pm; at the airport (tel. 302-28-32), open Monday through Saturday from 7am to midnight and on Sunday from 7am to 10pm.

Avis, Carrer de Casanova 209 (tel. 209-95-33), open Monday through Friday from 8am to 8pm, on Saturday from 8am to 7pm, and on Sunday from 8am to 1pm; at the airport (tel. 379-40-26), open daily from 7am to past midnight.

Europcar, Carrer de Consell de Cent 363 (tel. 317-58-76), open Monday through Friday from 8am to 2pm and 4 to 8pm, and on Saturday from 9am to 1pm; at the airport (tel. 317-84-30), open Monday through Saturday from 7am to midnight and on Sunday from 8am to 10pm.

Hertz, Tuset 10 (tel. 237-37-37), open Monday through Friday from 8am to 8pm, on Saturday from 8am to 1pm and 4 to 8pm, and on Sunday from 9am to 1pm; at the airport (tel. 370-57-72), open 24 hours daily.

As an example of **rental rates,** Avis daily rentals begin at 3,400 ptas. ($28.25) plus 25 ptas. (20¢) per kilometer; weekly rates start at 6,190 ptas. ($51.50) per day, with unlimited mileage. Rentals of two weeks or more are 5,510 ptas. ($46) per day, with unlimited mileage. Insurance and 12% IVA are extra. Be sure to shop around for the best rate at the moment.

---

4. Fast Facts

BUSINESS HOURS: **Banking hours** are generally Monday through Friday from 8:30am to 2pm and on Saturday from 8:30am to 1pm (in the summer, from 8:30am to 12:30pm). Some banks in the center of town stay open until 4:45pm. If you need to change money on Sunday or a holiday, you can do so at the following locations: Estación Término, Sección Cercanías (tel. 310-21-75), open daily from 7:30am to 11pm; Barcelona Estación Central-Sants (tel. 410-39-15), open in winter daily from 8am to 8pm, and in summer Monday through Saturday from 8:30am to 10pm and on Sunday from 8:30am to 2pm and 4:30 to 10pm; El Prat Airport (tel. 370-40-05), open in winter daily from 7am to 11pm, and in summer Monday through Saturday from 8am to 10pm.

Office hours vary widely but the norm is from 9am to 1:30pm and 4 to 7pm. Some offices have special summer hours from 8am to 3pm.

Shop hours also vary widely, with the norm being from 10am to 1:30pm and 5 to 8pm.

CONSULATES: The **U.S. Consulate** is at Via Laietana 33 (tel. 319-95-50); the **Canadian Consulate** is at Via Augusta 125 (tel. 209-06-34); and the **Consulate of the United Kingdom** is at Avinguda Diagonal 477 (tel. 322-21-51).

CREDIT CARDS: Most hotels, restaurants, and stores accept major credit cards. For assistance or information, call **American Express** (tel. 217-00-70), **Eurocard** (tel. 302-14-28), **VISA** (tel. 315-25-12), **MasterCard** (tel. 091/435-49-05 in Madrid), or **Diners Club** (tel. 091/247-40-00 in Madrid).

CURRENCY: The Spanish unit of currency is the **peseta (pta.),** which is issued in coin denominations of 1, 5, 10, 25, 50, 100, 200, and 500 ptas., and bills of 500, 1,000, 2,000, 5,000, and 10,000 ptas. The rate of exchange used to calculate dollar equivalents in this guidebook is 120 ptas. to $1 U.S., but given the constant state of flux of today's economies, prices (in both pesetas and dollars) should be considered as reference points rather than as statements of strict financial fact.

The Peseta and the Dollar

At this writing $1 = approximately 120 ptas. (or 1 pta. = 0.83¢), and this was the rate of exchange used to calculate the dollar values given in this book (rounded off). This rate fluctuates from time to time and may not be the same when you travel to Barcelona. Therefore the following table should be used only as a guide:

Ptas.	$ U.S.	Ptas.	$ U.S.
5	.04	1,500	12.50
10	.08	2,000	16.67
15	.13	2,500	20.83
20	.17	3,000	25.00
25	.21	3,500	29.17
30	.25	4,000	33.33
40	.33	4,500	37.50
50	.42	5,000	41.67
75	.63	6,000	50.00
100	.83	7,000	58.33
150	1.25	8,000	66.67
200	1.67	9,000	75.00
250	2.08	10,000	83.33
500	4.17	12,500	104.17
750	6.25	15,000	125.00
1,000	8.33	20,000	166.67

ELECTRICITY: In most cases, the local electricity is 220/230 volts; however, some hotels have 110/120V lines. Although Spain is increasingly standardizing on 220/230V, it is advisable to bring along a converter or dual-voltage appliances and adaptor plugs (most outlets accept only round-prong plugs).

EMERGENCIES: For **medical attention,** call 212-85-85 for a doctor or 417-19-94 for a nurse. If you require hospital attention, go to **Hospital de Sant Pau,** Avinguda S. Antoni Maria Claret 167 (tel. 347-31-33); **Hospital Clínic,** Carrer de Casanova 143 (tel. 323-14-14); or **Hospital de la Cruz Roja,** Dos de Maig 301 (tel. 235-93-00). For an **ambulance,** call 329-77-66 or 300-20-20.

For the **national police,** dial 091; for the **municipal police,** 092. In the event of **fire,** dial 080.

HOLIDAYS: Local holidays are celebrated with special flair (see "Special Events," Section 5 in Chapter V), but life as usual takes a breather on the following days: January 1 (New Year's Day), January 6 (Feast of the Three Kings), Good Friday, Easter Monday, May 1 (Labor Day), May 15 (Feast of the Pentecost), June 24 (Feast of St. John), August 15 (Assumption Day), September 11 (Catalunya Day), October 12 (Columbus Day), November 1 (All Souls' Day),

December 6 (Constitution Day), December 8 (Feast of the Immaculate Conception), December 25 (Christmas Day), and December 26 (Feast of St. Stephen).

LANGUAGE: Catalan is the indigenous language of Barcelona and Catalonia, and is the second official language of the region. As street, highway, and all other signs are increasingly appearing either solely in Catalan or in both Catalan and Spanish, you may get confused if your map or other orientational materials are not recent. Throughout this guidebook, as in the city itself, both languages are used and in most cases street names, important sights, and key terminology initially appear in Catalan with the Spanish or English indicated in parentheses. Subsequent mentions may be in Catalan or Spanish, depending on prevailing usage. (Also see the "Catalan Addresses" box in Section 2, "Orientation," above.)

LOST AND FOUND: If you've lost something, dial 301-39-23. If you've lost something on public transportation, contact the Metro office in the Plaça Catalunya across from Carrer Bergara (tel. 318-52-93).

MAIL: Post offices are generally open Monday through Friday from 9am to 2pm. The **central post office,** in Plaça Antonio López (tel. 318-38-31), is open Monday through Friday from 8:30am to 10pm, on Saturday from 9am to 2pm, and on Sunday and holidays from 10am to noon.

Postcards to the United States cost 64 ptas. (55¢); to Europe, 45 ptas. (35¢). Letters to the United States cost 69 ptas. (55¢); to Europe, 50 ptas. (40¢).

NEWSPAPERS: *La Vanguardia* and *El Periódico* are Barcelona's leading daily newspapers. *El País* is the nation's leading paper and offers a Barcelona edition. Most newsstands—and particularly those on Las Ramblas—sell the *Wall Street Journal, USA Today* (yesterday's, of course), *The Times* (of London), *The Daily Telegraph* (London), the *Financial Times* (London), and the *International Herald Tribune.*

PHARMACIES: When they close, all pharmacies are required to post a notice indicating the nearest pharmacy that is open. For the list of pharmacies open off-hours on any given day, check *La Vanguardia.*

POLICE: Should you need police assistance in English, the stations at Via Laietana 49 (tel. 302-63-25) and Carrer Ample 23 (tel. 318-36-89) offer the services of an interpreter during the summer months.

RELIGIOUS SERVICES: Most of the churches in Barcelona are Roman Catholic. Masses are generally held between 7am and 2pm and between 7 and 9pm on Sunday and holidays, and between 7 and 9pm on Saturday. This holds true for churches of historical and artistic interest as well. Mass in English is held at 10:30am on the first and third Sunday of the month at Paroisse Française, Anglí 15 (tel. 204-49-62), and Anglican Mass in English is celebrated every Sunday at 11am and every Wednesday at 11:30am at Saint George Church, Sant Joan de la Salle 41 (tel. 417-88-67).

SAFETY: Whenever you're traveling in an unfamiliar city or country, stay alert. Be aware of your immediate surroundings. Wear a moneybelt and don't sling your camera or purse over your shoulder; wear the strap diagonally across your body. This will minimize the possibility of your becoming a victim of crime. Every society has its criminals. It's your responsibility to be aware and alert even in the most heavily touristed areas.

In Barcelona, street crime is so rampant that the tourist office publishes a multilingual pamphlet entitled "Barcelona Con Toda Seguridad" ("Barcelona in Complete Safety"), which suggests precautions you should take as you tour the city. Most of the advice is common sense, but here are a few helpful hints to keep in mind: Reject any offers of flowers or other objects—often the motive is stealing, not selling. Be on guard against surprise attacks—chain- and purse-snatchers seem to come out of nowhere. If you are part of a group touring by bus, make sure that the driver stays on board to guard any items left inside. Make photocopies of all your personal documents and leave the originals at the hotel.

TAX: The value-added tax (VAT) is known as **IVA** in Spain and runs from 6% on restaurant bills to 33% on luxury items. Recovery of the tax is possible for non–EC residents on single purchases costing over 55,000 ptas. ($460) obtained in stores owned by companies rather than by private individuals. A special receipt is required for Customs and must be stamped upon departure. The refund is sent to the store, which then passes it on to you. The whole painstaking process may take up to a year. For further information, contact the Cámara Oficial de Comercio, Avinguda Diagonal 452 (tel. 415-16-00).

TELEPHONE: For local information, dial 003; for national assistance, dial 009. For operator-assisted calls from any phone other than a phone booth, dial 008 for Europe, 005 for everywhere else. The minimum amount for a local call from a booth is 25 ptas. (20¢).

To make an international call, dial 07, wait for the tone, and dial the area code(s) and number. Note, however, that an international call from a phone booth requires stacks and stacks of heavy 100-pta. coins.

Most hotels impose a surcharge on phone calls—some as much as 25%. As an alternative, international phone calls can be made at Carrer Fontanella 4, Monday through Saturday from 8:30am to 7pm.

TELEVISION: There are two national TV channels (1 and 2) in Spanish and two regional channels (3 and 33) in Catalan. There is also a channel broadcast from the Balearic Islands (in Spanish) and one from France (French). Spain has recently sanctioned private TV so there is much more to come.

TIME: Most of the year Barcelona is six hours ahead of the eastern United States. However, Spain switches to and from daylight saving time about a month before the United States, so during most of October and March the time difference is five hours and seven hours, respectively.

TIPPING: Tipping is by no means obligatory and large tips are not expected. A **bellhop** should get from 100 to 200 ptas. (85¢ to $1.75), depending on the number of bags. **Taxi drivers** don't get surly if you don't tip them, but 5% to 10% is customary. Virtually all **restaurants** include a service charge in the bill, so 5% usually suffices. At **bars and cafeterias,** tipping from 10 to 100 ptas. (10¢ to 85¢), depending on the amount of the bill, is the norm. Contrary to Stateside practice, the percentage left as a tip decreases as the amount of the bill increases.

TOURIST INFORMATION: For 24-hour information on what's happening in Barcelona, dial 010 if you're within the city limits, 318-25-25 if you're within the province, and 93/318-25-25 if you're elsewhere in Spain.

The **tourist office at El Prat Airport** (tel. 325-58-29) is open Monday through Saturday from 9:30am to 8:30pm (to 8pm in winter) and on Sunday and holidays from 9:30am to 3pm. **In-town tourist offices** are at Puerto de Barcelona (Moll de la Fusta) (tel. 310-37-16), open October 1 to June 14 daily from 9am to 3pm, and June 15 to September 30 daily from 8am to 8pm; in the vestibule of the Barcelona Estació Central-Sants (tel. 410-25-94), open daily from 8am to 8pm; in the vestibule at the Estació Barcelona-Término, Sector Cercanías (no phone), open June 15 to September 30 daily from 8am to 8pm; and at Gran Via de les Corts Catalanes 658 (tel. 301-74-43), open Monday through Friday from 9am to 7pm and on Saturday from 9am to 2pm.

The following **English-language publications** are available at the tourist offices: "Plano-Guía de Barcelona" and "Plano de Barcelona" (maps with sightseeing information); "Barcelona: A Guide to Congress & Convention Facilities"; "Barcelona—Shopping"; "Barri Gòtic"; "Modernisme"; and a monthly listing of cultural and entertainment offerings.

III

BARCELONA ACCOMMODATIONS

1. VERY EXPENSIVE HOTELS
2. MODERATE HOTELS
3. BUDGET LODGINGS
4. APARTMENT ACCOMMODATIONS

In anticipation of the 1992 Olympic Games and to accommodate the waves of business and tourist traffic preceding it, Barcelona hotels of every category are sprucing up. Since the Olympic Committee stipulated that hotel rates must be frozen two years before the games, a number of hotels upgraded their facilities and substantially raised their prices in anticipation. If not new or recently renovated, many of the hotels listed below are currently renovating or have plans to do so in the near future.

Barcelona's economic vigor has spawned several new hotels in recent years and will give rise to half a dozen more by 1992. But city officials wisely curbed the euphoric ambitions of many hotel entrepreneurs by limiting the number of new constructions to a dozen or so, realizing that demand will drop sharply after the games.

In the past, the slow times for Barcelona's hotels were the winter months, July, and August, but that has changed drastically with the increase in business bookings. Nowadays hotel space is at a premium year round, so you had best make reservations well in advance. Things are especially tight during the city's numerous trade fairs. Although you'll always be likely to find a bed in a pension or hostel, the moderate and luxury hotels fill up in a hurry.

With the exception of a handful of large, luxury hotels, most of Barcelona's hostelries are small by American standards—both in their total number of rooms and in the size of the rooms themselves. With the exception of the luxury hotels, double beds are scarce. If you want one, ask for a *cama de matrimonio* (literally, "marriage bed").

Spain's one- to five-star rating system is more a barometer of a hotel's physical dimensions and attributes than of its level of cleanliness or service. Typically, hotels of three stars or fewer don't have restaurants but may have a cafeteria or snack bar. Hotels of two stars or fewer often offer breakfast only.

The bulk of Barcelona's hotels cluster along either side of Las Ramblas and the Passeig de Gràcia south of Avinguda Diagonal, with a few scattered in the city's northern and western reaches. Since this is a compact city, none of the hotels mentioned below is inconvenient to the major sights. Consequently, they are grouped according to price rather than geographic location. For the purposes of this guide, "very expensive" hotels charge 14,000 ptas. ($117) and up for a double room; "moderate" hotels, 7,000 to 14,000 ptas. ($58 to $117); and "budget" lodgings, 3,000 to 7,000 ptas. ($25 to $58). *Note:* Unless otherwise indicated, all accommodations have private bath or shower and all rates given include service charge but *not* IVA.

1. Very Expensive Hotels

• **Hotel Ritz,** Gran Via de les Corts Catalanes 668, 08010 Barcelona (tel. 3/318-52-00). 150 rms. 11 suites. A/C TV TEL

This has been Barcelona's classic grande dame hotel since it opened in 1919. A member of both the Leading Hotels of the World and the HUSA Group, it attracts upper-echelon visitors from all walks of life. The public areas are outfitted with all the trappings of old-world elegance—hand-woven woolen rugs, brocaded curtains and upholstery, multicolored marble floors, and twinkling chandeliers.

The rooms are somewhat less sumptuous, but stylish and outfitted with all the modern conveniences. Nevertheless, the large baths, reproduction antique furnishings, decorative moldings, and floor-length windows denote another era. The deluxe doubles and suites feature a Roman bath, which amounts to a sunken tiled area with two steps leading down into it.

Dining/Entertainment: The back corner of the lobby lounge is devoted daily to high tea. Off the lobby, a winding staircase leads down to a cozy bar offering live piano music nightly except in July and August. The hotel's palatial Restaurant Diana serves an eclectic assortment of dishes, including curry chicken, steak tartare, lobster thermidor, and gratin de langostinos and setas al whisky (prawns au gratin with wild mushrooms in a whisky sauce). Candlelight dinners are accompanied by live piano music. The restaurant is open from 1:30 to 4pm and 8:30 to 11pm.

Services: 24-hour room service.

Facilities: Beauty parlor, sauna, massage.

RATES: 27,000 ptas. ($225) single; 38,000 ptas. ($317) double; 53,000 ptas. ($442) double with Roman bath; 66,000–200,000 ptas. ($550–$1,667) suite. *Metro:* Urquinaona (Line 1 or 4).

• **Ramada Renaissance,** Ramblas 111, 08002 Barcelona (tel. 3/318-62-00; for reservations, 3/318-44-32 or toll free 900/318-318 in Spain, or toll free 800/228-2828 in the U.S.). 203 rms, 7 suites. A/C MINIBAR TV TEL

Located just off the upper end of Las Ramblas, this is one of the rare American hotel chains in town. Bruce Springsteen slept here; so did Michael Jackson. Behind the vintage facade awaits the epitome of modern comfort and luxury.

The rooms are done in pleasant pastels and feature *real* hairdryers (not those boxes mounted on the wall), a constant air-renewal system, heated bathroom floors, sound insulation, and high-tech communication via radio, TV, video, and direct-dial telephones. For people who work in their rooms, the dimming desk lamp is a nice touch. Popular among business travelers are the 28 Renaissance Club executive rooms on floors 6 to 9 with their own reception area, bar, and restaurant. All sixth-floor rooms have large private terraces. The most sybaritic suite is no. 918 (its dual shower heads are a favorite with honeymooners). No-smoking rooms and special rooms for the disabled are available.

Dining/Entertainment: The lobby bar hums with live piano music from 7 to 11pm nightly. Adjacent to the bar is the airy (thanks to a skylight) El Patio restaurant, which serves an à la carte and buffet breakfast from 7 to 11am and is open for lunch, snacks, and dinner from 1pm to midnight. The menu is Continental with Spanish accents.

Services: Renaissance Club amenities include private check-in and check-out, terry-cloth bathrobes, Minitel, private elevator.

Facilities: Meeting rooms.

RATES: 16,500–19,000 ptas. ($138–$158) single; 19,500–21,000 ptas. ($163–$175) double; 28,000–168,000 ptas. ($233–$1,400) superior Renaissance Club rooms and suites. *Metro:* Liceu (Line 3).

• **Hotel Princesa Sofia,** Plaça Pius XII 4, 08028 Barcelona (tel. 3/330-71-11). 505 rms, 26 suites. A/C MINIBAR TV TEL

This businesslike hotel is at a distance from the central tourist area but very convenient for commerce. Designated an Olympic headquarters hotel, it will accommodate only Olympic personnel during the games. As it will be completely renovated by 1992, little can be said about its salient aspects at the moment.

Because the rooms are being completely redone, details will have to wait for our next edition. In the meantime, the old rooms, dating from the 1970s, are modern and functional and swarming with businesspeople, especially from Japan.

Dining/Entertainment: Le Gourmet restaurant offers gourmet French and Catalan fare. L'Emporda restaurant features Catalan (and, more specifically, Ampurdan) cuisine. Sandwiches and snacks are available 24 hours in the coffeeshop. Regine's disco and piano bar is in the hotel but has a separate entrance.

Services: Avis and Iberia office on premises, complimentary morning newspaper.

Facilities: Combination indoor/outdoor pool, solarium, sauna, gymnasium, hairdresser and barber, lobby shops (including Loewe and Gucci), extensive meeting and banquet facilities.

RATES: 18,000 ptas. ($150) single (15,000 ptas. [$125] in July and August); 26,500 ptas. ($221) double (22,300 ptas., $186, in July and August); 48,000–143,600 ptas. ($400–$1,197) suite. *Metro:* María Cristina (Line 3).

■ **Hotel Alexandra,** Carrer de Mallorca 251, 08008 Barcelona (tel. 3/215-30-52, or toll free 800/528-1234 in the U.S.). 75 double rms. A/C MINIBAR TV TEL

This small, three-year-old hotel, affiliated with the Best Western reservation system, is at once upscale and low key. Director Arcadio Recio cultivates an atmosphere of friendly efficiency. The vintage facade, torn down and faithfully reconstructed stone by numbered stone, houses a completely new interior. The sleek lobby and mezzanine bar, almost minimalist in their stark lack of paintings and other decorative items, feature sporadic flourishes of art deco. The hotel's design is the work of Joan Pera, an architect of the Gaudí school. Its clientele includes many American, German, and Japanese businesspeople.

The soundproofed rooms are sizable and stylishly appointed. Rooms that face the courtyard have oversize double beds; rooms that face the street have twin beds.

Dining/Entertainment: The breakfast buffet amounts to a first-rate brunch, complete with champagne and crema catalana, eggs, sausages, and pastries. There are also dietetic, Catalan, American, and continental breakfasts offered in the rooms. At lunch and dinner, the restaurant offers moderately priced meals prepared with market-fresh ingredients. Monday through Friday from 7 to 10pm there's live music in the mezzanine bar.

Facilities: Parking, meeting and banquet facilities.

RATES: 15,850 ptas. ($132) single use of double room; 19,800 ptas. ($165) double. *Metro:* Passeig de Gràcia (Line 3 or 4).

■ **Hotel Rivoli Ramblas,** Rambla dels Estudis 128, 08002 Barcelona (tel. 3/302-66-43). 90 rms (including suites). A/C MINIBAR TV TEL

Located in Las Ramblas, this hotel is quite new and dazzles the eye with its abundance of marble. Housed in an art deco building that has been totally modernized, its interior is elegantly uncluttered and boldly accented with splashes of bright color. The overall effect suggests a diet version of art deco.

The small but stylish soundproofed rooms are sunny and bright and outfitted with marble-top tables and desks. The artwork throughout is Catalan contemporary. Rooms on the Ramblas side are more expensive and have small balconies; rooms on the Ateneo side face a building that was painted with an abstract design expressly for the visual pleasure of hotel guests. Ask for a room on the seventh floor—a floor that contains the fewest rooms, each one having large terrace with a view of the cathedral. The rooms on the sixth floor also have spacious terraces. All suites have Minitel PCs, and the Suite Opera has antique furnishings, a mega-terrace, and a bath with a view.

Dining/Entertainment: In the lobby is the Blue Moon piano cocktail bar. On the mezzanine level, another small bar adjoins Le Brut restaurant, where all three meals offer buffet and à la carte service. The menu is a mixture of Catalan and Continental.

Facilities: Small fitness center with Jacuzzi, sauna, and tanning table; banquet and meeting rooms.

RATES: 13,000 ptas. ($108) single; 16,750–18,625 ptas. ($140–$155) double; 26,875–57,500 ptas. ($224–$479) suite. *Metro:* Liceu (Line 3).

■ **Hotel Condes de Barcelona,** Passeig de Gràcia 75, 08008 Barcelona (tel. 3/487-3737; or 3/215-7931 or 3/215-7981 for reservations). 100 rms (including suites). A/C MINIBAR TV TEL

Art nouveau outside and mildly art deco inside, this four-star hotel with five-star sophistication and glamour had to ask permission from the real Conde (Count) de Barcelona, King Juan Carlos's father, to use his aristocratic moniker. The count himself is now a frequent guest, as are the Baron von Thyssen and his Barcelona-born wife. Housed in the late 19th-century modernistic mansion designed by architect Josep Vilaseca for the Batlló family, the hotel retains the original facade and an interior stairway with rose-colored wainscoting.

Each pastel-pretty room has a balcony, and street-side rooms have double-glazed windows. The rooms on the fifth floor have wooden floors; all others are carpeted. The premier Suite Barcelona changes its decor every year, except for the pricey silk area rug and the chandelier that architect José Juanpera commandeered from his mother's home. Juanpera also designed the furniture throughout the hotel. Reproductions of Picasso, Dalí, and Sorolla are throughout. The hotel is currently expanding; by the 1992 Olympics, 80 additional rooms plus a business center should be complete.

Dining/Entertainment: In the lobby area, a small curved bar precedes the small, classically stylish Brasserie Condal, which features special regional dishes.

Facilities: Access to fitness club one block away.

RATES: 14,500 ptas. ($120) single; 18,200–20,700 ptas. ($152–$173) double; 23,900–39,100 ptas. ($199–$326) suite. *Metro:* Passeig de Gràcia (Line 3 or 4).

■ **Hotel Royal,** Ramblas 117-119, 08002 Barcelona (tel. 3/318-73-29). 108 rms. A/C MINIBAR TV TEL

At the lower end of the luxury scale in terms of price, this hotel offers a comfortable complement of amenities in a modern, no-nonsense setting.

The somewhat small rooms are attractive and functional. Some of the singles have showers only.

Dining/Entertainment: It offers a bar, cafeteria-pizzeria, and the cozy, rustic El Racó restaurant with an open grill and a mixed menu of Catalan and international cuisine.

Facilities: Garage, banquet and meeting rooms.

RATES: 9,300–10,300 ptas. ($78–$86) single; 14,700 ptas. ($123) double. *Metro:* Catalunya (Line 1 or 3).

2. Moderate Hotels

- **Hotel Regente,** Rambla de Catalunya 76, 08008 Barcelona (tel. 3/215-25-70). 78 rms. A/C MINIBAR TV

In a pleasant Eixample location, the Regente is a solid choice and is unusual in offering a small swimming pool and sunbathing area on the roof. The inviting lobby has Tiffany touches and an etched-glass doorway leading to a charming bar. The rooms are compact and modern, with double beds available in singles only. If you don't mind a bit of noise, you might consider a room with a terrace.

Facilities: Solarium, parking.

RATES: 9,425 ptas. ($79) single; 13,650 ptas. ($114) double. Rates higher during trade fairs. *Metro:* Passeig de Gràcia (Line 3 or 4).

- **Hotel Colón,** Avinguda Catedral 7, 08002 Barcelona (tel. 3/301-14-04); for reservations, contact Marketing Ahead, 433 Fifth Ave., New York, NY 10016 (tel. 212/686-9213). 200 rms (including suites). A/C TV TEL

Occupying a privileged spot opposite the 13th-century Gothic cathedral, the Colón feels like an amiable country home in both its public areas and its cheery, high-ceilinged guest rooms. The size of the rooms varies widely, so if space is important to you, make sure you say so. The suites are especially warm and bright. Although the Colón is located in prime tourist country, numerous business travelers also opt for its special charm. The hotel's grill room offers a comprehensive Continental menu.

RATES: 7,000 ptas. ($58) single; 12,500 ptas. ($104) double; 21,000–22,250 ptas. ($175–$185) suite. *Metro:* Jaume I (Line 4).

- **Hotel Gravina,** Carrer Gravina 12, 08001 Barcelona (tel. 3/301-68-68). 60 rms. A/C MINIBAR TV TEL

Opened in 1988, this three-star hostelry is among the few around town that are not being renovated. Conveniently situated between the Plaça Catalunya and Plaça de la Universitat, its classic exterior houses a bright, modern interior. The rooms are small with sparkling marble baths and double-glazed windows on the street side.

Facilities: Parking.

RATES: 7,900 ptas. ($66) single; 11,900 ptas. ($99) double. *Metro:* Universitat (Line 1).

- **Hotel Regencia Colón,** Carrer Sagristans 13-17, 08002 Barcelona (tel. 3/318-98-58); for reservations, contact Marketing Ahead, 433 Fifth Ave., New York, NY 10016 (tel. 212/686-9213). 55 rms. A/C MINIBAR TV

Related to the Hotel Colón—and virtually next door—the Regencia Colón's proximity to the Barri Gòtic, and its moderate prices, attract a large tour-group business. The recently renovated rooms are bright, cheerful, and sound-insulated. Some singles have a shower only.

RATES (INCLUDING BREAKFAST): 5,400 ptas
10,200 ptas. ($85) double; 13,900 ptas. ($116
Jaume I (Line 4).

- **Hotel Residencia Wilson,** Avinguda Diago
Barcelona (tel. 3/209-25-11). 55 rms. A/C MINIBAR TV

Convenient to both the business and tourist areas of town, this
three-star hotel has clean, comfortable, businesslike rooms. Breakfast is served in the first-floor cafeteria-bar.

RATES: 6,500 ptas. ($54) single, 9,600 ptas. ($80) double;
12,700 ptas. ($106) triple. Rates higher during trade fairs. *Metro:*
Diagonal (Line 3 or 5).

- **Hotel Rialto,** Carrer de Ferran 42, 08002 Barcelona (tel. 3/
318-52-12). 130 rms. A/C TV TEL

The Gargallo group of hotels offers three solid three-star
choices in the Barri Gòtic. All feature distinctively Spanish furnishings in the rooms and attractive, comfortable public areas. The
Rialto is the most expensive and spacious of the three and was completely modernized in 1985. In fact, the rooms are larger than
those of most hotels in this category. Keep in mind, though, that
the exterior rooms with balconies are noisier than the interior
rooms.

RATES: 6,650 ptas. ($55) single; 9,600 ptas. ($80) double.
Metro: Jaume I (Line 4).

- **Hotel Suizo,** Plaça del Àngel 12, 08002 Barcelona (tel. 3/315-
41-11). 48 rms. A/C TV TEL

This is the next best bet in the Gargallo group. Its recently renovated rooms all have small balconies and sound-insulated sliding
glass doors. The cafeteria-bar next to the reception area offers breakfast and tapas in a charming bistro atmosphere with a wooden bar,
etched glass, brass fixtures, and marble tables.

RATES: 6,300 ptas. ($53) single; 9,200 ptas. ($77) double.
Metro: Jaume I (Line 4).

- **Hotel Gótico,** Carrer Jaime I no. 14, 08002 Barcelona (tel. 3/
315-22-11). 70 rms. A/C TV TEL

Located on one of the Barri Gòtic's main arteries, the Gótico
is a notch below the Suizo when it comes to charm and is somewhat noisier, but it's still a solid choice in the heart of the medieval
city.

RATES: 6,300 ptas. ($53) single; 9,200 ptas. ($77) double.
Metro: Jaume I (Line 4).

- **Hotel Oriente,** Ramblas 45-47, 08002 Barcelona (tel. 3/302-
25-58). 150 rms. TEL

This 150-year-old hotel is conveniently located, but request a
room away from Las Ramblas for peace and quiet. The rooms are
comfortable, though rather dimly lit, and the baths are modern. Unlike most three-star hotels, the Oriente has a restaurant, a vestige of
the hotel's five-star days when Las Ramblas was Barcelona's most
prestigious neighborhood. Both the restaurant and the large, somewhat palatial TV/sitting room retain the grandiosity of those glory
days.

TES: 5,400 ptas. ($45) single; 8,900 ptas. ($74) double.
o: Liceu (Line 3).

Hotel Residencia Regina, Carrer Bergara 4, 08002 Barcelona (tel. 3/301-32-32). 103 rms. A/C MINIBAR TV TEL

Near Plaça Catalunya, this Best Western affiliate is a very comfortable choice at a moderate price. Its recently renovated rooms are quite large, though the baths are a bit small. Doubles on the street side have a balcony; doubles in the back have a small sitting area.

RATES: 6,400 ptas. ($53) single; 9,500 ptas. ($79) double. Prices higher during certain trade fairs. *Metro:* Catalunya (Line 1 or 3).

- **Hotel Mesón Castilla,** Carrer Valdonzella 5, 08001 Barcelona (tel. 3/318-21-82). 60 rms. TEL

From the outside this former apartment building near the Plaça Catalunya looks like a displaced Castillian structure. On the inside it's undergoing a complete renovation. To assure that you get one of the redone rooms, ask to stay on the fourth or fifth floor; the renovated rooms all have air conditioning. Each floor, though, has a pleasant sitting area, and the first floor has a large TV room with a beamed ceiling. The furnishings throughout are in the sturdy, stoic Castillian vernacular. The buffet breakfast is more substantial than the usual croissant and coffee.

Facilities: Parking on premises.

RATES (INCLUDING BREAKFAST): 5,400 ptas. ($45) single; 8,100 ptas. ($68) double. Rates higher in July and August and during trade fairs. *Metro:* Universitat (Line 1).

- **Hotel Montecarlo,** Rambla dels Estudis 124, 08002 Barcelona (tel. 3/317-58-00). 70 rms (plus new ones to be added during current renovation). A/C TV TEL

Beyond the Montecarlo's Felliniesque portal adorned with chandeliers and imposing statues awaits a certain mundane modernity, except for the baroque sitting room one flight up. The rooms are simple, clean, and comfortable. Those facing Las Ramblas have small balconies and double-glazed windows to dampen the noise.

Facilities: Parking on premises.

RATES: 5,100 ptas. ($43) single; 7,500 ptas. ($63) double; 8,700 ptas. ($73) triple; 9,450 ptas. ($79) quad. *Metro:* Liceu (Line 3).

- **Hotel Gaudí,** Carrer Nou de la Rambla 12, 08001 Barcelona (tel. 3/317-90-32). 71 rms. TEL

Across from Gaudí's Palau Güell, this hotel is rather quiet, but be cautious when returning late at night as it's just off Las Ramblas. The rooms have white floors and light-wood furnishings that make them bright and cheery; air conditioning is being added. Although it's a three-star property, it has a simple, pleasant restaurant primarily offering Continental fare.

RATES (INCLUDING BREAKFAST): 4,900 ptas. ($41) single; 7,100 ptas. ($59) double. *Metro:* Liceu (Line 3).

3. Budget Lodgings

• **Hotel Residencia Internacional,** Ramblas 78-80, 08002 Barcelona (tel. 3/302-25-66). 60 rms.

Popular with students, the Internacional offers a great location (across from the Liceu Theatre) and cleanliness, but not excessive comfort. Perhaps this will change after the planned renovation. All rooms have either a bath or a shower. Room 210 has an exceptionally large bath and a view of Las Ramblas. Also overlooking Las Ramblas is the large, friendly breakfast room by the reception area. Show this guidebook when you check in there and you'll get a 10% discount.

RATES (INCLUDING BREAKFAST AND IVA): 4,500 ptas. ($38) single; 6,800 ptas. ($57) double. Prices higher in August and during trade fairs. *Metro:* Liceu (Line 3).

• **Hotel Cataluña,** Carrer de Santa Anna 24, 08002 Barcelona (tel. 3/301-91-20). 40 rms. TEL

About a block east of the upper Ramblas, this spotless budget choice offers complete baths in all rooms (some with a truncated tub). Colorful rugs brighten the halls. The rooms are furnished simply, but everything is well maintained.

RATES (INCLUDING BREAKFAST AND IVA): 3,900 ptas. ($33) single; 6,700 ptas. ($56) double. *Metro:* Catalunya (Line 1 or 3).

• **Hotel Cortés,** Carrer de Santa Anna 25, 08002 Barcelona (tel. 3/317-91-12). 54 rms. TEL

Just off Las Ramblas, the Cortés is popular with American students on youth tours. All the rooms are clean and have modern tile baths.

RATES (INCLUDING BREAKFAST AND IVA): 3,750 ptas. ($31) single; 6,350 ptas. ($53) double. *Metro:* Catalunya (Line 1 or 3).

• **Hotel San Agustín,** Plaça San Agustín 3 (at Carrer Hospital), 08001 Barcelona (tel. 3/318-17-08). 78 rms (some with bath).

Close to Las Ramblas, but at a quiet remove, this was once a convent and has been a hotel for over 100 years now. It's currently being renovated; the redone rooms have gleaming white walls, rustic ceiling beams, and air conditioning. Highly unusual for a two-star hotel is the large, commendable restaurant offering daily fixed-price lunch and dinner menus with a choice of appetizers, entrées, and desserts. When the renovation is completed, this should prove to be one of the best of the budget choices in town.

RATES (INCLUDING BREAKFAST): 3,500 ptas. ($29); 5,300 ptas. ($44) double. *Metro:* Liceu (Line 3).

• **Hotel Pelayo,** Carrer de Pelai 9-1°.1ª, 08001 Barcelona (tel. 3/302-37-27). 15 rms. A/C TEL

If your idea of a traveler's bargain is a clean, comfortable room in a central location, you'll be happy here. Located between the Plaça Catalunya and the Plaça de la Universitat, this hotel is tucked away at the back of a vintage building and is a little tricky to find.

After you go through the large portal entrance and walk all the way to the rear, go up one flight of stairs to the elevator and press no. 1. The hotel's friendly reception area looks like somebody's living room and will dispel any doubts the recessed entrance may have raised. Flowers and plants everywhere give the place a very homey feeling. All rooms have baths (some with a truncated tub), and most rooms look out onto a courtyard. Some doubles offer a small sitting room.

Services: Laundry.

RATES: 2,200 ptas. ($18) single; 4,100 ptas. ($34) double with a double bed, 4,600 ptas. ($38) with two beds, 7,000 ptas. ($58) double occupied by four people. *Metro:* Catalunya (Line 1 or 3).

■ **Hotel Residencia Cosmos,** Carrer dels Escudillers 19, 08002 Barcelona (tel. 3/317-18-16). 67 rms (most with toilet and bath but some with shower only).

Located near the lower end of Las Ramblas, the Cosmos offers no-frills budget digs amid undecorated halls. The white walls of the rooms themselves, however, do much to brighten the clean but rather cramped quarters.

RATES (INCLUDING BREAKFAST): 2,460 ptas. ($21) single; 4,050 ptas. ($34) double. *Metro:* Drassanes (Line 3).

■ **Hotel Residencia Neutral,** Rambla de Catalunya 42, 08007 Barcelona (tel. 3/318-73-70). 28 rms (with varying degrees of in-room plumbing). TEL

A budget choice in a luxury area, the Neutral's entrance is one flight up. Colorful antique floor tiling helps brighten the high-ceilinged rooms furnished with assorted odds'n'ends. The rooms are small, but the breakfast room, with its impressive coffered ceiling, and the TV room, adjacent, are spacious.

RATES (INCLUDING IVA): 1,800 ptas. ($15) single; 2,900–3,500 ptas. ($24–$29) double, depending on the extent of the bathroom fittings. *Metro:* Catalunya (Line 1 or 3).

---

4. Apartment Accommodations

■ **La Equitativa,** Passeig de Gràcia 44 (at the corner of Consell de Cent), 08007 Barcelona (tel. 3/215-93-00). 42 tourist apartments (some air-conditioned).

An alternative for couples or families, these clean, spacious apartments in a prime Eixample location accommodate two to five people. Each comes with a fully equipped kitchen. The dormitory-style furnishings are strictly functional. Reception is on the fifth floor.

Services: Maid and laundry service.

RATES (INCLUDING IVA): 6,200–13,100 ptas. ($52–$109) from June to September, 5,900–12,500 ptas. ($49–$104) from October to May. *Metro:* Passeig de Gràcia (Line 3 or 4).

IV

BARCELONA DINING

1. VERY EXPENSIVE RESTAURANTS
2. MODERATE RESTAURANTS
3. BUDGET RESTAURANTS
4. DINING AROUND TOWN
5. SPECIALTY DINING

Catalan cuisine in all its diversity is the culinary highlight of Barcelona. Drawn from areas whose climate and topography run from the alpine in the Pyrenees to the Mediterranean along the coast, the Catalan kitchen employs a wide variety of fresh ingredients and is complemented by a similarly wide variety of regional wines. Typical dishes include *paella a la parellada,* with rice, fish, shellfish, chicken, and beef; *zarzuela,* a mixture of fish and shellfish in a rich sauce (some variations on this theme are *suquet de peix* and *caldereta marinera*); *escudella i carn d'olla,* chickpeas or beans stewed with different kinds of sausage, meatballs, chicken, and vegetables; *peus de porc,* or "pig's trotters," cooked in a rich sauce; and *faves,* broad beans stewed with *butifarra,* a tasty local sausage. Catalunya is also the land of mushrooms, with over 100 varieties of *setas* (the generic term for wild, gourmet mushrooms).

Cuisines from other areas of Spain, however, are also well represented in the city. And when it comes to foreign fare, Italian and French restaurants predominate, although there are a smattering of Middle Eastern and Asian offerings as well as a few vegetarian restaurants. Cafeterias and snack bars typically offer extensive and varied menus and a selection of economical *platos combinados* composed of meat, a potato and a vegetable, and usually a fried egg.

Many of the more prestigious restaurants around town have recently taken to charging a "cover" (*pan y cubierto*) of 100 to 200 ptas. (75¢ to $1.50) for bread and, it seems, the sheer privilege of eating there—a regrettable practice that appears to be spreading through all the ranks of Barcelona restaurants. Sometimes the menu lets you know it's coming, but sometimes it doesn't. Although restaurants are increasingly offering menus in English, this practice is not yet widespread. Those eateries most frequented by tourists, of course, have always done so, while the city's luxury restaurants have polyglot waiters to do the translating for you.

The Spanish eat later than Americans and other Europeans; most Barcelona restaurants are open from 1 to 4pm and 8pm to midnight. In deference to the growing influx of foreign businesspeople and tourists, however, more and more restaurants are keeping longer hours. For the purposes of this guide, entrées at a "very expensive" restaurant can be as high as 6,500 ptas. ($54.25); at a "moderate" restaurant, as high as 3,700 ptas. ($30.75) but usually a bit lower; and in a "budget" restaurant, as high as 1,500 ptas. ($12.50) but as low as 300 ptas. ($2.50). Where prices are indicated for "meals" in this chapter, they refer to an average three-course meal without wine. As with the hotels, service is usually included in the prices but IVA is *not*. Many restaurants offer very economical fixed-price three-course luncheon menus, including bread and house wine. At cafeterias, tapas bars, and other informal establishments, it often costs less to eat at the bar than at a table.

---

1. Very Expensive Restaurants

- **Restaurante Reno,** Tuset 27 (tel. 200-91-29). *Prices:* Entrées 1,600–6,500 ptas. ($13.50–$54.25); six-course degustation menu 5,500 ptas. ($45.75).

One of Barcelona's top restaurants, Reno is one of three Spanish restaurants (the other two are in Madrid) to be listed in the prestigious French *Traditions & Qualité* guide. Founded in 1954 by Antonio Juliá Rafecas, father of the current proprietors, its decor is fashionably contemporary with lots of wood, plants, and black-leather benches and chairs. The clientele is subdued and sophisticated. The china is Villeroy & Boch.

Chef-owner José Juliá Bertrán describes his cuisine as "rooted in Catalan but prepared in the French manner." Many of his dishes are a cross between the two cuisines, or common Catalan recipes spruced up for a night on the town. Although he abhors categories, he places his menu between the classical and the nouvelle because he believes in sauces that are light and subtle. The seasonal menu changes four times a year. For an appetizer, try the cold langostinos (prawns) from the Catalan region—they're succulent and sweet. As a main course, the pimientos con salsa negra (red peppers with a delicate black sauce based in squid's ink) or arroz con chipirones (a juicy rice dish with baby squid in a fish-broth–based sauce). Or try the distinctive solomillo (filet mignon) served with a sweet-and-sour sauce of honey and sherry vinegar. In the summer there's a salad of green beans topped with thinly sliced lobster and dressed with delicate olive oil that has been steeped with truffles for two weeks to give it a distinctively delicate flavor. The tartare de salmon is made of raw salmon with a pinch of smoked salmon (prepared in-house) and salmon roe. The extensive wine list embraces over 400 different vintners with the emphasis on Catalan and French wines, in keeping with the cuisine. A squadron of attentive waiters virtually makes a ritual of the meal.

Open: Sun–Fri 1–5pm (kitchen closes at 3:30pm) and 8:30pm–1am (kitchen closes at 11pm). *Closed:* Three weeks in Aug. *Reservations:* Imperative. CATALAN/FRENCH

- **El Dorado Petit,** Dolors Monserdá 51 (tel. 204-51-53). *Prices:* Entrées 1,800–6,500 ptas. ($15–$54.25); six-course degustation menu 5,200 ptas. ($43.25).

Perhaps the restaurant with the most inviting entranceway in all of Barcelona, El Dorado Petit is situated in the northern reaches of the city in a fin-de-siècle house that in its youth was a summer retreat from the heat of the city. The plain but gracious decor exudes a corresponding breeziness.

Owner Luis Cruañas characterizes the seasonal menu as "Mediterranean" since it is based on the finest and freshest ingredients the area has to offer. For starters, there's a shrimp salad with champagne vinegar, remarkable for the tenderness and sweetness of the shrimp brought in from Cruañas's home village on the Costa Brava. ("These are the best in the world," he says.) The menu is highly imaginative, with such dishes as canelones de cigalas a la crema de "russinyols" (canelones stuffed with prawns and topped with a wild-mushroom sauce) or raviolis stuffed with shrimp and Iranian caviar. There are also dishes built around baby squid and baby octopus. Also recommended is the San Pedro (a Mediterranean fish) baked with rosemary and served with a dry white wine sauce. Hard to resist is the tantalizing selection of unique ice creams, sorbets, and pastries.

Open: Mon–Sat 1–4pm and 9pm–midnight. *Closed:* Several weeks in Aug, Fri–Mon of Holy Week, and several days at Christmas. *Reservations:* Imperative. MEDITERRANEAN

- **Restaurant Quo Vadis,** Carrer del Carme 7 (tel. 302-40-72). *Prices:* Entrées 875–2,800 ptas. ($7.25–$23.50).

Quo Vadis was founded 34 years ago by the father of the current owner, Marti Forcada. The understated elegance of the polished-wood bar and dining areas have a men's-club feel about them. A single flower on each table adds a grace note of femininity. Lone travelers will be interested to know that there are some tables for one.

Located near the Boquería Market, Quo Vadis builds its meals around the day's prime produce. The menu is mainly Catalan with some representative dishes from other parts of Spain—for example, cochinillo tostado (suckling pig)—and more universal fare like grilled chateaubriand and chuletitas de cabrito lechal a la milanesa ("suckling lamb" chops). House specialties include a potpourri de setas (wild mushrooms sautéed with garlic and parsley) usually available from September to January, filete de toro (yes, that's right, from the bull), and espaldita de cabrito asado (roasted lamb's back). Look for game in the fall.

Open: Mon–Sat 1:15–4pm and 8:30–11:30pm. *Closed:* Holidays and Aug. *Reservations:* Advised. CATALAN/CONTINENTAL

- **Orotava,** Carrer de Consell de Cent 335 (tel. 302-31-28). *Prices:* Meals begin at 6,000 ptas. ($50).

This Eixample restaurant has character—both in its decor and in the ingratiating exuberance of its owner, José María Luna. Celebrating its 60th anniversary, it is the successful legacy of Luna's father. The Madame Sousatzka decor, laden with brocades and lamps trailing strung beads or glass crystals, is studded with several original Miró paintings dedicated to the restaurant and its honored owners. In the downstairs dining area several Picasso ceramics are on casual display.

Billing itself as "the small restaurant for the grand gourmet," Orotava has an ample menu concentrating on seafood and game. Luna himself makes a point of greeting everyone and pointing out what he considers particularly good that day. Standard dishes include partridge with wild mushrooms and venison in a delicate cream sauce, served with raspberry and apple marmalades. Luna is especially proud of his "Cobonoff," a kind of seafood tartare he invented and calls "a symphony of seafood that is a guaranteed aphrodisiac." It blends seven kinds of fish and is topped with caviar and served with whole-wheat bread. The vieira al cava (scallops with a dash of sparkling cava wine) is another culinary trademark, as is the baby octopuses prepared with garlic and parsley that were once served to Prince Juan Carlos before he became king of Spain. On Tuesday guests are treated to a magic show during dinner and on Friday and Saturday to live piano music (no additional charge).

Open: Mon–Sat 1–4pm and 8pm–midnight. *Reservations:* Imperative. SEAFOOD/GAME

- **Botafumeiro,** Gran de Gràcia 81 (tel. 218-42-30). *Prices:* Meals begin at 5,000 ptas. ($41.75); five-course degustation menu 3,000 ptas. ($25).

Botafumeiro, housed in a modernist building of the late 19th century, is truly a contender for best seafood restaurant in the land. Among its repeat clientele is the King of Spain. As you enter, you can appraise the fresh marine life, flown in primarily from Galicia, in northern Spain. An appropriate nautical decor prevails, and patrons may eat at the long wooden bar (complete with tablecloth) if they wish. In the restaurant proper, the pink linen tablecloths and napkins are imported from France.

Chef-owner Moncho Neira is from Galicia, and this is his fifth successful restaurant in the city. The lobsters, shrimp, mussels, and other assorted shellfish are usually served steamed, boiled, or grilled. "In preparing mariscos," says Neira, "you need simple recipes that permit the full realization of their flavor without masking it in any way." Some of the fish, however, do come with their own delicate sauces, such as the mero al champagne (grouper in champagne) and the lubina a la sidra (sea bass in cider sauce). The menu is in half a dozen languages.

Open: Tues–Sat 1pm–1am and Sun lunch. *Closed:* Holy Week and Aug. *Reservations:* Imperative. SEAFOOD

- **La Odisea,** Carrer Copons 7 (tel. 302-36-92). *Prices:* Meals average 4,500 ptas. ($37.50); degustation menu 4,600 ptas. ($38.25).

As its name suggests, La Odisea is an adventure. Chef Antonio Ferre Taratiel is also a part-time poet, and the restaurant's decor is sophisticatedly bohemian—the attractive contemporary art on the walls is the work of talented friends. At lunch, businesspeople abound; at dinner, numerous artists and writers.

A native of Aragón, Taratiel carefully studied Catalan cuisine to create a menu that he calls "Mediterranean." Though the offerings vary, some standard entrées include the crema de cangrejos (cream of crab) appetizer, the solomillo villetes con hortalizas al Calvados (steak filet with vegetables in a Calvados sauce), and the hígado de pato con manzana (duck liver with apple). The extensive wine list includes a large selection of regional cavas (sparkling wines) and French champagnes, as well as numerous Rioja reds.

Open: Mon–Fri 1:30–4pm and 9pm–midnight, Sat 9pm–midnight. *Closed:* Holidays, and Aug. *Reservations:* Advised. MEDITERRANEAN

- **Azulete,** Via Augusta 281 (tel. 203-59-43). *Prices:* Meals average 5,000 ptas. ($41.75).

A long taxi ride from the center of town, Azulete attracts a crowd as breezy and spirited as the place itself, which features a glass-enclosed garden with exuberant greenery adjacent to a restored beaux arts house whose ground-level salon is now an elegant bar.

Chef Victoria Roqué has assembled a diverse nouvelle menu that draws from various cooking traditions, among them French and Chinese. A salad of raw lubina (sea bass) with a delicate mustard sauce is a refreshing starter on a summer evening, as are the cold cream-of-spider-crab soup, the sliced lobster-and-monkfish salad with tomato sauce seasoned with thyme, and the artichokes stuffed with crab. As a main course, you might want to try the traditional Catalan stewed rabbit with butifarra, the veal with wild mushrooms, the monkfish in champagne sauce, or if you're adventurous, the Peking-style lamb brains. A selection of sorbets and fruit desserts such as baked apple with honey ice cream, figs with honey-and-raspberry sauce, and strawberries tops off the meal.

Open: Mon–Fri 1:30–3:30pm and 9–11:30pm, Sat 9–11:30pm. *Closed:* Aug 1–15. *Reservations:* Essential. ECLECTIC

- **Restaurant Passadis del Pep,** Plaça del Palau 2 (tel. 310-10-21). *Prices:* Meals average 6,500 ptas. ($54).

No sign indicates the presence of this "insider's" restaurant at the end of a rather run-down corridor leading off a large portal. Located in the port area, Passadis del Pep is small with a decor devoid of pretentious frills. The lack of fanfare extends to the menu and wine list as well—there are none. Both at lunch and dinner you are simply presented with that day's offering of fine, fresh fish and seafood, and there is never a doubt that it will be superb. The selection of wines is ample and equally reliable.

Open: Mon–Sat 1:30–3:30pm and 9:30–11pm. *Closed:* Holidays, and sometimes in Aug. *Reservations:* Obligatory. SEAFOOD

---

2. Moderate Restaurants

▪ **Los Caracoles,** Carrer dels Escudellers 14 (tel. 302-31-85). *Prices:* Meals average 1,700 ptas. ($14.25).

Los Caracoles is to Barcelona restaurants what Las Ramblas is to Barcelona sights—a must for the visitor. Located just off the Ramblas, it is full of the kind of character that comes only with time. Run by the same family since it was established in 1835 as a bodega selling wine—the original barrels are part of the current decor—and snails (caracoles), it evolved into a restaurant. Outside, you'll see chicken roasting over a wood fire; as you enter you'll pass through the kitchen where large pots simmer with snails and mussels. Among the patrons whose photos line the walls are John Wayne, President Nixon, Dalí, Christian Dior, and Cole Porter.

The snails and spit-roasted chicken are, of course, the house specialties. But there is much, much more, and it's all good.

Open: Daily 1pm–midnight. SPANISH

▪ **Restaurant 7 Portes,** Passeig de Isabel II no. 14 (tel. 319-30-33). *Prices:* Meals average 2,700 ptas. ($22.50).

Founded in 1836, this Barcelona institution buzzes at midday with brokers from the nearby stock exchange; at night, you'll find just about everybody else. It's a classic place, complete with high ceilings and waiters wearing the long, white aprons of yore.

Paella in several variations (with rabbit, with sardines, spicy) is the specialty of the house, but the extensive menu goes on to offer a broad selection of meat and fish dishes as well. The wine list contains a healthy sampling of regional cavas.

Open: Daily 1pm–1am. *Reservations:* Recommended if you're in a hurry. SPANISH

▪ **Cafè de L'Academia,** Carrer Lledó 1 (Plaça Sant Just) (tel. 315-00-26). *Prices:* Salads 475–600 ptas. ($4–$5); entrées 450–1,450 ptas. ($3.75–$12).

Off a quiet plaza in the Barri Gòtic, ensconced within Gothic walls of amber stone, L'Academia is very popular with the government officials who work nearby. Although the menu is exclusively in Catalan, it's well worth struggling with the language to savor the low-priced gourmet fare.

The empredat de fesolets amb tonyina (white-bean-and-tuna salad) and pollastre de pagés (a typical Catalan dish of roast chicken with prunes and pine nuts) are highly recommended. The luscious desserts are on tempting display. Since the place has only about a dozen tables, reservations are strongly recommended, although unannounced patrons are happily accommodated with place settings at the bar.

Open: Mon–Fri 8am–4pm. *Closed:* Aug. *Reservations:* Strongly recommended. CATALAN

■ **Mordisco,** Carrer de Roselló 265, at the corner of Passeig de Gràcia (tel. 218-33-14). *Prices:* Salads 400–650 ptas. ($3.25–$5.50); main dishes 450–1,450 ptas. ($3.75–$12).

Mordisco's decor of rust-yellow walls and avant-garde art seems slightly tongue-in-chic. Two long, narrow tables accommodate singles who don't mind dining in the company of strangers. The management considers its cuisine "capricious" and states plainly on its calling card that it's not in the Michelin guide.

Specialties include a variety of stuffed rolls—hot and cold—and local bread toasted with tomato and topped with sausage, cheese, or ham. Beyond that, there's the usual roundup of meat entrées. Great for off-hour snacking.

Open: Mon–Sat 8:30am–2am (kitchen closes at 1:30am). SPANISH

■ **El Gran Colmado,** Carrer de Consell de Cent 318 (tel. 302-26-26). *Prices:* Entrées 700–2,100 ptas. ($5.75–$17.50).

Colmado is Catalan for grocery store, and in part that's what this is. The other part is a very fine restaurant—the tables are set in the grocery store aisles. The Catalan chef seemingly invents new dishes daily, but all are firmly rooted in the regional culinary traditions. A long, oval table seating more than a dozen people is popular with single diners who don't wish to eat alone. If you're interested in a picnic, purchase your provisions here and head for the Parc de la Ciutadella.

Open: Mon–Sat 1:30–4pm and 7pm–midnight for meals; Mon–Sat 10am–12:30am for grocery shopping. *Closed:* Holidays. CONTEMPORARY CATALAN

■ **Flash-Flash,** La Granada del Penedés 25 (tel. 237-09-90). *Prices:* tortillas 290–885 ptas. ($2.50–$7.50); main dishes 495–1,650 ptas. ($4.25–$13.75).

A trendy spot where the Barcelona elite meet to grab an informal bite, Flash-Flash is in the business end of town. Primarily this is a *tortillería,* a restaurant specializing in omelets. You can have yours with potatoes ("a la española"), beans, capers, butifarra (Catalonian sausage), sweetbreads, all manner of vegetables, shrimp, cod, tuna, or various combinations thereof. Team your choice with a salad for a perfect light meal. Heartier eaters can select among steak, veal, hamburgers, and half a dozen daily specials.

Open: Daily 1:30–5pm and 8:30pm–1:30am. CATALAN

■ **Durán Durán,** Alfonso XII no. 39-41 (tel. 201-35-13). *Prices:* Appetizers 550–1,840 ptas. ($4.50–$15.25); main dishes 995–2,150 ptas. ($8.25–$18).

Slightly off the beaten track, Durán Durán is worth seeking out. Though the owner, Señor Durán, dislikes culinary labels, he characterizes his menu as Catalan-French (although there are some Italian overtones).

House specialties are amanida de salmó fumat i poma (smoked salmon and apple salad), timbal d'alberginies, panses, pinyons i crema de pebrot (a savory pastry with eggplant, raisins, pine nuts, and sweet-pepper sauce), homemade duck pâté, veal filet with duck-liver pâté, magret of duck with sweet-and-sour figs, and roast leg of lamb. Durán is especially proud of the botifarra dolça amb allioli de codonys (sweet Catalan sausage with quince allioli), a traditional Catalan dish rarely found in Barcelona. When this sausage is cooked, the sugar caramelizes, making for a crispy sweet entrée. Durán Durán is also one of the few Barcelona restaurants to offer a selection of gourmet coffee and tea.

Open: Mon–Sat 1–4pm and 9–11:30pm. *Closed:* Holidays and Aug. CATALAN

• **Paradis Barcelona,** Passeig Manuel Girona 7 (tel. 203-76-37). *Prices:* Buffet 1,975 ptas. ($16.50) Mon–Sat and 2,450 ptas. ($20.50) Sun and holidays; appetizers 550–1,600 ptas. ($4.50–$13.25); main dishes 850–3,600 ptas. ($7–$30).

Located in a modern building near the Hotel Princesa Sofia, Paradis Barcelona offers both buffet dining in a gracious, cafeteria-like setting and à la carte service in the elegant intimacy of its small adjoining restaurant. The outstanding buffet, where the meat of your choice is grilled before your eyes, runs the full gamut from salads to desserts. The presentation and quality of the fare are excellent. Specialties in the à la carte restaurant include pimientos del piquillo rellenos con brandada (roasted red peppers stuffed with cod), arroz negro con chipirones y gambas (rice with shrimp and baby squid in its own ink), and merluza a la sidra (hake in a cider sauce).

In 1989 Paradis Barcelona opened its first foreign outpost, in New York at 145 E. 50th St. (tel. 212/754-3333), where the same care is taken with the fine Catalan cuisine and the stylish decor largely imported from Catalonia.

Open: Mon–Sat 1–4pm and 8–11:30pm, Sun 1–4pm. *Closed:* Christmas Eve. CATALAN

• **Brasserie Flo Restaurante,** Carrer Junqueres 10 (tel. 317-80-37). *Prices:* Main dishes 900–3250 ptas. ($7.50–$27).

Near the Palau de la Música and not far from the Catedral, a passage flanked with Spanish tiles leads to a bit of Paris at the Brasserie Flo. The wooden floor, plants, statues and busts, and vintage French posters and photos conspire to create a bistro ambience. Specialties are duck pâté and choucroûte.

Open: Daily 1–4:30pm and 8pm–1am. FRENCH

• **Giardinetto Notte,** La Granada del Penedés 22 (tel. 218-75-36). *Prices:* Appetizers 575–1,500 ptas. ($4.75–$12.50); main dishes 950–1,875 ptas. ($8–$15.50).

This "night garden" is intimately lit and features lots of wood and dark-green walls and upholstery. The menu is a blend of Catalan, traditional Spanish, and Italian influences. Pasta dishes include tagliatelle with tuna, tomato, capers, olives, and oregano. The risotto with crab and shrimp and the carpaccio are good too.

Open: Mon–Sat 8pm–3am. *Closed:* Aug. ITALIAN

• **Network,** Avinguda Diagonal 616 (tel. 201-72-38). *Prices:* Main dishes 700–1,800 ptas. ($5.75–$15).

Network is a trendy spot that bills its fare as "cocina mundana" (literally, worldly cuisine). Those who read Spanish will enjoy the wry, self-directed humor sprinkled throughout the menu. Rock music permeates the cavelike atmosphere punctuated with TVs at each table and several more suspended over the large central bar. Dishes include tempura, guacamole and shrimp, German potato salad, chicken curry salad, burgers, barbecued chicken, fettuccine, filet mignon, spareribs, chicken wings, and carpaccio.

Downstairs are a bar and billiard tables. Rather quiet at lunch, Network gains momentum as the night goes on.

Open: Daily 1–4pm and 7:30pm–2am. CONTINENTAL

• **Tramonti 1980,** Avinguda Diagonal 501, across the street from Network (tel. 410-15-35). *Prices:* Pastas 600–1,200 ptas. ($5–$10); main dishes 900–2,000 ptas. ($7.50–$16.50).

Named after the Italian village where the owner, Giuliano Lombardo, and his brother Franco, the chef, hail from, this is one of the best Italian choices in the city. White wrought-iron furnishings impart an outdoorsy feel to the dining area. The clientele includes many artists and athletes, and most of the eccentric knickknacks and works of art on display are gifts from patrons. The spaghetti with sepia en su tinta (cuttlefish in its own ink) is a hybrid Italian-Catalan dish. There is also a choice of risotti.

Adjacent to the bar is a small sitting area perfect for a pre-dinner drink accompanied by a small plate of imported parmesan cheese.

Open: Daily 1–4pm and 9–11pm. *Closed:* Christmas Day. ITALIAN

• **Restaurant Llivia,** Carrer Copons 2 (tel. 318-10-78). *Prices:* Main dishes 750–2,200 ptas. ($6.25–$18.25).

Although both the menu and the wine list are limited, the selections are a good value for the money. And be sure to ask about the daily market-fresh specials. The navajas a la plancha (grilled razor clams) in a delicate garlic-butter sauce and the brocheta de solomillo (filet mignon shish kebab) are excellent. Anchoas (anchovies) are a Catalan specialty and are especially good here. Downstairs is a small tapas bar.

Open: Mon–Sat 1–4pm in summer, also 8–11pm in winter. *Closed:* Holidays. CATALAN

• **Restaurante El Cus/Cús,** Plaça Cardona 4 (tel. 201-98-67). *Prices:* Main dishes 650–2,400 ptas. ($5.50–$20).

Chef-owner Omar Difallah, a native of Algiers, has created a Moorish outpost in Barcelona with colorful blue, white, and yellow tiles and woven rugs, leather cushions, brassware, photos, and Algerian art. Couscous served with vegetables or a selection of meats is the main attraction, seconded by grilled meats.

Open: Tues–Sun 1:30–3:30pm and 8:30pm–midnight. NORTH AFRICAN

■ **Restaurant Font del Gat,** Passeig Santa Madrona s/n (no street number), Montjuïc (tel. 424-02-24). *Prices:* Main dishes 1,000–3,000 ptas. ($8.25–$25).

Housed in a 100-year-old building built by Puig i Cadafalch, the Font del Gat purveys Catalan and Continental cuisine. Posted at the doorway is an extensive "standard" menu (in Spanish only); a separate menu with English translations offers seasonal dishes. For an appetizer, try the habas a la catalana (Catalan beans). As a main course, the zarzuela is a good choice, or perhaps sole prepared as you like it. For a special treat, in season, consider the rabbit ampurdan style, grilled with white beans.

Note: If you don't have a car, you'll have to call for a taxi to take you back to the center of town, as taxis don't cruise the Montjuïc area. The nearest bus stop is also quite a hike.

Open: Daily 1–4pm and 6–9pm. CATALAN/CONTINENTAL

■ **Restaurante El Turia,** Carrer Petxina 7 (tel. 317-95-09). *Prices:* Main dishes 300–1,800 ptas. ($2.50–$15).

Tucked away on a narrow street off Las Ramblas, this small, cozy restaurant is very rustic with its low, beamed ceiling, white-washed walls, and decorative ceramics.

The cuisine is Spanish with such notable Catalan influences as the esqueixada de bacalao (an appetizer composed of raw codfish, black olives, and hard-boiled eggs dressed with olive oil and salt), the conejo al allioli (rabbit with a garlic mayonnaise), or the conejo al escabeche (rabbit marinated in vinegar and spices). The flan is ample and light.

Open: Mon–Sat 1–4:30pm and 8:30–11:30pm. SPANISH/CATALAN

■ **Restaurant Can Pescallunes,** Carrer Magdalenes 23 (tel. 318-54-83). *Prices:* Meals average 3,000 ptas. ($25).

The French bistro decor of Can Pescallunes echoes the French accents of its otherwise largely Catalan menu. (The menu, by the way, is available in English.) The brandada de bacalao (puréed cod-fish with raisins and pine nuts), steak tartare, and jarret de ternera con setas (veal stew with wild mushrooms) are some of the dishes available year round. Other house specialties include monkfish with clams and tomatoes, chateaubriand with béarnaise sauce, sole cooked in cider, and dessert crêpes with Cointreau.

Open: Mon–Sat 1–3:30pm and 8:30–10:30pm. *Closed:* Sat in June and July, holidays, and Aug. CATALAN/FRENCH

■ **Roig Robi,** Séneca 20 (tel. 218-92-22). *Prices:* Appetizers 750–1,850 ptas. ($6.25–$15.50); main dishes 1,450–2,650 ptas. ($12–$22).

Tucked away on an afterthought of an alleyway north of Avinguda Diagonal, Roig Robi is a fine place to dine. Chef-owner Mercé Navarro draws from the Catalan and French kitchens—and even more so from her own imagination—to offer a menu commensurate with the season.

A popular favorite is the merluza al Roig Robi (hake prepared with a tomato sauce and topped with lightly fried zucchini strips).

For an appetizer, try the fideos "rossos" con almejas (thin noodles fried and cooked in savory fish broth and served dry with small clams). Another fine appetizer that is a variation of the traditional Catalan esqueixada is the salad of raw codfish and pasta. All the desserts are homemade.

Open: Mon–Sat 1:30–4pm and 9–11:30pm. *Closed:* Holidays, Christmas and New Year's weeks, Holy Week, and one week in Aug. CATALAN/FRENCH

- **Escola de Restauració i Hostalatge Barcelona,** Carrer Muntaner 70-72 (tel. 253-29-03). *Prices:* Meals average 3,000 ptas. ($25).

A nonprofit organization that is a joint effort of the city's hotel and restaurant guilds, the Escola runs this friendly, modern, moderate-size restaurant as a training ground for the chefs, bartenders, waiters, and sommeliers of tomorrow. Here these professionals-to-be practice what they have already learned very well, carefully supervised by the professors. Behind the restaurant are the actual classrooms, where the students study their respective arts for three years.

The menu is seasonal: in the summer it includes such dishes as sopa frappe de mar i muntanya (a gazpacho enriched with seafood) and macedonia de mars sobre salsa d'eriço (a seafood medley over sea-urchin sauce); in winter and fall, look for game, such as venison, rabbit, and partridge; in spring, the freshest of vegetables. Even the breads and desserts—including the ice cream—are made here.

Open: Mon–Fri 1:30–3pm and 9–11pm. *Closed:* Aug. CATALAN

- **Reial Club Marítim de Barcelona,** Moll d'Espanya s/n (no street number) (tel. 315-02-56). *Prices:* Appetizers 725–1,800 ptas. ($6–$15); main dishes 1,400–3,700 ptas. ($11.50–$30.75).

You must take a taxi to this restaurant located at the end of a pier next to the nautical club. Despite its location, it attracts lots of businesspeople at lunchtime. But then again, it's always worth going out of your way for a good meal with a fine view, and this is the only restaurant open to the public with a view of the harbor, the Columbus monument, and lots of luxurious yachts.

The restaurant offers an abbreviated standard menu of grilled fish and meats and an extensive daily menu that is market fresh. The innovative dishes are grounded in the Catalan kitchen but have a nouvelle twist—the prawn flan with tarragon vinaigrette is a tasty example. After the meal, sample the coffee of the month.

Open: Tues–Sat 1:30–4pm and 9–11:30pm, Sun 1:30–4pm. *Closed:* Aug. NOUVELLE CATALAN

- **La Perla Nera,** Via Laietana 32-34 (tel. 310-56-46). *Prices:* Pizzas under 1,000 pesetas ($8.25); main dishes up to 2,000 ($16.50).

Imagine a rustic Italian trattoria installed in a modern cafeteria and you have a good idea of La Perla Nera. Its specialty is pizza prepared in a wood-burning oven. The standard array of pasta dishes are offered as well. Both the owner and the chef are Italian.

Open: Daily 1–4pm and 8–11pm. *Closed:* several days at Christmas. ITALIAN

3. Budget Restaurants

- **Mas i Mas Cafè,** Carrer de Córsega 300 (tel. 237-57-31). *Prices:* 875–1,500 ptas. ($7.25–$12.50).

Right off the Rambla de Catalunya, this is a simple, pleasant, friendly spot for a pick-me-up snack or inexpensive meal. Wooden tables and chairs flank a long bar trimmed with wood. Tapas include assorted tortillas and salads running from 150 to 250 ptas. ($1.25 to $2) per plate. At lunch there is a daily menu for 875 ptas. ($7.25) plus an à la carte selection of dishes with Italian, Basque, and French accents. The dinner menu features an additional dozen or so daily specials.

Open: Mon–Fri 7am–2am, Sat–Sun and holidays 6am–2am; lunch is 1–4:30pm, and dinner, 9pm–1:30am. SPANISH

- **Henry J. Bean's Bar and Grill,** La Granada del Penedés 14-16 (tel. 218-29-98). *Prices:* 600–1,400 ptas. ($5–$11.50).

Step right up and see a culinary culture warp—an Englishman's idea of an American bar and grill in the heart of Barcelona. The atmosphere is English pub, the food American fast, and the clientele multinational and lively. Celebrity photos and assorted American posters and ads from the 1950s grace the walls. At the bar they serve Budweiser and American tapas (nachos, potato skins, garlic bread, and breaded mushrooms). During the 7-to-9pm happy hour, drinks and tapas are half price. The salad bar—a rare find in Spain—offers less variety than Americans are used to, but Henry J.'s hamburguesa super (cheeseburger with french fries), barbecued ribs with cole slaw and french fries, and spicy chili con carne will make you feel at home. Desserts include mud pie, pecan pie, and cheesecake.

Open: Mon–Thurs 12:30pm–1am, Fri–Sat and holidays 12:30pm–1:30am. AMERICAN

- **Moka Restaurant Cafeteria,** Ramblas 126 (tel. 302-68-86). *Prices:* 450–1,400 ptas. ($3.75–$11.50).

This clean, airy, well-lit place features salads, pizzas, pastas, and platos combinados. Regular entrées cover the full range of fish and meats. The menu of the day costs 725 ptas. ($6), including bread and wine.

Open: Sun–Fri 8am–1:30am, Sat 8am–2pm (Christmas Day 7pm–1:30am). CONTINENTAL

- **Zi Teresa,** Infanta Carlota 155 (tel. 410-27-04). *Prices:* 600–1,500 ptas. ($5–$12.50).

Pastas and individual-size, thin, crispy pizzas in 18 varieties are the culinary mainstays here, but there is also a selection of fish and meat entrées. Soccer photos line the wall. It's a good place to grab a quick bite.

Open: Daily 1–4pm and 8pm–midnight. ITALIAN

- **Can Tripes,** Carrer Sagues 16 (tel. 200-85-40). *Prices:* 350–995 ptas. ($3–$8.25).

This super-budget bet is the place to go for mom's cooking Catalan style. Quaintly decorated with decorative tiles and plaid tablecloths, it's rustic and friendly. The savory escudella is a cross between soup and stew with garbanzos, beans, and potatoes.

Open: Daily 1pm–midnight (lunch served 1–4pm and dinner 9–11pm). *Closed:* Holy Thursday, Good Friday, and Dec 25–26. SPANISH/CATALAN

■ **Self Naturista,** Carrer de Santa Anna 11-15 (tel. 318-23-88). *Prices:* 300–1,000 ptas. ($2.50–$8.25).

Off the upper Ramblas, this self-service vegetarian restaurant is extremely cheap and extremely good. The ample selection of salads, main courses, and desserts varies daily, and there is a healthy choice of fresh fruit juices. Seating is McDonald's style. The daily fixed-price menu is only 495 ptas. ($4).

Open: Mon–Sat 11:30am–10pm. *Closed:* Holidays. VEGETARIAN

■ **Restaurante Egipte,** Jerusalem 3 (tel. 317-30-33). *Prices:* 450–1,500 ptas. ($3.75–$12.50).

Despite this restaurant's name, the cuisine is primarily Spanish and Catalan, and it's the closest thing to fast food in a true restaurant setting that I've come across. It's also a very good value. Because of its popularity, however, the service is somewhat impatient. At lunch there is a daily menu with a choice of appetizers and main courses for 645 ptas. ($5.50). The gazpacho and chicken with mustard-herb sauce are very good. Downstairs, the tables for two are old sewing-machine bases topped with marble. Upstairs, at the larger tables, the ambience is a bit more intimate.

Open: Mon–Sat 1–4pm and 8:30pm–12:30am. *Closed:* Holidays, and Mon in July and Aug. CATALAN/SPANISH

■ **Ca La Maria Restaurant,** Carrer dels Tallers 76 bis (tel. 318-89-93). *Prices:* 875–1,200 ptas. ($7.25–$10).

Colorful tiles and wood decorate the entrance of this eatery near the Plaça de la Universitat. A great value for its combination of fine food and pleasant ambience, Ca La Maria features meat and fish dishes that are primarily Catalan. As there are only 18 tables, it's wise to make a reservation.

Open: Tues–Sat 1:30–4pm and 8:30–11pm, Sun 1:30–4pm. *Closed:* Aug. *Reservations:* Advised. CATALAN

■ **Govinda,** Plaça Villa de Madrid 4-5 (tel. 318-77-29). *Prices:* 390–1,750 ptas. ($3.25–$14.50).

Located in a quiet plaza east of the upper Ramblas, this rather curious restaurant is strictly vegetarian and largely Indian, but also has on its menu an enchilada and numerous pizzas. The fixed-price luncheon menu at 690 ptas. ($5.75) is Spanish, however. The house specialty is the thali, a round tray with various Indian dishes that constitute a meal. Other fine features include a very appetizing salad bar, a selection of Indian breads and desserts, and fresh fruit and vegetable juices.

Open: Mon–Sat 12:30–4pm and 8:30pm–midnight. *Closed:* Most of Aug. INDIAN/VEGETARIAN

4. Dining Around Town

AT LA BOQUERÍA

It's only fitting that in this fine market, along Las Ramblas near the Gran Teatre del Liceu, there should be two fine Barcelona eateries.

One is **Bar Pinocho** (tel. 317-17-31). As you enter the market, take a right at Frutos Secos Morilla and it's right there. There is no sign—just a picture of Pinocchio. There is also no menu. The owner, Juanito, will gladly let you sample what's on the stove conjured from the abundant fresh ingredients all around. Even a simple amanida (salad) is a treat here. As there is only room for eight on the counterside stools, you'll probably have to eat and run. Meals average under 1,000 ptas. ($8.25). This is also a good place to come for breakfast.

Open Monday through Saturday from 6am to 6pm. Closed holidays and the first two weeks in August.

The second market eatery is **Restaurante Garduña,** Carrer Morera 17-19 (tel. 302-43-23), located at the back of the market. At the entrance is a tapas bar. Inside, a casual rusticity prevails, with half a dozen tables with checkered tablecloths downstairs and two more formal dining rooms upstairs. Downstairs the walls are filled with autographed photos of satisfied celebrity customers. The menu includes a selection of grilled seafood and over a dozen daily specials—again, all is market-fresh. There is also a sampling of rice and pasta dishes, as well as a respectable wine list. Meals average 1,800 ptas. ($15).

Open Monday through Saturday from 1 to 4pm and 8pm to midnight.

ON THE MOLL DE LA FUSTA

The Moll de la Fusta is a pier where formerly they loaded and unloaded wood (*fusta*). Now it's a waterfront promenade with a choice of eateries.

Most notable among them is **Gambrinus** (tel. 310-55-77), at the eastern end. You can't miss it—just look for the wavy roof topped by the giant prawn designed by Olympic-mascot creator Xavier Mariscal. Although advertised as a place to enjoy tapes marines (seafood tapas), this is more of a restaurant than a tapas bar. In the summer you can eat al fresco in the shadow of hand-painted umbrellas. In the winter you must limit yourself to the indoor restaurant whose bar resembles the prow of a ship complete with a plastic "smokestack." The cuisine is principally Catalan. English-language menus are available. For starters, try the toasted bread with tomato and cured ham for 750 ptas. ($6.25), half a dozen oysters for 1,200 ptas. ($10), or one of the cold salads, such as octopus, seafood, or smoked salmon, for about 600 ptas. ($5). Entrées run to 2,800 ptas. ($23.25) for an assorted fish platter or paella for two. You can also come here just to sit and have a drink by the sea. It's open daily in summer from noon to 3am, with the kitchen operating from noon to 4:30pm and 8pm to 2:30am; in winter, from noon to 4:30pm and 8pm to 1am.

Also along the waterfront is the moderately priced, more informal **Blau Mari** (tel. 310-10-15), owned by the proprietors of Roig Robi (mentioned previously). The emphasis here is on seafood tapas, oysters, and rice dishes. Open in summer daily from 11:30am to 2am and in winter from 1 to 5pm and 9pm to midnight.

Distrito, the bar next door, offers croissants and pizzas. It's open daily from 11:30am to 2am.

IN BARCELONETA

The Passeig Nacional and the Passeig Maritim, along the beach, are lined largely with mediocre restaurants, some of which aggressively solicit your patronage. Natives throng here on Sunday in summer to swim and sunbathe. If you're at the beach and want to have lunch, you can enjoy a meal at one of the restaurants with tables right on the beach—among them, El Salomete, La Gaviota, and Casa Paulino.

IN EL CORTE INGLÉS

El Corte Inglés, the large department store in Plaça Catalunya, offers an extensive and appetizing luncheon buffet for 2,075 ptas. ($17.25) in its ninth-floor cafeteria Monday through Saturday from 12:30 to 4pm. An added treat is the view of the city—in summer you can eat on the outdoor terrace. There is also counter service for snacks, drinks, and sandwiches. More formal dining is offered in the adjacent Spanish restaurant, Las Trebedes (sorry, no view), open from 1 to 4pm, where meals average about 3,500 ptas. ($29.25).

---

5. Specialty Dining

FOR TAPAS

- **Bar Naviera,** Ramblas Canaletas 12 (tel. 301-92-28).

This place near Plaça Catalunya offers a wide selection of tapas from 300 to 600 ptas. ($2.50 to $5) and *raciones* (slightly larger portions) for 850 to 1,600 ptas. ($7 to $13.25). The shellfish tapas are especially good; try the three varieties of pulpo (octopus) dishes.

Open: Daily 8:30am–1:30am.

- **El Xampanyet,** Carrer Montcada 22 (tel. 319-70-03).

This small, very inexpensive place near the Picasso Museum serves a sparkling wine, from which it gets its name, and specializes in a variety of seafood tapas from various parts of Spain.

Open: Tues–Sat noon–4pm and 6:30–11:30pm, Sun noon–4pm. *Closed:* Aug.

- **Alt Heidelberg,** Ronda Universitat 5 (tel. 318-10-32).

Near Plaça de la Universitat, this tapas bar/restaurant is quite popular and rightly so—its food is good and very reasonable. There is an extensive selection of tapas for under 400 ptas. ($3.25), and a large selection of sandwiches, including hamburgers and hot dogs (known here as "frankfurt"). As the name suggests, the emphasis is on German specialties, such as Bratwurst, German salads, and choucroûte (sauerkraut) with bacon, sausage, and potatoes. The choice of beers includes Guinness.

Open: Daily 8:30am–2am.

■ **Cervesería José Luis,** Avinguda Diagonal 520 (tel. 200-83-12).

If you don't mind paying as much for tapas as some people pay for a meal, you'll probably appreciate the sophistication of this place where you can readily pick from the display of tempting tapas lining the blond-wood bar. A glass of cava and a small slice of bread topped with cured ham cost me 600 ptas. ($5), but the quality is first-rate. Understandably, José Luis attracts the same kind of upscale crowd here as do its counterparts in Madrid and Seville.

Open: Mon–Fri 8:30am–1am, Sat–Sun noon–1am.

■ **Nou Celler,** Carrer de la Princesa 16 (tel. 319-90-24).

This is a typical tasca with wine barrels and wooden tables seasoned with carved graffiti. It offers hot sandwiches, potato salad, sautéed mushrooms, squid, meatballs, mussels, and other assorted tapas at its bar and restaurant tables (where prices are slightly higher). Tapas average about 300 ptas. ($2.50) a plate.

Open: Mon–Fri 8am–9pm, Sun 8am–4pm. *Closed:* End of June to mid-July.

■ **El Bodegón,** Carrer de Mallorca 197, at the corner of Aribau (tel. 253-10-17).

El Bodegón is a small, modern tapas bar with several tables and an outdoor terrace in summer. Seafood and salads are the specialties, with a tasty tapa of salpicón de mariscos (seafood salad) going for 375 ptas. ($3). The salads are on display, making it easy to choose among the octopus, potato, or beet selections. Around the corner is El Bodegón Restaurant, a more formal version of the same establishment.

Open: Mon–Fri 1pm–1am. *Closed:* Part of Aug.

FOR BREAKFAST

Breakfast in Spain is grabbing a cup of coffee and a croissant or roll. If you want a full breakfast with eggs and toast, you'll have to stick to the hotels.

For breakfast or a quick caffeine pick-me-up during the day, stop in at the **Mesón del Cafè,** Llibretería 16 (tel. 315-07-54). Near the cathedral in the Barri Gòtic, this tiny place founded in 1909 looks like a bar but specializes in coffee and cappuccino with whipped cream instead of steamed milk. There are few stools so you'll most likely have to eat breakfast standing. It's open Monday through Saturday from 7am to 12:30am. Closed holidays and the month of August.

The **Xocolatería Santa Clara,** just down the street in Plaça Sant Jaume, also offers cappuccino and a wonderfully rich, thick hot chocolate (topped with whipped cream, if you want). For breakfast or a snack, select among the tasty pastries on the counter. Open daily from 8am to 9:30pm.

In the Eixample, the **Forn de Sant Jaume,** Rambla de Catalunya 50 (tel. 216-02-29), specializes in croissants, plain or stuffed with your choice of chocolate, cheese, foie gras, or ham. Open Monday through Friday from 9am to 9pm and on Saturday from 9am to 1pm and 5 to 9pm.

FOR THE SWEET TOOTH

The **Gelateria Italiana Pagliotta,** Carrer Jaime I no. 15 (tel. 310-53-24), in the Barri Gòtic, makes its own ice cream and has the best horchata (a refreshing drink made from the chufa nut) in town. It also serves cappuccino. Open March to October (more or less) daily from 8am to 11pm.

Forn de Sant Jaume, Rambla de Catalunya 50 (tel. 216-02-29), also offers homemade horchata, ice cream, and chocolates. There is also a cafeteria next door (see "For Breakfast"). Open daily (except Christmas night) from 9am to 10pm.

COOL FOR KIDS

McDonald's has two Barcelona outposts: Carrer de Pelai 62, near Plaça Catalunya (tel. 318-29-90), open Sunday through Thursday from 10am to midnight and on Friday and Saturday from 10am to 1am; and Creu Coberta 90 (tel. 421-97-57), open Monday through Thursday from 11am to 11pm, on Friday from 11am to midnight, on Saturday from 11am to 1am, and on Sunday from 11am to midnight.

Burger King also has two outposts: Rambla Canaletes 135, near Plaça Catalunya (tel. 302-54-29), and Passeig de Gràcia 4, the opposite side of Plaça Catalunya (tel. 317-18-57), both open Monday through Thursday from 11am to midnight, on Friday and Saturday from 11am to 1:30am, and on Sunday from noon to midnight.

WHAT TO SEE AND DO IN BARCELONA

Barcelona consistently gets rave reviews from visitors enthralled with the sheer spectacle of its everyday life. Even if you don't set foot in a single museum, or take in any of the must-see sights, the city will charm you with its impressive architectural displays and its unmistakable Mediterranean flair. As elsewhere in the Mediterranean, life in Barcelona unfolds in the streets. Foremost among these streets is Las Ramblas, the central, tree-lined boulevard where life *is* street theater. But while Barcelona is an extremely attractive city capable of entertaining passersby for hours on end, it is much more than a pretty urban face. Its ranks of monuments and museums reveal great historic depth and cultural complexity; its trendy "designer" bars and enduring opera house demonstrate a flair for fun of all kinds; and its chic shops and boutiques purvey a cosmopolitan sense of style and cutting-edge design that point the way to tomorrow.

1. Sightseeing Tours

BUS TOURS

Julia Tours, Ronda Universitat 5 (tel. 317-64-54 or 318-38-95), and **Pullmantur,** Gran Via de les Corts Catalanes 635 (tel. 317-12-97 or 318-02-41), offer a variety of guided bus tours in English. The daily half-day city tour for 2,400 ptas. ($20) takes in the main thoroughfares of the city, the Barri Gòtic, the cathedral, City Hall, the Poble Espanyol (Pueblo Español), and the view from Montjuïc. The daily (except Monday) full-day "Barcelona al completo" tour (with lunch) for 5,800 ptas. ($48.25) takes in the main thoroughfares, the Gothic Quarter, the Columbus Monument, Montjuïc, the stadium and Olympic buildings, the Poble Espanyol, several Gaudí works, and the Picasso Museum; for an additional 1,000 ptas. ($8.25) you can sample a special gastronomic menu featuring typical foods of the region. Other daily tours ranging from 2,400 to 7,800 ptas. ($20 to $65) include "Gaudí y Picasso"; "Panorámica de noche y flamenco," featuring a flamenco performance; "Noche flamenca con cena," featuring dinner and a flamenco performance; "Gala en Scala con cena," which takes in the dinner/cabaret show at the Scala (see Section 9, "Nightlife") and requires a jacket and tie; and "Gala en Scala," which is the same show without dinner but still requiring jacket and tie. During the bullfight season (April to the beginning of October) the "Panorámica y toros" tour is offered every Sunday and weekdays when there is a bullfight. You will be given the option of a *sol* (in the sun) or *sombra* (in the shade) seat. Unless you're a real sun worshipper, opt for the latter.

AERIAL TOURS

Both the Montjuïc cable car and the one crossing the harbor from Montjuïc to Barceloneta are fine ways to survey the city, sea, and surrounding mountains from on high. The former, as you approach the castle, provides a partial glimpse of the Olympic installations on your right behind the Palau Nacional, while in the distance the Sagrada Familia protrudes like a crown from the urban landscape. The latter provides a view of Las Ramblas and the port.

For a look at the city and the sea from the mountains, go to the top of Tibidabo, recently dubbed the "Muntanya Màgica." The ascent combines a smörgåsbord of transports beginning with the **Ferrocarrils de la Generalitat** from the Plaça Catalunya station (use your T-2 ticket). Next, the quaint, colorful **tramvía blau** (also T-2 ticket), an old-fashioned streetcar that travels Avinguda Tibidabo with its stately mansions (many now house offices or luxury apartments). On your left you'll pass El Asador de Aranda, an expensive restaurant in a stunning modernist building. After the tramvia azul, you continue in the funicular costing 150 ptas. ($1.25) one way, 275 ptas. ($2.30) round-trip, to the amusement park (see Section 4, "Kids' Barcelona," below), Sacred Heart

Church, and a nice overlook. To the left of the main altar in the church there is access to the elevator that will take you to the base of the Christ statue, the highest vantage point of all; the fee is 50 ptas. (40¢). The Bar Tibidabo here serves good sandwiches, or, if you wish, go around the back to Restaurante La Masía (tel. 417-63-50), whose moderately priced menu offers quality Catalan fare averaging about 2,200 ptas. ($18.25) a meal; open in winter Monday through Saturday from 1 to 4pm and June to September from 1 to 4pm and 8:30 to 11:30pm, and all year on Sunday from 1 to 4pm.

2. The Top Attractions

Museu Picasso, Carrer de Montcada 15-19 (tel. 319-63-10).

This is Barcelona's most popular attraction, and with good reason—it reveals much about this multitalented artist that many of us never knew. Here you will see a boundless artistic vision evolve from adolescence through a long, prolific career, whose creative span extends well beyond the cubist style. All of us have seen bits and pieces of Picasso's oeuvre over the years, but here the scope of his work becomes a coherent whole, and the man and his art take on greater depth.

Ensconced in two Gothic mansions, this intimate museum of small rooms and cozy corners invites lingering over the paintings, drawings, engravings, ceramic creations, and other assorted artistic reflections displayed chronologically to trace the artist's development.

Among the individual highlights are: the portrait of Picasso's aunt, Tía Pepa, and sketches of his friends Sabartés and Junyer, all of which reveal something more of Picasso the man; *Science and Charity,* a strikingly vivid work produced by the artist at age 16, using his father as a model for the doctor; the famous "Las Meninas" series; and interesting works from his blue period.

Open: Tues–Sat 10am–8pm. *Admission:* 400 ptas. ($3.35) for adults; children under 16, free. *Metro:* Jaume I (Line 4). *Bus:* 16, 17, 22, 45.

Catedral, Plaça de la Seu s/n (no street number) (tel. 315-35-55).

This Gothic cathedral reflects the splendor of medieval Barcelona. Construction began at the end of the 13th century and was completed around the middle of the 15th (except for the main facade, which dates from the 19th century). Built on top of the remains of a Roman temple, a Moorish mosque, and a Romanesque cathedral, it contains three artistically lit naves, 29 side chapels, a central choir impressively adorned with medieval and Renaissance designs, soaring Gothic arches, and 10 columns around the main altar. Steps lead from the altar down to the crypt of Santa Eulalia, Barcelona's patron saint, whose white alabaster sepulchre is of 14th-century Italian craftsmanship. In the Chapel of the Most Holy Sac-

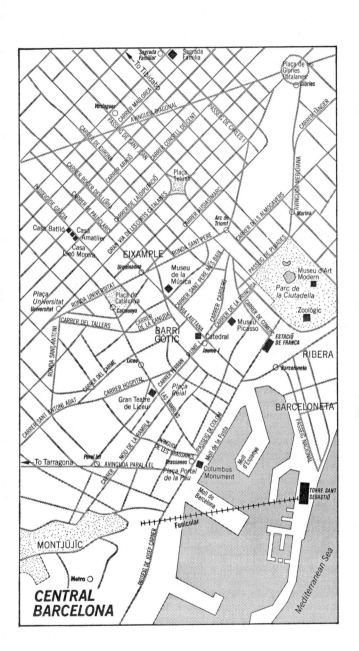

To Tibidabo
Sagrada Familiar
Sagrada Familia
Plaça de les Glòries Catalanes
Glòries
CARRER TANGER
Verdaguer
CARRER MALLORCA
AVINGUDA DIAGONAL
PASSEIG DE SANT JOAN
CARRER CONSELL DE CENT
PASSEIG DE CARLES
CARRER DE GIRONA
CARRER ARAGÓ
AVINGUDA MERIDIANA
CARRER ROGER DE LLÚRIA
Plaça Tetuán
CARRER AUSIAS MARC
Marina
CARRER DE PAU CLARIS
PASSEIG DE GRÁCIA
CARRER DE LA DIPUTACIÓ
GRAN VIA DE LES CORTS CATALANES
Arc de Triomf
CARRER DELS ALMOGÀVERS
Casa Batlló
Casa Amatller
Casa Lleó Morera
RONDA SANT PERE
CARRER DE LA PRINCESA
PASSEIG DE PUJADES
EIXAMPLE
Urquinaona
Museu de la Música
Museu d'Art Modern
Plaça Universitat Universitat
RONDA UNIVERSITAT
Plaça de Catalunya
CARRER SANT PERE MÉS BAIX
Parc de la Ciutadella
Catalunya
CARRER CARDENER
Zoològic
CARRER DEL TALLERS
CARRER DE LA CANUDA
VIA LAIETANA
CARRER DE COMERÇ
CARRER SANT ANTONI
BARRI GÒTIC
Catedral
Museu Picasso
ESTACIÓ DE FRANCA
CARRER DEL CARME
CARRER FERRAN
Jaume I
RIBERA
Liceu
Barceloneta
RONDA SANT ANTONI
CARRER HOSPITAL
Plaça Reial
BARCELONETA
CARRER SANT ANTONI ABAT
Gran Teatre de Liceu
LES RAMBLES
PASSEIG NACIONAL
PASSEIG DE COLOM
Moll de la Festa
MOLL DE LA RAMBLA
AVINGUDA DE LES DRASSANES
Moll d'Espanya
Paral.lel
Drassanes
To Tarragona
AVINGUDA PARAL.LEL
Plaça Portal de la Pau
Columbus Monument
Moll de Barcelona
TORRE SANT SEBASTIÓ
PASSEIG DE JOSEP CARNER
Funicular
MONTJUÏC
Metro
Mediterranean Sea
CENTRAL BARCELONA

rament, to the right of the main entrance, is the *Cristo de Lepanto*. Legend has it that the figure's twisted torso dodged a bullet during the Battle of Lepanto when it graced the prow of Juan de Austria's flagship. Along one of the cathedral's lateral walls are the sepulchres of Ramón Berenguer I, the Count of Barcelona, and his wife, Almodis, founders of the city's Romanesque cathedral in 1058.

In the Sala Capitular of the cathedral's cloisters is a small museum whose focal point is Bartolomé Bermejo's late 15th-century painting *La Pietat* (the pietà). The museum is open daily from 11am to 1pm; admission is 25 ptas. (20¢).

The vaulted galleries of the cloisters themselves enclose a garden with palm trees, magnolias, and medlars; an unusual fountain erupting from a moss-covered rock; and a small gaggle of geese.

Note: Though you can enter the cathedral in jeans and modest shorts, bare shoulders must be covered with a shawl.

Open: Daily 7:30am–1:30pm and 4–7:30pm. *Admission:* Free. *Metro:* Jaume I (Line 4). *Bus:* 16, 17, 19, 22, 45.

Sagrada Familia, Carrer de Mallorca 401 (tel. 255-02-47).

An ambitious work-in-perpetual-progress, this unique, modernistic rendition of a cathedral that, if finished, will be Europe's largest, is perhaps Barcelona's best-known landmark. Work on it began in 1882; two years later Gaudí took over and projected a monumental temple of immense proportions (the dome is slated to be 525 feet high) and profound religious symbolism. The ornamentation—composed of symbols within symbols, crosses within crosses, and effusive motifs drawn from nature—drips whimsically down the facades like caramelized sugar. But to date, it is still only a shell of a cathedral and controversy swirls around what's missing. When Gaudí died in 1926, he left no detailed plan for the cathedral's completion. Ever since, construction has continued by fits and starts financed by donations. Some people claim that no one can imitate Gaudí's free interpretation of Gothic motifs— and no one should even try. It's rather like having Leonard Bernstein complete Schubert's *Unfinished Symphony,* they say. But the cranes have become a permanent fixture and the work continues. Within one of the towers is an elevator that ascends to a magnificent urban panorama.

Installed in the cathedral's crypt is the Museo del Templo Expiatorio de la Sagrada Familia, which chronicles the cathedral's evolution in blueprints, models, and drawings. Admission is 250 ptas. ($2.10).

Open: Daily, Oct–June 9am–7pm and July–Sept 9am–8pm. *Admission:* 300 ptas. ($2.50); elevator 75 ptas. (65¢). *Metro:* Sagrada Familia (Line 5). *Bus:* 19, 34, 43, 50, 51, 54.

Museu d'Art de Catalunya (Museum of Catalan Art), Palau Nacional, Parc de Montjuïc (tel. 423-18-24).

After ascending some 200 stairs from Plaça Espanya, visitors are rewarded not only with an impressive museum but with a fine view of the city. The source of a good deal of municipal and regional pride, the museum's attractive, uncluttered, and informative displays of Catalan artistic expression are installed in a building constructed for the 1929 World's Fair. Also represented are such high-caliber non-Catalan artists as El Greco, Velázquez, Zurbarán, and Tintoretto.

The collections primarily reflect three historic eras: the Romanesque, the Gothic, and the 16th to the 18th century. Most outstanding among them is the Romanesque collection containing numerous statues, sculptures, frescoes, and murals hailing from village churches throughout the region. The Gothic section contains not only important Catalan paintings and sculptures, but also pieces from other regions of Spain. The works from the Renaissance, baroque, and neoclassical eras are more fragmentary but include some exemplary works from the Spanish, Flemish, and Italian schools.

Also housed in the same building is an interesting Museu de Ceràmica (Ceramics Museum), which features Spanish pottery dating from the 13th to the 20th century.

Open: Tues–Sun 9am–2pm. *Admission:* 400 ptas ($3.35); free for children under 13, and free for all the first Sunday of every month. *Metro:* Espanya (Line 1 or 3). *Bus:* 61.

Fundació Joan Miró, Plaça Neptú, Parc de Montjuïc (tel. 329-19-08).

Acclaimed for artistic expression both outside and inside, this museum was designed by Josep Lluis Sert to house in permanent tribute the work of the prolific Catalan abstractionist Joan Miró. The nucleus of the collection follows his work from 1914 to 1978 and includes many highly original sculptures, paintings, and multimedia tapestries. The Mediterranean feel of the boxy, white building gives added punch to Miró's exuberant use of primary colors. Temporary exhibitions of other contemporary artists are also featured here on a regular basis.

The museum restaurant with outdoor terrace offers entrées under 1,000 ptas. ($8.50).

Open: Tues–Sat 10am–7pm (to 7:30pm on Thurs), Sun and holidays 10:30am–2:30pm. *Admission:* 300 ptas. ($2.50) for adults, 150 ptas. ($1.25) for students. *Directions:* Montjuïc funicular, or bus 61 from Plaça Espanya.

3. More Attractions

Gran Teatre del Liceu (Gran Teatro del Liceo), Carrer de Sant Pau 1 bis (tel. 318-92-77); enter at Carrer San Pablo 1 bis, around the corner from the main facade on Las Ramblas.

Barcelona's majestic opera house dates from the 19th century and nowadays often resounds with the native talents of Montserrat Caballé and José Carreras. A study in Victorian opulence, the theater features blue silk walls in the entrance hall, a sweeping staircase leading to a salon of mirrors, and one of Europe's largest stages, soon to be even larger. A massive expansion and remodeling program will be ongoing from July 1990 to January 1992—unfortunately, the theater will be closed.

Tours: Guided half-hour tours in English Mon–Fri at 11:30am and 12:15pm. *Admission:* 200 ptas. ($1.65). *Metro:* Liceu (Line 3).

Columbus Monument, at the harbor end of Las Ramblas (tel. 302-52-24).

This Barcelona landmark commemorates Columbus's triumphant return after his first successful expedition to the New World. After sailing into the harbor, he delivered reports of his discoveries to Queen Isabella in the Gothic Quarter's Salon de Tinell.

The monument itself contains a small, tubular elevator that ascends 60 meters (200 ft.) to Columbus's feet, where a tiny platform offers a partially obstructed view of the sea and city.

Open: Easter week 10am–8pm, June 15–Sept 30 daily 9am–8:30pm, and the rest of the year daily 10am–2pm and 3:30–6:30pm. Ticket sales stop a half hour before closing. *Admission:* 175 ptas. ($1.45) for adults, 50 ptas. (40¢) for children ages 4 to 12 and senior citizens over 60; children under 4, free. *Metro:* Drassanes (Line 3).

Santa María del Mar, Plaça Santa María (no phone).

This is not a church you need go out of your way for, but since it's close to the Museu Picasso, drop in and see its lovely rose window and stained-glass display.

Open: Daily 10am–12:15pm and 5–7pm (except when a mass is being celebrated). *Admission:* Free. *Metro:* Jaume I (Line 4).

Museu Textil i d'Indumentaria, Carrer de Montcada 12 (tel. 210-45-16).

Occupying two 13th-century Gothic palaces near the Museu Picasso, this museum contains a fascinating collection of textiles. Both ancient pieces (Egyptian and Spanish-Arabic) and a spectrum of fabrics, garments, and accessories dating from the Gothic period to the 20th century can be found here. Particularly impressive is the assemblage of clothing and accessories from the 18th to the 20th century and the interesting lace collection (including a lovely array of Chantilly lace shawls) stretching from the 16th century forward.

Open: June–Sept, Tues–Sun 10am–2pm and 4:30–7pm; Sept–June, Tues–Sun 9am–2pm and Tues–Sat 4–7pm. *Admission:* 200 ptas. ($1.65). *Metro:* Jaume I (Line 4).

Museu Monestir de Pedralbes, Baixada del Monestir 9 (tel. 203-92-82 or 204-27-47).

A jewel of Catalan Gothic art, this monastery was founded in 1326 by Queen Elisenda of Montcada and her husband, King Jaume II. Among its more noteworthy features are the three-story cloisters and the chapel's outstanding mural paintings by Ferrer Bassa.

Open: Tues–Sun 9:30am–2pm. *Closed:* Weekday holidays. *Admission:* 200 ptas. ($1.65) for adults, free for children under 13. *Bus:* 22, 64, 75, BC, BI, or SJ.

Museu Palau Reial de Pedralbes, Avinguda Diagonal 686 (tel. 203-75-00 or 204-63-19).

This vintage 1920s palace was given to King Alfonso XIII by the people of Barcelona. Full of remarkable furniture, paintings, carpets, sculptures, and personal mementos of the royal family, it's a poignant reminder of the years preceding the brutal Civil War. The classically simple facade is embellished with trompe l'oeil. The well-manicured gardens are frequented by people just out for a stroll or relaxing with a newspaper on one of the numerous benches. At one end of the garden is the Coach Museum, a collection of vintage carriages.

Open: Tues–Fri 10am–1pm and 4–6pm, Sat–Sun and holidays 10am–1:30pm. *Admission:* 200 ptas. ($1.65) for adults, free for children under 13. *Metro:* Palau Reial (Line 3). *Bus:* 7, 75, BC, BI, or SJ.

Pabellon Mies Van der Rohe, Montjuïc (tel. 423-40-16).

Reconstructed several years ago on its original site, this pavilion was designed by Mies van der Rohe as the German entry to the 1929 World's Fair. It features a bronze copy of a Georges Kolbe sculpture and the famous "Barcelona chair," also designed by the architect.

Open: Daily 10am–6pm. *Admission:* Free. *Bus:* 61.

Fuentes de Montjuïc (Montjuïc Fountains)

One of Barcelona's most unique spectacles is the Fuentes de Montjuïc when illuminated. A masterpiece of engineering by Carles Buigas, the fountains were built for the 1929 World's Fair. They're illuminated October to May on Saturday and Sunday from 8 to 11pm (from 9 to 10pm with music) and June to September on Thursday, Saturday, and Sunday from 9pm to midnight (from 10 to 11pm with music). Make an effort to see them with the musical accompaniment—it transforms the play of water and colored lights (in 50 different and extraordinary formations) into a dramatic ballet.

Parc de la Ciutadella, southeast corner of the Barri de la Ribera.

Occupying the former site of the city's citadel, Parc de la Ciutadella packs a lot into a small space. Among its noteworthy attributes are some remnants of its military past—among them a chapel, the governor's palace, and the arsenal—the zoo (see Section 4, "Kids' Barcelona," below), the Museu d'Art Modern (see below), and a lake with rowboats.

Last remodeled for the Universal Expo of 1888, the park's grand cascade, lake, flower beds, and abundant trees make a tranquil sanctuary in a dense metropolis. Here, too, installed in the Domenech i Montaner building that housed the 1888 Expo's café-restaurant, is the Museo de Zoología (exactly what it sounds like—a zoological museum). Another modernistic touch is Llimona's *El*

Desconsol sculpture in the middle of the pool in front of the Parliament. But the park's most monumental feature is the effusive fountain (you can't miss it) by Gaudí.

Open: Daily 24 hours. *Admission:* Free. *Metro:* Ciutadella (Line 4).

Museu d'Art Modern, Parc de la Ciutadella (tel. 319-57-28).

The Museu d'Art Modern primarily contains the work of Catalan painters. Especially eye-catching is a courtyard sculpture of wooden poles and mobiles by Josep Guinovart i Bertran. You will also find Modernist furniture, with some particularly nice pieces by Puig i Cadafalch.

Open: Mon 3–7:30 pm, Tues–Sat 9am–7:30pm, Sun and holidays 9am–2pm (ticket sales stop a half hour before closing). *Admission:* 400 ptas. ($3.35). *Metro:* Ciutadella (Line 4).

Poble Espanyol (Pueblo Español), Montjuïc.

This microcosm of Spain was conceived for the 1929 World's Fair and constructed as a permanent open-air museum of Spanish architecture and handcrafts. As you look around, you'll find it hard to believe that most of what you see is simulated stone, brick, and rock. But nowadays the Poble Espanyol is much more than a museum. In fact, it's almost a village in its own right, with artisans working in their shops and frequent "fiestas" that evoke the spirit of local village fairs. In recent years it has also become a favored leisure retreat for Barceloneses, who especially flock here on summer evenings to enjoy the cooler Montjuïc air and the various nightclubs, music bars, flamenco performances, jazz "caves," restaurants—in short, over 40 different nightspots.

Open: Daily 9am–4am. *Admission:* 400 ptas. ($3.35) for adults, 200 ptas. ($1.65) for children ages 7 to 14; children under 7, free. *Directions:* From Plaça Espanya, a free double-decker bus shuttles visitors back and forth.

Parc Güell, Carmel Mountain, Gràcia (tel. 214-64-46 or 317-52-21).

From 1910 to 1914, Gaudí worked here to compose a garden suburb of 60 homes and the requisite supporting services such as roads, markets, and schools. Commissioned by the financier Eusebi Güell, the project was aborted after only two houses and a smattering of public areas had been built. In 1922 the city acquired the land and turned it into a park. One of the two finished houses, where the architect lived from 1906 to 1926, is devoted to the Casa-Museo Gaudí and contains a selection of furniture designed by him. The house itself, however, is the work of Ramón Berenguer.

The entrance stairway to the park itself is adorned with a colorful lizard fountain, and inside you *must* visit the surrealistic Hall of a Hundred Columns (all Doric and slightly askew) and the proposed market area above it (ringed with benches covered with mosaics fashioned of broken ceramics). From here you can see Barcelona stretch away to the sea.

Open: Parc Güell: winter, daily 10am–6pm; summer, daily 9am–8pm. Gaudí museum: winter, Sun–Fri 11am–2pm and 4–

6pm; summer, Sun–Fri 10am–2pm and 4–7pm. *Admission:* Parc Güell, free; Gaudí museum, 100 ptas. (85¢). *Directions:* Bus 24 or 25, but my advice is to take a cab.

4. Kids' Barcelona

Golondrinas (tel. 310-03-82).

Both children and adults enjoy the 30-minute round-trip boat ride from the Barcelona Pier (in front of the Columbus Monument) to the breakwater.

Departures: Winter daily every 30 min 10:30am–1pm and 3–5pm; summer daily every 30 min 10am–8pm. *Price:* 175 ptas. ($1.45).

Zoo, Parc de la Ciutadella (tel. 309-25-00).

If you think you've seen it all as far as zoos are concerned, you'll be pleasantly surprised by Copito de Nieve, the only albino gorilla in captivity and the headliner among this zoo's outstanding cast of primates. With over 7,000 animals in residence and a petting zoo, children will find hours of educational entertainment here.

Open: Winter, daily 10am–5pm; summer, daily 9:30am–8pm (tickets sold until 7:30pm). *Admission:* 600 ptas. ($5) for adults, free for children under 3. *Metro:* Ciutadella (Line 4).

Parc d'Atraccions (Amusement Park), Montjuïc (tel. 242-31-75).

For children there are 40 rides and open-air concerts in summer; for adults there is a panoramic view of the city and port.

Open: June 24–Sept 11, Tues–Fri 6:15pm–midnight, Sat 6:15pm–1am, Sun and holidays noon–midnight; the rest of the year, Sat–Sun and holidays noon–8pm. (Note: Hours of operation vary greatly from season to season and year to year, so call before you go.) *Admission:* 300 ptas. ($2.50), or a global ticket good for all rides 1,100 ptas. ($9.15). *Directions:* Funicular from the Paral.lel Metro stop.

Parc d'Atraccions (Amusement Park), Cumbre del Tibidabo s/n (no street number) (tel. 211-79-42).

More rides for the kids and another spectacular view for the parents.

Open: Jan–Mar and Oct–Dec, Sat and Sun 11am–8pm; summer, Mon–Sat 4:30pm–12:30am, Sun and holidays noon–12:30am; during Christmas and Easter school vacations, also open weekdays. (Note: The hours are equally volatile here as at the Montjuïc park, so call before you make the trek.) *Admission* (includes three attractions): 300 ptas. ($2.50), or a global ticket good for all rides 1,200 ptas. ($10), 950 ptas. ($7.90) if you arrive 4 to 6 hours before the park closes). *Directions:* Ferrocarrils de la Generalitat to the tramvía blau to the funicular (an amusing ride in itself!).

5. Special Events

The *sardanas* is a sedate, regional folk dance very popular with the local citizenry who gather regularly to keep the tradition alive. Watch them in Plaça Catedral on Saturday at 6:30pm and on Sunday at noon; at Plaça Sant Jaume on Sunday and holidays at 7pm in the summer and 6:30pm in the winter; at Plaça Eivissa on Sunday at noon; at Plaça Sant Felip Neri the first Saturday of the month at 6pm; at Parc de l'Escorxador on Sunday at noon; and at Parc de la Guineueta, also on Sunday at noon.

Although **bullfights** are not quite the passion here that they are in other parts of Spain, they're a national pastime that I recommend if you want to gain some insight into the Spanish temperament. Watching the crowd is almost as much a spectacle as the sport itself and will distract you, if you wish, at the "moment of truth"—when the torero zeroes in for the kill. Barcelona's bullfight season runs from March to September, with corridas held on Sunday at 5:30pm at the Plaça de Toros Monumental, Gran Via de les Corts Catalanes 743 (tel. 245-58-04). Advance tickets may be purchased at Muntaner 24 (tel. 253-38-21).

As a prelude to the 1992 Summer Olympic Games, Barcelona is staging a series of **exhibitions** celebrating a different theme each year. The arts are being featured in 1990. The future is the focus for 1991, with exhibits highlighting the most advanced contributions in the areas of design and communications. Contact any Spanish National Tourist Office for information on current exhibits (see Chapter I).

The night of June 23 Barcelona celebrates the **Verbena de Sant Joan,** with bonfires in the city's streets and plazas. It is customary to eat the coca, a special sweet made from fruit and pine nuts, and attend the festivities on Montjuïc, which culminate with an impressive display of fireworks.

Every year during the second half of June, Barcelona holds its **Festival de Flamenco** at the Casa Macaya, Passeig Sant Joan 108, and in the Poble Espanyol. For information, call 317-57-57.

Every year during the last week of June and the first week of July, Barcelona holds its **Festival de Cine de Barcelona.** Activities include bestowing awards on Europe's best cinematic efforts, screenings of the latest films and documentaries, and tributes to certain film genres and filmmakers. Tickets are sold at the corner of Rambla de Catalunya and Aragó. For information, call 215-24-24.

During the week of September 24 the city holds a variety of celebrations in honor of the **fiestas de la Mercé,** Barcelona's most important popular festival. Concerts and theatrical performances animate the plaças de Sant Jaume, de la Catedral, del Rei, Sot del Migdia, Escorxador, and Reial, and parades of giants, devils, dragons, and other fantastic creatures wind through the streets of the old city districts. Marking the end of the festivities is a pageant of music and fireworks.

During the month of November, the annual **Festival Internacional de Jazz de Barcelona** is held in the Palau de la

Música Catalán, Amadeu Vives 1, and in the Palacio de Deportes, Lleida 40. For information, call 302-68-70.

6. Strolling Around Barcelona

LAS RAMBLAS

Las Ramblas, one of the world's most fascinating promenades, not only attracts the full spectrum of humanity but offers numerous architectural and cultural tidbits. Let's begin this two- to three-hour tour at the port where a replica of Columbus's caravel, the **Santa María,** is anchored opposite the monument to its famous captain. For 150 ptas. ($1.25) you can board the ship and get a sense of the hardships endured in the discovery of the New World. For 100 ptas. (85¢) more you can listen to a recording in English that details the history of the original boat and this particular replica. Summer visiting hours are daily 9am to 9pm; winter, daily 9am to 6pm.

Just opposite the *Santa María* is the **Columbus Monument** (see Section 3, "More Attractions," above) and to the left as you look up the Ramblas is the **Museu Maritim (Museo Marítimo),** Porta de la Pau 1 (tel. 301-64-25), installed in the Drassanes (medieval shipyards of the 13th century). It's open Tuesday through Saturday from 9:30am to 1pm and 4 to 7pm and on Sunday from 10am to 2pm; admission is 150 ptas. ($1.25). Most outstanding among its collection of seafaring paraphernalia is a reconstruction of *La Galera Real* of Don Juan de Austria, which took part in the Battle of Lepanto, and a map from the hand of Amerigo Vespucci.

Now we enter **Las Ramblas** proper, a long boulevard that ascends to Plaça Catalunya in five seamless segments. The first is the Rambla de Santa Monica, the seedy end of Las Ramblas, lined with sex shops, assorted soothsayers, and a smattering of respectable newspaper kiosks and terrace bars. To the right down the Passatge de la Banca is the **Museu de Cera** (Wax Museum) and its sister wax museum, **Expomuseu,** both open daily from 11am to 8pm. Admission to the Wax Museum is 360 ptas. ($3) for adults, 180 ptas. ($1.50) for children ages 5 to 11 and senior citizens. Admission to Expomuseu is 280 ptas. ($2.25), 140 ptas. ($1.15) for children ages 5 to 11 and senior citizens. A combination ticket is 500 ptas. ($4) and 250 ptas. ($2), respectively.

At Plaça del Teatre begins the Rambla dels Caputxins, where the terrace bars continue and more souvenir shops appear. To the left down Carrer Nou de La Rambla, at no. 3, is the **Museu de les Arts de l'Espectacle** (tel. 317-39-74), now a misnomer as the theatrical arts exhibits have been removed to reveal the greater glory of Gaudí's architectural hand. This is the Palau Güell he built in the 1880s for his patron Eusebi Güell. It is very Gothic, melodramatic, and even somewhat foreboding; the carved ceilings are especially notable. The building still houses the archives and a library of the theater arts. It's open Monday through Saturday (except holidays) from 11am to 2pm and 5 to 8pm; admission is 100 ptas. (85¢).

On the other side of Las Ramblas is the indented Plaça Reial, its yellow facades and courtyard palms reminiscent of Seville. Along its periphery are numerous cafés; at its center, a fountain with surrounding lamps by Gaudí. Take care here at night—it's an unsavory area filled with pickpockets, prostitution, drugs.

Back in Las Ramblas, you'll notice some white chairs lined up along the curbs. If you decide to sit, you may be asked to pay a token fee. Across from the Gran Teatre del Liceu is the **Cafeteria de La Opera.** Over 100 years old, this café's former cachet lingers in the etched mirrors and elaborate mural paintings adorning its walls, but as with Las Ramblas itself, its original luster has tarnished considerably. Once a hotbed of intellectual discussion, it is now a place where people of diverse classes and ages and varying degrees of indigence and elegance come to sip coffee side by side.

The **Gran Teatre del Liceu** (Gran Teatro del Liceo; see Section 3, "More Attractions," above) is a magnificent opera house, built in 1847 and then rebuilt after a fire in 1861–62. Though modest outside, inside it's a glittering feast of Victorian gilt, glass, velvet, and blue silk walls. Especially masterful are the ceiling paintings. Guided tours are conducted in various languages. But from July 1990 to January 1992 the theater will be closed for a massive expansion and remodeling program.

The Rambla de Sant Josep, primarily dedicated to the sale of plants and flowers, begins at the Plaça de la Boquería where on the right you'll find the facade of Josep Vilaseca's modernist **Casa Bruno Cuadros.** It dates from the 1890s and displays a protruding green dragon and other Asian designs. In the middle of the center sidewalk is a mosaic by Miró. A little farther up on the left is **La Boquería** (Mercat Sant Josep), one of the world's great produce markets.

The Rambla dels Estudis, where birds and fish and an occasional large turtle are sold, begins at Carrer del Carme (on the left) and Carrer de la Portaferrissa (on the right). The new Ramada Renaissance and Rivoli Ramblas hotels along this stretch have toned the place up considerably.

The fifth and final section, Rambla de Canaletes, lined with banks, better shops, and an abundance of snackbars, begins its brief sprint to the Plaça Catalunya at the Carrer del Santa Anna. Take Carrer Canuda leading off to the right to the Plaça de la Vila de Madrid, where you'll find some steps leading down to Roman tombs.

BARRI GÒTIC (THE GOTHIC QUARTER)

The following two-hour walking tour of the Barri Gòtic takes in the quarter's most important structures. The tour begins at **Plaça Nova,** where several circular and square towers incorporate Roman bases made up of large stone blocks. The upper portions, constructed of smaller stones, date from the 12th century. As you pass from the plaza onto Carrer de Bisbe (toward the port) you are crossing the threshold that was the city's oldest entrance gate. The first

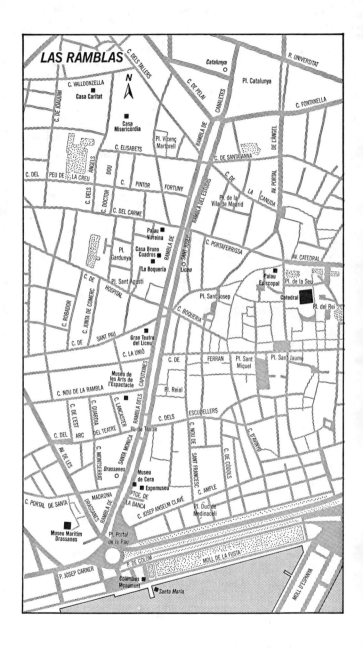

building on the right is the **Palau Episcopal** (Bishop's Palace), whose 18th-century portal opens onto an attractive courtyard with Romanesque construction below and Gothic above. At the top of the stairway leading off the courtyard is a patio with a 13th-century Romanesque mural and a splendid coffered ceiling. The courtyard is open to the public daily from 10am to 1:30pm, but even if the gate is closed you can peek into the courtyard and see the incongruous central fountain that dates from this century.

Leaving the Palau Episcopal and walking straight ahead onto Carrer Santa Llúcia you'll see the **Casa de L'Ardiacá** on your left. Although it was originally built atop the Roman wall, it exhibits a Gothic-Renaissance styling dating from its 15th-century reconstruction and expansion. You can visit the courtyard here as well, which contains a single palm tree, a murmuring fountain, and beautiful *azulejos* (tiles) that, despite their addition as recently as 1920, do not detract from the overall sense of history. Once the archdeacon's residence, this structure now houses the city archives.

Across the way on the right, the **Capilla de Santa Llúcia** (open daily from 8am to 1:30pm and 4 to 7:30pm) is a vestige of the 11th-century Romanesque cathedral built by Count Ramón Berenguer I. Exiting the chapel at the far side, you will find yourself in the **cathedral** cloisters, whose moss-covered fountain, white geese, and soaring palms exude a singular charm. Entering the cathedral through the door by the fountain you will find the tombs of Count Ramón Berenguer I and his wife, Almodis, on your right. (For more details on the cathedral and cloisters, see Section 2, "The Top Attractions," above.)

Upon exiting the cathedral through the main entrance, turn right up Carrer dels Comtes. Look up and you'll see some classic Gothic gargoyles. As you turn right down Carrer de la Pietat behind the cathedral, the medieval atmosphere intensifies. Leading off to the left is Carrer Paradís where, at no. 10 in the **Centre Excursionista de Catalunya,** you can see from the courtyard four remaining columns of the city's largest Roman temple, honoring Augustus (a model of which can be seen in the Museu de la Historia de la Ciutat).

Return to Carrer de la Pietat and continue to the left behind the cathedral. On your left you'll pass **Casa dels Canonges,** the former residence of the canons and now home to a number of regional government offices. One of them, no. 8, whose entrance is on Carrer Bisbe, is the official residence of the president of the Generalitat, but it is rarely used. Continuing along Carrer Bisbe to Plaça de Sant Jaume, you'll pass along the Gothic side of the **Palau de la Generalitat,** seat of the regional Catalan government, whose main 16th-century Renaissance facade faces the plaza itself and displays a distinctive statue of Sant Jordi. Across the square is the **Casa de la Ciutat** (City Hall), whose 19th-century neoclassical facade supersedes a Gothic one. Again, the side wall along Carrer de la Ciutat is older and more interesting in its Gothic styling. Above its doorway is an unusual image of the Archangel San Rafael sprouting bronze wings. Inside both of these governmental buildings are

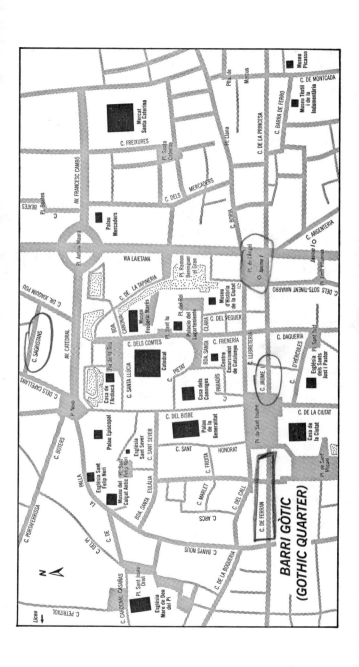

magnificent salons that were once open to the public but are now off-limits for security reasons.

To the left off Carrer de la Ciutat runs the narrow Carrer d'Hercules, which leads into Plaça Sant Just and its **Església dels Sants Just i Pastor.** On Saturday and Sunday the main entrance of this church is open to the public from 9am to 1pm and 5 to 9pm. If you wish to go inside any other days, you must go around to the gate at the back of the church (at the end of the brief Carrer de Rera Sant Just); ring the bell if no one is there to open the door for you. The same visiting hours apply. This church was built above an old church in the 14th century and contains a single nave with side chapels. Most notable is a curious Byzantine capital with a Greek inscription and the 16th-century retablo in the San Félix chapel. An image of the Virgen de Montserrat presides at the altar.

Back in the Plaça Sant Just, notice the upper-crust 18th-century houses with their decorative relief work. Now turn left onto Carrer Daguería and cross Carrer Jaume I and Carrer de la Llibreria and continue along Carrer Frenería. Turn right onto the Baixada de San-ta Clara and you'll soon find yourself in the remarkable **Plaça del Rei.** It's lined with palatial medieval structures that will make you feel that you've stepped back in time. To do so within the context of a museum, turn right on Carrer del Veguer to the **Museu de l'Historia de la Ciutat** (tel. 315-11-11), open Tuesday through Sat-urday from 9am to 8pm and on Sunday from 9am to 1:30pm; admission is 200 ptas. ($1.65). The museum is housed in the 15th-century Casa Clariana Padéllas, which was moved stone by stone from its original site on Carrer Mercaders. Inside, below ground level, are the excavated remains of the Roman and Visigothic cities that were the seeds of Barcelona, along with mosaics, statuary, and pediments of those eras, and a model of the supposed layout of the city. The museum's upper floors are a veritable maze of municipal memorabilia with some dioramas of Barcelona as it looked in days gone by.

You can enter the **Palacio Real Mayor,** former residence of the Condes de Barcelona and the kings of Aragón, through this muse-um (unless, as frequently happens, there is a special exhibition on). Begun in the 11th and 12th centuries, the palace evolved to its pres-ent aspect by the end of the 14th century. Rumor has it that one wing was once given over to the Inquisition, but we do know for certain that in its majestic **Salón del Tinell** Isabella and Ferdinand received Columbus—with six Native Americans in tow—upon his return from the New World. The palace's **Capilla de Santa Agueda,** built atop the Roman wall, is distinguished by a slender bell tower that is an extension of a Roman tower. Within, the chap-el's single nave is adorned with polychromatic wood, its altar with a beautiful 15th-century retablo.

Returning to the Plaça del Rei, go back to the Baixada de Santa Clara and turn right on Carrer dels Comtes. On the right you can enter the courtyard of the Arxiu de la Corona d'Aragó in the old **Palacio del Lugarteniente.** Note the elaborate coffered ceiling above the stairs.

Alongside the cathedral in the Plaça de Sant Iu is the **Museu**

Frederic Marés (tel. 315-58-00), open Tuesday through Saturday from 9am to 2pm and 4 to 7pm, and on Sunday and holidays from 9am to 2pm; admission is 200 ptas. ($1.65). It houses the collection of, obviously, Frederic Marés, a Catalan sculptor who, at this writing, is in his 90s. At the far end of the exterior courtyard is a section of Roman wall. The lower floors of the museum contain Punic, Hellenistic, and Roman artifacts; a vast array of religious carvings and sculptures from the 12th to the 16th century; and assorted Gothic and baroque objets d'art. As you ascend to the upper floor, you go from the solemn to the frivolous, for here is a collection of items so vast and varied that one wonders how the man could have amassed all this in a mere nine decades. On display is virtually everything from cigar wrappers to cameras, clocks, parasols, belt buckles, and tiaras.

"Footnote": If you're not too tired by now, go back around the cathedral via Carrer de la Pietat and Carrer Bisbe and make a left onto Carrer Sant Sever. Make your first right on Carrer Sant Felip Neri into the plaza of the same name, where you will find the **Museu del Calçat Antic** (Museum of Antique Shoes) (tel. 302-26-80). Founded by the local shoemaker's guild, it contains extraordinary samples of footwear ranging from a 1st-century A.D. Roman slave's sandal to shoes donated by modern-day celebrities. The museum is open Tuesday through Sunday from 11am to 2pm. Admission is 100 ptas. (85¢).

MODERNIST BARCELONA

We know it as art nouveau, the Germans call it *Jugendstil,* the Finns call it National Romantic, and the Spanish (more specifically, the Catalans) call it modernism. All these terms refer to an essentially organic architectural vernacular loosely grounded in the Gothic tradition and inspired by forms found in nature.

The best way to survey the broad scope of forms and fantasy embraced by this turn-of-the-century genre is to have a look at the numerous examples of modernist architecture sprinkled throughout Barcelona's Eixample area. The city's three most important modernist stylists were Domenech i Montaner, Gaudí, and Puig i Cadafalch. Because most of their buildings are now apartment houses or offices, they are not readily accessible to the general public; however, a discreet glance at their interiors is often possible. The following walking tour should take between one and two hours.

One representative work by each of these architects can be seen along Passeig de Gràcia between Carrer Consell de Cent and Carrer Provença. The first, at Consell de Cent, is **Casa Lleó Morera,** designed in 1905 by Domenech i Montaner in a floral modernist mode. Today it houses the Patronato de Turismo and the chic Loewe, whose installation unfortunately disfigured many of the modernist elements on the ground and first floors. Enter portal no. 35 next to Loewe for a look at the floral decoration of the staircase.

Casa Amatller at Passeig de Gràcia 41 (tel. 216-01-75), dating from 1900, is the work of Josep Puig i Cadafalch superimposed on an older structure. It combines grace notes of Dutch Gothic (note the finish of the facade) with elements of Catalan architecture (note the style of the arches) and the typical, naturalist elements of modernism (note the sculptures, ceramics, and wrought iron). Enter the **Institut Amatller d'Art Hispanic** (Amatller Institute of Hispanic Art) on the first floor for a look at the neo-Gothic interior decoration. Open Monday through Friday from 10am to 2pm and 4 to 8pm; admission is free.

Next door is the **Casa Batlló,** built by Gaudí on top of an existing structure between 1905 and 1907. A fine example of the integration of nature and architecture, it rises organically from its stone base through the bony forms of its windows to a rolling crown recalling a mountain. The impact is enhanced by the brilliant, polychromatic exterior, which takes on an added sheen on rainy mornings. Now it's the province of an insurance company, but you can go in and catch a discreet glimpse of the sinuously molded interior staircase off the entranceway and other decorative Gaudí flourishes beyond the double doors to the left.

Gaudí

By all accounts, Gaudí was an odd man, moody, unassuming, and quite austere in his personal habits. All effusiveness, it seems, was reserved for his work. An individualist with his own way of doing things, Gaudí took nine years to finish the architectural studies that others typically completed in five. But from the beginning he immersed himself in every aspect of the building trade and ultimately designed everything from doorknobs to the towering spires of his highly ambitious 20th-century cathedral, the Sagrada Familia.

Within Catalan modernism, Gaudí's work stands out as singularly organic and brilliantly creative in its use of ornamentation. Through his relationship with the Güells, a family of industrialists who commissioned him to do numerous works, he gained prestige among Barcelona's bourgeoisie. From 1878 until his death in 1918, Eusebi Güell was Gaudí's principal patron.

Gifted as both interior designer and architect, Gaudí was able to integrate all the elements of his structural compositions into organic, unified wholes. Whether he was working with wrought iron, furniture, stained glass, sculpture, mosaics, stone, or brick, he drew his inspiration from nature's forms, colors, and light. "The spirituality of Gaudí's work comes from the material aspect of Nature understood as the work of God, who is the Great Architect of the world," Joan Bassegoda Nonell wrote in *A Guide to Gaudí* (Edicions de Nou Art Thor). A deeply religious man, Gaudí's spiritual and creative convictions converged most intensely during his involvement with the cathedral.

Born Antoni Gaudí Cornet in 1852, he died in 1926 after being struck by a tram, leaving behind no definitive plans for the completion of his masterwork.

EIXAMPLE

At the corner of Carrer Provença is **Casa Milá** (popularly known as "La Pedrera") (tel. 215-33-98), the butt of many jokes in its youth but now considered one of Gaudí's—and modernism's—most singular works. Gaudí's last completed work, it was built between 1905 and 1910 and resulted in a lawsuit with Señora Milá, who complained that the finished product did not conform to the plans she'd been shown. Of course it didn't, but Gaudí was nonetheless vindicated. The house, which evolved according to Gaudí's improvisatorial whims, takes the use of the curve to the limit in its endless interior and exterior undulations. Free half-hour guided visits of "La Pedrera" in various languages are offered Monday through Friday at 10am, 11am, noon, and 1, 4, 5, and 6pm; on Saturday at 10am, 11am, noon, and 1pm; and on Sunday at 11am, noon, and 1pm. Since a maximum of 25 people may visit at once, you might want to call ahead. Currently you visit only the interior patio and the roof (six floors up) with its singular assemblage of chimney turrets—some clustered like a small squadron of helmeted knights, others spiralling upward in a twisting mosaic of stone. From here you also have a good view of Barcelona and, as Gaudí no doubt intended, the Sagrada Familia.

La Pedrera now houses an assortment of apartments, offices, and even a school; but the Caixa de Catalunya, which recently took it over, plans to restore it and open up much of it as a museum.

Continue along Passeig de Gràcia to Avinguda Diagonal. At Diagonal 373 is Puig i Cadafalch's 1904 castlelike **Palau Quadras,** which now houses the Museu de la Música. The elaborate sculpture work of the facade brings a hint of baroque to the overall Gothic and naturalist tenor of the design. If you want to pay the 200 ptas. ($1.75) to enter the museum (open Tuesday through Sunday from 9am to 2pm), you can see the hand of Cadafalch in the decorative elements on the first floor.

Just across the way at no. 442 is the **Casa Comalat,** the work of Salvador Valeri dating from 1911. The back of the building on Carrer Córsega is more interesting, with its bulging undulations and colorful ceramics clearly inspired by Gaudí.

A little farther east along Avinguda Diagonal, at the corner of Roselló, is the **Casa Terrades,** also known as the **Casa de les Punxes.** A Puig i Cadafalch structure of 1904 to 1905, its brickwork and spires are reminiscent of Saarinen's National Museum in Helsinki.

Although the walking tour ends here, Gaudí devotees might want to take Metro Line 3 to Fontana to have a look at **Casa Vincens,** Carrer Carolines 22. This was Gaudí's first important work after graduating as an architect and shows the Arab influence characteristic of his early work. As it is a private home, you can only view it from the outside.

---

7. For Business Travelers

As one of Spain's leading commercial and industrial cities, Barcelona is becoming an increasingly important destination for business travelers as well as for tourists. In convention and meeting facilities it ranks among the top 10 cities in Europe, and every month the city hosts several large-scale national and international trade fairs and numerous small-scale company meetings and conventions.

"Thanks to its industrial structure, longstanding manufacturing tradition, and geographical location, Barcelona—less than 150 miles from the French border—is an outstanding target for international investment," notes Jordi Pujol, Honorable President of the Regional Government of Catalonia since 1980. Within an economically unified Europe, Barcelona is clearly jockeying for position. Today many of Catalonia's financial resources derive from foreign investment. Since the 1970s the French and Germans have injected large amounts of capital, and currently 85% of all Japanese investment in Spain is concentrated in Catalonia. In recent years Kuwaiti money has also chosen Barcelona as its operational base in Spain. The planned International Business Center in the port of Barcelona being designed by I. M. Pei, the renowned American firm responsible for the pyramid in the center of the Louvre, is an indicator of the city's growing economic importance.

Here is a sampling of the international trade fairs held in Barcelona every year: Pielespaña (leather fashions), Gaudí Hombre (ready-to-wear men's fashions), Gaudí Mujer (ready-to-wear women's fashions), Rodatur (tourism industry), Construmat (construction industry), Sonimag (audio-visual and electronics industries), Barnajoya (jewelry industry), and Muestra de Tejidos (textiles).

SPECIAL FACILITIES

Those attending conventions, trade fairs, or simply spending a few days in the city on business, might consider soliciting a temporary **taxi "credit card"** for convenience and ease in getting around town and keeping track of expenses. For information, call 336-00-00. To arrange for a participating cab, call 330-08-04, 358-11-11, 212-22-22, or 300-38-11.

Feria de Barcelona, Avinguda Reina María Cristina, 08004 Barcelona (tel. 3/423-31-01; Telex 53117/50458 FOIMB-E; fax 3/423-86-51).

This attractive convention complex graced with two Venetian towers occupies more than 240,000 square meters (more than 2.6 million sq. ft.) and offers a dozen pavilions just 10 minutes from the airport by car and 10 minutes on foot from the after-hour diversions of the Poble Espanyol. During the Olympic Games it will serve as the communications center, with pavilions being used for some of the competitions. The Palacio de Congresos is the best equipped of the pavilions. Come July 1992 the distinctive towers of the Feria de Barcelona will be a recurring image on TV screens around the world.

Poble Espanyol, Avinguda Marqués de Comillas s/n (no street number), Montjuïc (tel. 325-78-66).

Ideal for combining daytime business with nighttime diversion, this recreation "village" offers three conference rooms that can accommodate 300, 800, and 900 people. (For more details, see Section 2, "The Top Attractions," above.)

Gran Casino de Barcelona, Sant Pere de Ribes (tel. 893-36-66).

About 25 miles out of Barcelona, this casino offers banquet and conference facilities in addition to baccarat and roulette. (See Section 5, "Sitges," in Chapter VI.)

RESOURCES

The **Barcelona Convention Bureau,** a department of the Patronato de Turismo, helps companies plan successful meetings and conventions. It can also help arrange meeting rooms and auditoriums, hotels in and around the city, banquet facilities, professional services, transportation and excursions, inspection visits, and special programs for companions. For detailed information, contact the Barcelona Convention Bureau, Passeig de Gràcia 35, 08007 Barcelona (tel. 3/215-44-77; Telex 59327 PMTB E; fax 3/215-42-76).

For full-service catering ranging from the formal to the downright amusing, call **Paradis Service,** Capitán Arenas 3-5, Esc. A bajos, local 1, 08034 Barcelona (tel. 3/205-04-11; Telex 99406; fax 3/204-78-10).

---

8. Shopping

Fashion and design have long been in the forefront of Barcelona's cultural and commercial activities, and the city, always open to foreign influences through its Mediterranean gateway, cultivated a notably strong streak of independence and boldness during the Franco years. Today the ranks of local designers of clothing, chairs, and complete interior environments are growing quickly, and although this is no Paris when it comes to designer name recognition and sheer numbers of shops, what you will find here is the best of the latest and a glimpse of what awaits on the horizon.

In a city with Barcelona's historic pedigree, one would expect the emphasis to be on the arts and crafts of yesteryear, yet quite the opposite is true. Here the aim is to look for the newest of the new. In fact, innovative design is such a vital aspect of Barcelona life that the *Guía del Ocio,* in its listing of bars, often cites the designers responsible for fashioning their distinctive atmospheres. And as you stroll along any of the main shopping thoroughfares mentioned below you'll see stores not only selling the latest designs in everything from coffeemakers to couches, but you'll see the application of designing vision in the window displays and shop installations.

Most shops are open from 10am to 1pm and 4:30 to 8pm. However, department stores and certain shopping centers and stores, especially in the city center, no longer close at lunch. Although consumer prices in Barcelona have catapulted in recent years, the annual sales, which run from the second week of January to the end of February and during the months of July and August, provide ample opportunity for bargain hunting.

SHOPPING AREAS AND CENTERS

The **main shopping streets** in the old town are Las Ramblas, Avinguda Portal de l'Angel, Carrer Portaferrissa, Carrer del Pi, Carrer de la Palla, and Carrer Pelai. In the Eixample they are Passeig de Catalunya, Passeig de Gràcia, and Rambla de Catalunya. In the northern reaches of town, Avinguda Diagonal, Plaça Francesc Macia, Bori i Fontesta, Valvet, Via Augusta, Travessera de Gràcia, Carrer de Balmes, and Carrer Muntaner.

Most purchases are subject to a VAT (value-added tax), here called **IVA,** ranging from 6% to 33% and more, depending on the degree of luxury of the item. Nonresidents can recover this tax under certain circumstances, but it's a cumbersome and protracted process (see Section 4, "Barcelona Fast Facts," in Chapter II).

The big department stores of Barcelona are **El Corte Inglés,** Plaça Catalunya 14 (tel. 302-12-12) and Avinguda Diagonal 617-619 (tel. 322-40-11); and **Galerías Preciados,** Avinguda Portal de l'Angel 19-21 (tel. 317-00-00) and Avinguda Diagonal 471-473 (tel. 322-30-11). Both are open Monday through Friday from 10am to 8pm and on Saturday from 10am to 9pm.

El Bulevard Rosa, Passeig de Gràcia 55 (tel. 309-06-50), was Barcelona's pioneer shopping mall, and suffice it to say that a shopping mall is a shopping mall is a shopping mall—wherever it may be. Its 102 diverse shops are open Monday through Saturday from 10:30am to 8:30pm. Above this cornucopia of consumer abundance is **El Bulevard dels Antiquaris** with over 70 shops selling art and antiques including paintings, jewelry, ivories, bronzes, furniture, toys, watches, porcelains, silver, dolls, African art, and coins. Open in summer Monday through Friday from 9:30am to 8:30pm; in winter, on Monday from 4:30 to 8:30pm and Tuesday through Saturday from 10:30 am to 8:30pm. Although the gallery itself is open all day, some shops do close for three hours at midday.

Not surprisingly, El Bulevard Rosa proved popular enough to spawn offspring at Avinguda Diagonal 470 and Avinguda Diagonal 611-615 (same phone as above), next door to El Corte Inglés. The former has some 40 shops, notable among them Beverly Feldman for stylishly outrageous shoes and Tráfico de Modas for contemporary fashions; the latter has some 100 establishments, including Sharper Image, the Body Shop, and a second El Gran Colmado restaurant (see Section 2 in Chapter IV, "Barcelona Dining").

Another popular shopping gallery is **Diagonal Center,** Avinguda Diagonal 584 (tel. 209-65-97), with 59 stores open Monday through Saturday from 10:30am to 2pm and 4:30 to 8:30pm.

The **Drugstore** (not a pharmacy) at Passeig de Gràcia 71 (tel. 215-70-74), near the Hotel Condes de Barcelona, is a complex of 12 shops open 24 hours daily and contains a restaurant, cafeteria, bar, supermarket, tobacco shop, bookstore, gift shop, photographic shop, and video games. A similar array of shops and services is available at the 22 establishments that comprise **VIP'S,** Rambla de Catalunya 7 (tel. 301-73-98), open Monday through Thursday from 8am to 1:30am, on Friday from 8am to 3am, on Saturday from 9am to 3am, and on Sunday from 9am to 1:30am.

A ROUNDUP OF SHOPS

Arts and Crafts

Artespaña, Rambla de Catalunya 75 (tel. 215-61-46).

Artespaña is a national network of stores promoting Spain's great variety of quality handcrafts. Typically, these stores offer everything from ceramics to furniture, but this particular one features furniture and decorative items for the home. The quality is first class and the styling most attractive.

Open: Mon–Sat 10am–1:30pm and 5–8pm. *Metro:* Passeig de Gràcia (Line 3) or Diagonal (Line 3).

La Manual Alpargatera, Aviño 7 (tel. 301-01-72).

For almost 50 years this store has been purveying baskets, handbags, hats, and other assorted articles woven of straw, palm, or reeds. In the back of the store at a table brimming with spools of ribbon sits a woman making some of the wares you see. Judging by the way they are overflowing the shelves, she must be very productive indeed. As you walk in, you'll see the left wall stacked to the ceiling with espadrilles, which you can have made to order in as little as one day or as much as a week, depending on the intricacy of the styling. Proudly displayed above the cashier's counter is the photo of one celebrated customer—Jack Nicholson.

Open: Mon–Sat 9am–1:30pm and 4:30–7:30pm. *Closed:* Holidays. *Metro:* Liceu (Line 3).

Gòtic, Avinguda Catedral 3, opposite the cathedral (tel. 318-06-27).

Although located in the heart of tourist territory, this shop offers more than the standard souvenir trinkets. Its artistic ceramic creations come from all parts of Spain and include Mallorcan reproductions of Roman glassware, Arab-style ceramics from Granada, the black-and-white statuary of Ibizan artist Luis Amor, the distinctive blue-and-white Sargadelos ceramics from Galicia, and of course, Lladró from Valencia.

Open: Mon–Sat 10am–2pm and 4–8pm. *Closed:* Holidays. *Metro:* Jaume I (Line 4).

Mils, Passeig de Gràcia 11 (tel. 315-37-65).

This rather chic shop also carries Lladró and features some of the more elaborate figurines in the line. The entrance is on Condal Corner, an upscale shopping mall near Plaça Catalunya.

Open: Mon–Fri 9:30am–1:30pm and 4–8pm, Sat 10am–1:30pm and 5–8:30pm. *Closed:* Sat in Aug. *Metro:* Catalunya (Line 1 or 3).

Julio Gomez, S.A., Las Ramblas 104 (tel. 301-33-26).

Considering that it doesn't rain all that much in Barcelona, this specialty shop selling umbrellas of its own manufacture (see them being made in the back of the store) seems eccentrically out of place. For 100 years it has been selling not only umbrellas (which you can have custom-made), but canes and flirtatious Spanish fans and parasols. All sales are rung up on a beautiful antique cash register that's probably every bit as old as the store itself.

Open: Mon–Sat 9:30am–1:30pm and 4–8pm. *Closed:* Sat afternoon in July and Aug. *Metro:* Liceu (Line 3).

Fashion and Design

Beverly Feldman, Carrer de Mallorca 259, next door to the Hotel Condes de Barcelona (tel. 487-03-83).

If you're really into shoes (women's only), you'll have to set foot in here. Feldman is an American shoe designer who has lived and worked in Spain for over 20 years and whose shoes also sell Stateside at such upmarket outlets as Neiman-Marcus, I. Magnin, and Saks Fifth Avenue (where, by the way, they are considerably cheaper). Here, however, you can select from her *entire* collection of up-to-the-minute footwear fantasy.

Open: Mon–Sat 10am–2pm and 4:30–8:30pm. *Metro:* Passeig de Gràcia (Line 3).

Aldolfo Domínguez, Passeig de Gràcia 89 (tel. 215-13-39).

Those who watched "Miami Vice" will recognize the designing hand of Adolfo Domínguez, who dressed Don Johnson to kill during that show's second season. Although most noted for redefining the "classic" look of today's chic male, Domínguez also offers designs for women on the upper floor of this store whose angular, unadorned decor echoes the stark lines of his fashions.

Open: Mon–Sat 10am–2pm and 5–8pm. *Metro:* Passeig de Gràcia (Line 3).

Aramis, Rambla de Catalunya 103 (tel. 215-16-69).

If your tastes run to the classically traditional and money is no object, Aramis can dress you in Ungaro and Valentino, among other elite designer rubrics. The store's Ralph Lauren-esque decor tells the fashion story. And King Juan Carlos has been known to shop here while in town.

Open: Mon–Sat 10am–1:45pm and 4:30–8pm. *Metro:* Passeig de Gràcia or Diagonal (Line 3).

Groc, Rambla de Catalunya 100 bis (tel. 215-74-74).

Just across the street from Aramis, Groc showcases the creations of Toni Miró, who has been a major player in the Barcelona fashion world for some 20 years. His success, of course, commands its price. The shop is classically modern in keeping with the classical lines of Miró's designs and offers ready-made or custom-made fashions in such natural fibers as linen, cotton, and silk. The offering runs the full gamut from casual wear to ball gowns, and all items in the store, including the shoes, are Miró's creations. Women go up one flight from street level; men go down.

Open: Mon–Sat 10am–2pm and 4:30–8pm. *Closed:* Sat afternoon the women's section, Mon morning the men's; also Aug.

b.d Ediciones de Diseño, Carrer de Mallorca 291 (tel. 258-69-09).

Installed in a turn-of-the-century modernist building designed by Lluís Domenech i Montaner, b.d Ediciones de Diseño is a notable showcase for Barcelona design both inside and out. Spread over two vast floors are the latest statements in furniture, lamps, and other household accoutrements by leading contemporary Spanish and foreign designers, among them English Jane Dillon; Italians Vittorio Gregotti, Ettore Sottsass, and Alessandro Mendini; Portuguese Alvaro Siza Vieira; American Robert Stern; and Spaniards Miguel Milá, Enric Soria, Jorid Garcés, André Ricard, Pep Bonet, Cristián Cirici, Lluís Clotet, Pepe Cortés, Xavier Mariscal, Pete Sans, Oscar Tusquets, and Mireia Riera. But b.d Ediciones is also in the business of manufacturing reproductions of historic furniture by such masters as Gaudí, Domenech i Montaner, Terragni, MacKintosh, and Schindler. Apart from its own production, b.d imports and distributes exceptional design objects such as those by Alvar Aalto, Josef Hoffman, Le Corbusier, Mies van der Rohe, Breuer, and more. (Some of the designs it carries are on permanent exhibition in the Philadelphia Museum of Art, the Victoria and Albert Museum in London, and New York's Museum of Modern Art.) b.d will ship purchases home for you. Travelers who live in the Chicago area should note that they can buy some b.d products more cheaply there.

Open: Mon–Fri 10am–1:30pm and 4–8pm, Sat 10am–1:30pm. *Closed:* Holidays and Aug. *Metro:* Verdaguer (Line 4 or 5).

MARKETS

La Boquería, also known as the Mercat de Sant Josep, along Las Ramblas near the Gran Teatre del Liceu, is one of the world's cleanest, most extensive, and most fascinating produce markets and, as such, is a Barcelona sight in its own right. Beyond its great gates of glass and iron dating from 1914 await aisle upon aisle of attractively displayed produce from both sea and land and all manner of prepared provisions, vying for the attention of a highly discerning and demanding clientele. Within the market itself are some choice places to have a meal or a snack (see Section 4 of Chapter IV, "Barcelona Dining").

Antique lovers will enjoy the open-air **mercado gótico de antiguedades** (Gothic antique market), Plaça Nova, next to the Gothic cathedral (tel. 317-19-96), that springs up every Thursday from 9am to 8pm, except during the month of August. Here you'll find everything from antique buttons and lace to vintage armoires. Remember to bargain.

The **feria de artesanado** is an open-air crafts fair held the first Sunday of every month from 10am to 3pm, except August and September. Among the handmade goods typically offered here are ceramics, glass, wrought iron, enamelware, knits and weaves, and textiles.

9. Nightlife

While Barcelona offers the full range of evening entertainment from plays to cabarets, those who don't speak Spanish will find their options somewhat restricted by the language barrier. Even movies are typically dubbed rather than subtitled.

Of course, ballets, operas, and concerts transcend the language barrier, and the season for these events runs from September to early July. For the latest information on concerts and other musical events around town, call the **Amics de la Música de Barcelona** (literally, Barcelona's "Friends of Music") at 302-68-70 Monday through Friday from 10am to 1pm or 3 to 8pm. For information on performances by the Ballet Contemporáneo de Barcelona, call 322-10-37.

On a trendier note, "designer" bars have been the rage in Barcelona for several years now, with each new offering aspiring to ever-greater heights of originality. A recent penchant for claiming innovative kinship with the "in" spots of New York City seems to me to sell Barcelona short, for when it comes to cutting-edge designs for night living, a strong case can be made for Barcelona's own unmistakable brand of Catalan chutzpah. Of course, drinks in these ultra-trendy bars cost several times what they do in the down-home bar next door. Since many of these chic spots come and go in the flicker of a neon light, ask around for the shining star of the moment.

For the most comprehensive listing of evening activities, including restaurants, television programming, clubs, and discos, pick up a copy of the weekly **Guía del Ocio** at any newsstand. Although it's in Spanish, such readily recognizable cognates as "Cocteles," "Bares," and "Champañerías" should help you negotiate a path. A more upscale guide to nightlife is the monthly **Vivir en Barcelona.** For a guide to the thriving gay scene, pick up a map of gay Barcelona with a list of bars, clubs, hotels, and contacts at **SEXTIENDA,** Carrer Rauric 11.

Barcelona's nightlife often greets the dawn. The distinction between a music-bar and a disco, for example, resides partially in a closing time of 2am or 3am versus 5am (with a corresponding difference in price), and some semi-legal clubs actually open between 5am and 9am on weekends.

THE PERFORMING ARTS

Gran Teatro del Liceu, Sant Pau 1 bis (tel. 318-92-77).

This 19th-century opera house is a splendid setting for opera and ballet performances, as well as a sight in itself (see Section 3,

"More Attractions," above). The opera season runs from early February to June, and ballet performances are held in October and November. Do note, though, that the opera house will be closed for expansion and remodeling from July 1990 to January 1992.

Tours: Given Mon–Fri at 11:30am and 12:15pm; cost is 200 ptas. ($1.75).

Open: Box office Mon–Fri 10am–1pm and 4–7pm, Sat 10am–1pm; evening performances begin at 9pm, matinees at 5pm. *Prices:* 495–7,900 ptas. ($4–$65.75) for opera performances, 375–6,000 ptas. ($3–$50) for concerts and recitals, 280–4,500 ptas. ($2.25–$37.50) for ballet performances. *Metro:* Liceu (Line 3).

Palau de la Música Catalán, Amadeu Vives 1 (tel. 301-11-04).

This magnificent modernist concert hall is among the world's finest. The work of Catalan architect Lluís Domenech i Montaner, it was inaugurated in 1908 and is considered his most important structure. Its distinctive facade is a tour de force of brick, mosaic, and glass recalling in part the sensuous, rhythmic flow of Arab art. But it is the drama and elegance inside that truly set this hall apart from its peers worldwide. The harmonious interplay of ceramic mosaics, colored crystals, and a central skylight build to the stunning crescendo of carvings that frame the stage.

Throughout the year a variety of concerts and recitals by leading orchestras and artists are held here. Prices range from $4.50 to $36.

Metro: Urquinaona (Line 4).

MOVIES

Most first-run movies are dubbed into Spanish. The following cinemas often show English-language movies, but they are usually masterpieces from the past:

Capsa, Pau Claris/Carrer d'Aragó (tel. 215-73-93).
Casablanca I & II, Passeig de Gràcia 115 (tel. 218-43-45).
Moderno, Carrer Gerona 175 (tel. 257-76-41).
Rex, Gran Via de les Corts Catalanes 463 (tel. 223-10-60).
Sala X (erotica), Plaça Buensuceso 3 (tel. 318-12-91).
Sala X (erotica), Carrer d'Aragó 197 (tel. 253-97-45).
Verdi I & III, Verdi 32 (tel. 237-05-16).

Admission runs 275 to 500 ptas. ($2.25 to $4.25). Check the *Guía del Ocio* for shows, times, and nearest metro stop.

THE CLUB AND MUSIC SCENE

Scala, Passeig de Sant Joan 47-49 (tel. 232-63-63).

This dazzling dinner/cabaret extravaganza is a cross between a lavish Las Vegas revue and "The Ed Sullivan Show," except that many of the chorus girls appear topless from time to time. I've seen everything here from a live elephant on stage to acrobatics on ice. Although staunch feminists might take offense at some of the bare-breasted numbers, I find the shows quite energetic, entertaining, and admirable for the sheer complexity of the stage management, which includes countless backdrops, moving stages, and on-stage fountains. The show lasts about two hours and entails over 60 entertainers.

The Scala's three-tiered dining area offers four different three- or four-course menus plus an à la carte selection. The red-and-gold decor has baroque aspirations that have been held in check just this side of ostentatious.

Prices: Dinner menus 6,400–8,100 ptas. ($53.25–$67.50) per person; drinks and the show only 3,600 ptas. ($30) for the evening show and 2,750 ptas. ($23) for the late-night show (one drink included); afternoon matinee performances, 2,200 ptas. ($18.25), 1,400 ptas. ($11.75) for senior citizens; luncheon performances, 3,900 ptas. ($32.50). Two shows nightly (except Mon in winter) at 8:15pm (with dinner and dancing) and 12:15am (drinks and the show). Sun and Tues afternoon matinee performances at 4:30pm, and an additional luncheon performance Sun at 2:30pm.

Regine's, Avinguda Juan XXIII s/n (no street number) (tel. 339-71-08).

This Barcelona branch of the sophisticated, international Regine's network can be entered either from the street or through the Hotel Princesa Sofia. Upstairs there's a piano bar and downstairs a disco.

Open: Mon–Sat 9pm–4 am or later (the piano music stops at 3:30am); the disco is open 11pm–4:30am or later. *Closed:* Holidays. *Prices:* 1,300-pta. ($10.75) cover charge includes one drink. *Metro:* María Cristina (Line 3).

Tablao Flamenco Cordobés, Las Ramblas 35 (tel. 317-66-53).

Even in its native Andalucía, flamenco is a folk art that responds poorly to the rigors of regular nightly performances. But Luis Amade, a former guitarist with the José Greco flamenco troupe, does an admirable job of presenting it fairly authentically here. Located at the lower end of Las Ramblas (an iffy area at night), his club has a discrete entrance with a gurgling fountain behind a stairway that evokes the sound of a Seville plaza. Upstairs is a spacious bar, and everywhere is an abundance of brightly colored Moorish tiles.

The performance, which takes place in a suitably intimate setting, begins bombastically with highly stylized flamenco executed to recorded music, but then gradually converges over the course of an hour and a half to the more traditionally authentic *cuadro flamenco,* comprising guitarists, singers, and dancers.

Prices: Two performances nightly: 3,000 ptas. ($25) for the 10pm show, 2,750 ptas. ($23) for the 11:45pm show, one drink included; reserve ahead. *Closed:* Jan–Feb. *Metro:* Drassanes (Line 3).

El Tablao de Carmen, Poble Espanyol (tel. 325-68-95).

This is unquestionably the best flamenco show in town. The performances are consistently high caliber, the food is good, the atmosphere is intimate, and the service is friendly.

Open: The club itself is open 9pm–3am. There are two dinner shows, Tues–Thurs at 10:30pm and 12:30am; Fri and Sat (and

Mon when it's a holiday eve) at 11pm and 1am; Sun at 6:30 and 10:30pm. *Prices:* Dinner and show 3,700 ptas. ($30.75); a drink and the show 2,200 ptas. ($18.25); Sun and holidays, reduced admission for the 6:30pm show. *Directions:* From Plaça Espanya, a free double-decker bus shuttles visitors back and forth to the Poble Espanyol.

La Cava del Drac, Tuset 30 (tel. 217-56-42).

This dark, café-style basement club below the cafeteria of the same name is small and intimately suited to the jazz performances it offers from September to the end of June. On Tuesday it's the blues, Wednesday it's a jam session, Thursday it's Dixieland, and Friday and Saturday—all that jazz.

Open: Performances Tues–Fri begin at 11pm, Sat at 8pm. *Closed:* Holidays. *Prices:* cover of 400–1,100 ptas. ($3.25–$9), depending on the caliber of the performers. *FF.CC. Generalitat:* Provença.

Bikini, Avinguda Diagonal 571 (tel. 230-51-34).

On my last visit, this "in" spot near the Hotel Princesa Sofia offered a smörgåsbord of activities popular with a predominantly young crowd. Among them, an open-air patio bar (in summer), a disco dance floor, a salsa dance floor, and mini-golf. No pretensions here—in fact, it looks rather like converted basement space. The crowd seemed still to be enjoying itself on the dim, smoke-filled dance floors. Live entertainment Tuesday, Wednesday, and Thursday.

Open: Mon–Thurs 11:30pm–4:30am, Fri and Sat 11:30am–5am; mini-golf 5pm–2 or 3am. *Prices:* No cover. *Metro:* María Cristina (Line 3).

Tango, Diputación 94 (tel. 325-37-70).

A typically dark nightspot with two bars and a large dance floor, Tango features live orchestras playing Latin rhythms interspersed with recorded music of diverse rock vintages.

Open: Daily 6pm–9:45pm and 11:30pm–4am (6:30am on Fri nights and 4:45am on Sat nights). *Prices:* Cover charge 1,000 ptas. ($8.25) for men and 800 ptas. ($6.75) for women, including one drink.

La Paloma, Tigre 27 (tel. 301-68-97).

Both accomplished ballroom dancers and those with two left feet will enjoy this most campy of dance halls. Since 1903 (with a ponderous baroque decor dating from 1915), La Paloma has been catering to hoofers from all walks of life. The large, central chandelier, even unlit as it usually is, imparts a certain passé elegance to the cavernous space. The music is always provided by live orchestras. Local tradition calls for Barcelona wedding parties to make a stop here sometime during the night; other celebrations, from birthday parties to bachelor parties to retirement parties, are regularly announced between dance numbers. Even if you don't like dancing, stop in for the local color.

Open: Thur–Sun with sessions 6–9:30pm and 11:30pm–3:30am. The first features softer, more tranquil music; the latter is a little more lively. *Prices:* 250–400 ptas. ($2–$3.25), depending on the day and time. *Metro:* Universitat (Line 1).

A CASINO

Gran Casino de Barcelona, Sant Pere de Ribes (tel. 893-36-66).

About 25 miles out of Barcelona near Sitges, this casino is housed in a Romantic structure of the 19th century and offers the full range of games of chance in a grand setting studded with elegant rugs, chandeliers, and scalloped curtains. The sedate, sophisticated atmosphere is completely devoid of the boisterous frenzy of most gambling dens. In the casino's restaurant you can enjoy the five-course menu of the day for 2,700 ptas. ($22.50) or order à la carte from a Continental selection, with meals averaging about 5,000 ptas. ($41.75). After dinner, nongamblers can enjoy the downstairs disco. From mid-July through August there are also open-air cabaret performances; for information about these, call 893-15-04.

Open: June 1–August 30, daily 6pm–5am; the rest of the year, Sun–Thurs 5pm–4am, Fri and Sat 5pm–5am. *Closed:* Christmas Eve. *Prices:* You'll need your passport to get in and admission is 550 ptas. ($4.50), even if you're only planning to have dinner (served 9pm–2am) or go to the disco. Restaurant reservations are recommended on Fri and Sat and throughout Aug.

THE BAR SCENE

In summer, the lower end of the Rambla de Catalunya blossoms with umbrella'd café-bars lining its central sidewalk. Drinks, snacks, and assorted ice-cream treats are served until the wee hours. Great for late-afternoon coffee klatsches or late-night drinks. Here are some more suggestions:

Universal, Carrer Mariã Cubí 182-184 (tel. 200-74-70).

In the vanguard of avant-garde designer displays, Universal's postmodern punk decor is so minimalist it seems threatened with extinction. Stark, dark, and severe in its sparseness, the high-ceilinged space calls to mind a converted warehouse. The music is loud, and the visual sense is stimulated by slides projected on the far brick wall. The crowd is young; the wooden theater seats lining the walls, old.

Open: Daily 11pm–3am. *FF.CC. Generalitat:* Gràcia.

Ticktacktoe, Carrer Roger de Llúria 40 (tel. 318-99-47).

This multidimensional, ultramodern nightspot is part bar, part restaurant, and part billiard hall. The prime attraction, however, is Manuel Ybargüengoitia's ingenious decor featuring unique lamps, an abstract marble whale behind one bar, and another bar in the contours of a woman's breast. The crowd is mostly mid-20s to mid-30s and drawn from the fashion and sports worlds as well as from the VIP heights of other walks of life.

The music bar airs up-to-the-minute sounds and is often the venue for fashion shows and book or record launches. The moderately priced restaurant has a menu that varies daily with the market offerings. Upstairs, when you are standing at the sinks in the bathroom, there is a surprising view of the bar below.

Open: Bar: Mon–Thurs 7pm–2:30am, Fri and Sat 7pm–3am; restaurant: 1:30–4pm and 8:30pm–1am. *Closed:* Holidays, and most of Aug. *Metro:* Passeig Gràcia or Urquinaona (Line 3).

Velvet, Carrer de Balmes 161 (tel. 227-67-14).

Installed in a modernist structure, the ultra-chic Velvet has a small dance floor and two bars lined with buttock-shaped bar stools. There is no sign marking its dual entrances—one an arched pavement dotted with plants and the other a ramp.

The crowd here varies with the day of the week and the time of year, but is primarily older and seasoned with the occasional celebrity. Alfredo Arribas is the architect behind this distinctive design statement, where again even the bathrooms are worth a visit.

Open: Mon–Thurs 7:30pm–4:30am, Fri and Sat 7:30pm–5am, Sun 7pm–4:30am. *FF.CC. Generalitat:* Provença.

Tilos, Passeig de los Tilos 1 (tel. 203-75-46).

This is *not* a fancy designer bar but rather a converted mansion and garden that are particularly pleasant in summer when the front and backyards and balconies and terraces of the two-story house sprout outdoor bars and tables. Especially pleasant is the fact that you can actually converse above the background rock music. An ideal place for a pre-dinner drink or post-dinner or post-disco nightcap.

Open: Daily 7pm–3am. *Metro:* Palau Reial or María Cristina (Line 3).

CHAMPAÑERÍAS

These establishments specializing in cavas from Catalonia and the occasional foreign champagne run from the very sophisticated to the mundane. No doubt you'll find one among the selection below to suit your taste and mood of the moment.

La Cava del Palau, Verdaguer i Callis 10 (tel. 310-09-38).

This "champagne" bar has evolved from a small place specializing in *cava catalana* to a very sophisticated space carrying 40 different regional cavas, 40 French champagnes, and some 350 different appellation wines—mostly from Spain, some from France, and several from Chile. And plans are to expand the offering still further.

Connoisseurs of sparkling wines will want to try the *brut natures,* elaborated without the traditional *licor de expedición* and thus, as the name suggests, the driest and most natural of all cavas. If you like drinks so dry they evaporate on contact, you'll love *brut nature.*

To accompany their cavas and wines, La Cava del Palau serves a choice selection of *raciones* (somewhat larger than a tapa portion) of Spanish and foreign cheeses, French pâtés, and caviar for up to 3,500 ptas. ($29.25) a plate. Most raciones, however, average about 800 ptas. ($6.75), and the glasses of cava, served in fine fluted glasses, average about 550 ptas. ($4.50).

Although this bar can accommodate up to 300 people, its multilevel layout provides intimacy no matter where you sit. It usually fills up after 11pm and is especially packed after concerts at the nearby Palau de la Música.

Open: Mon–Sat 7pm–2:30am, with live piano music starting at 11:30pm. *Closed:* Holy Week and Aug. *Metro:* Urquinaona (Line 3).

La Xampanyería, Carrer de Provença 236, at the corner of Enric Granados (tel. 253-74-55).

The "blue lagoon" of champagne bars, this place attracts a lively, mixed crowd, especially after midnight on weekends. Twinkling above its undulating, marble-top bar are small lights that suggest stars. In addition to over 40 types of cavas—including half a dozen French champagnes—it serves pâtés, cured ham, and chocolates averaging about 800 ptas. ($6.75) a ración. A glass of cava averages 450 ptas. ($3.75).

Open: Mon–Sat 7pm–3am. *Closed:* Holidays and Aug. *FF.CC. Generalitat:* Provença.

Xampanyería Ca "La Monyos," Carrer Muntaner 18, at the corner of Gran Via de les Corts Catalanes (tel. 254-53-58).

This is the place to come and sip cava in a more informal, cafeteria-like setting. There are over 40 varieties of Catalan cava and a token selection of French champagnes to choose from. Nibbles and snacks include a selection of canapes, tapas, sandwiches, pizzas, and crêpes.

Open: Sun–Thurs 7am–1:30am, Fri and Sat 7am–2:30am. *Metro:* Universitat (Line 1).

FOR GAY MEN

SEXTIENDA, Carrer Rauric 11, was the first gay shop in Spain and bills itself as the "gay information center." It offers a free map listing bars, discos, restaurants, saunas, and other places around town where gay people congregate. Open Monday through Saturday from 10am to 8:30pm; closed holidays.

ONE-DAY EXCURSIONS FROM BARCELONA

Beyond Barcelona is the Catalan region it captains. Home to some six million inhabitants (about half of whom live in the greater Barcelona area), it offers great scenic variety, with 580 kilometers (365 miles) of Mediterranean coastline, impressive mountain ranges, and inland plains. Bordered by France to the north, Aragón to the west, and Valencia to the south, it is slightly larger than Belgium. Its geographic parameters hark back to the counties created by Charlemagne along the southern edge of his empire in the late 8th century as a buffer against Muslim incursions.

Two hundred years after Charlemagne, the Catalan counts, coalescing around the House of Barcelona, broke with the French kings. In 1137 Catalonia merged with the Kingdom of Aragón. And in the following century James I brought Mallorca and Valencia into the Catalan fold. In 1283 the parliamentary courts were consolidated, and in 1359 the Generalitat, Catalonia's permanent political delegation, was instituted.

Regional expansion continued to the 15th century, embracing Sicily, Athens, Sardinia, and Naples. Then, in the latter half of the 15th century, Mediterranean dominance waned and Catalonia-Aragón joined with Castilla—but without relinquishing its own political integrity. In the early 18th century, however, that integrity was abrogated by Philip V, and not until 1931 was the Generalitat revived under the Second Spanish Republic, only to be annihilated again soon in the aftermath of the brutal Spanish Civil War (1936–39).

During the ensuing 40 years of Franco's rule, all manifestations of Catalan identity were rigorously suppressed; but with the rebirth of the Generalitat at the head of the newly autonomous regional Catalan government in 1979, Catalan patriotism resurfaced with a good deal of pent-up zeal. Catalan once again became an official language, and the historic Catalan flag with four red stripes on a yellow background (which Catalans say was the inspiration for the flag of Spain) was resurrected.

As Catalonia rode the tumultuous tides of its political history, its artistic and cultural traditions were fed by the hybrid mix of conquerors and merchants carried here by the Mediterranean Sea. Thus Tarragona is today a showcase of Roman remains, and the medieval heart of Girona (Gerona) reflects the passing presences of Romans, Moors, and Jews. Marvelous monasteries and cathedrals, financed with the fruits of vigorous trade, rose up throughout the region, reaching their crowning glory in the Monastery of Montserrat, spiritual home of Catalonia.

In the 11th and 12th centuries, masterpieces of Romanesque art began to dot the countryside, and in the 13th, the Gothic style, essentially an urban phenomenon, echoed in stone the general economic and cultural prosperity of its time. Eclipsed by other centers of European power during the Renaissance and baroque eras and then swallowed up by a greater Spain, Catalonia offers but a smattering of artistic specimens from these and the neoclassical periods. But as the 20th century dawned, Catalan culture boldly reasserted itself in the modernist tradition, fueled by the innovative visions of such architectural geniuses as Gaudí and Domènech i Montaner. Carrying the rekindled torch of Catalan culture on through the 20th century were such grand artistic talents as Salvador Dalí, Joan Miró, and Antoni Tàpies.

Touring Catalonia by car allows you to combine some of its principal destinations with visits to interesting sidelights along the way, so the itineraries below are geared toward travelers with their own set of wheels. However, the major cities and sights mentioned can also be reached by train or bus; information on these alternative travel options is given.

1. Montserrat Monastery

GETTING THERE

Julià, Plaça Universitat 12 (tel. 318-38-95), offers half-day bus tours to Montserrat Monastery leaving daily all year long at 9:30am, and from April 1 to August 30 daily at 3:30pm as well. The cost is 3,100 ptas. ($25.75). You can also get here by taking the FF.CC. de la Generalitat (commuter train line) from Plaça d'Espanya station to the cable car serving the top of the mountain;

round-trip train fare is 430 ptas. ($3.50); round-trip cable-car fare is 575 ptas. ($4.75). For details, call FF.CC. de la Generalitat at 205-15-15.

However, if you go by car, you'll be able to add to your itinerary a visit to an interesting Gaudí church in Santa Coloma de Cervelló, about 20 kilometers (12.5 miles) from Barcelona, and lunch at a converted Catalan country mansion.

EN ROUTE

To visit Gaudí's crypt of the parish **Church of the Sacred Heart** in Santa Coloma de Cervelló, follow the Avinguda Diagonal out of town in the direction of the airport until it becomes the A-2 heading toward Tarragona. Take the "Cinturó Litoral" exit toward Sant Boi de Llobregat and then follow the road toward Sant Vincenç dels Horts. Just before the railroad crossing, take a left (a sign on the side of the building points to the Cripta Güell). Continue straight for about half a mile, and when you come to a small incline, you'll find the church on the right. (If you want to visit just the church and not continue on to the Montserrat Monastery, you can take the FF.CC. de la Generalitat from Plaça d'Espanya to Santa Coloma de Cervelló.)

Here in the village of Santa Coloma de Cervelló, the financier Güell and several associates established a velvet factory and constructed a village for the workers, commissioning Gaudí to design its church. After eight years the project was abandoned and only the crypt of the church had been finished. Nevertheless, it is one of Gaudí's most admired and studied works and anticipates a good many elements of his Sagrada Familia.

Perched atop a small hill amid pine trees, this round, mostly brick structure with a portico of sloping columns and vaults today functions as the village church. In the cavelike interior gloom, the flower-shaped stained-glass windows virtually shine like stars. In reinterpreting the traditional Catalan vault, Gaudí renders it in the form of hyperbolic paraboloids. Of special note inside are the unique benches of wood and wrought iron also of Gaudí design.

The church is open for visits Monday through Saturday from 10:15am to 1:30pm and 4 to 8pm, and on Sunday and holidays from 10am to 2pm. But since this is a functioning church, the hours may vary, and it's advisable to call ahead (have someone at the hotel do it for you if you don't speak Spanish) and confirm the hours. Even if the church isn't open when you get there, however, the exterior is well worth the slight detour en route to the Monastery of Montserrat.

Upon leaving the church, retrace your route to the railroad tracks on the San Vincenç dels Horts road (which becomes the N-11) and continue straight on through that village and through Martorell for a total of about 38 kilometers (24 miles). At this point you'll see a sign indicating Manresa and Montserrat to the right. Up until now you will have been traveling through a highly industrialized area, but here the scenery changes abruptly. The 14 kilometers

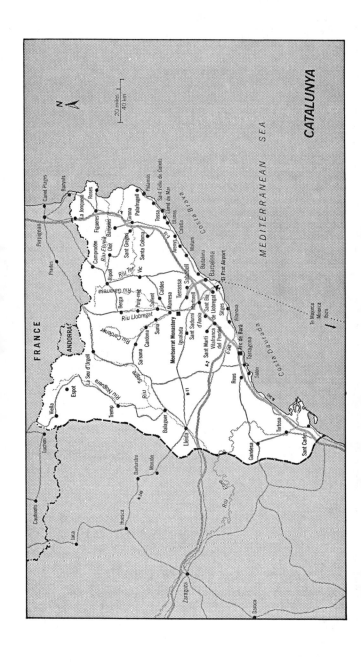

(9 miles) leading up to the monastery wind through pine forests and eerie rock formations resembling sculptured towers. Those familiar with the Meteora in Greece will notice a great scenic similarity.

As you ascend, the vista expands below. In all, it's about 52 kilometers (32 miles) from the Colonia Güell to the monastery, and the drive takes just over an hour in light traffic. Parking at the monastery costs 200 ptas. ($1.75), and on Sunday when the mountaintop is awash with day-trippers and faithful worshippers you may have a bit of a walk from your car.

EXPLORING THE MONASTERY AND ENVIRONS

The complex of the Montserrat Monastery is vast, containing a basilica with the venerated Black Virgin, a museum, numerous hostels for pilgrims, restaurants, and a wealth of souvenir shops and food stalls. The jagged mountain itself ("Montserrat" means "serrated mountain") is 10 kilometers (7 miles) long and 5 kilometers (3.5 miles) wide. Its highest peak, Sant Jeróni, is 1,235 meters (4,075 feet). The monastery itself is situated at 725 meters (2,393 feet). One of its noted institutions is the 50-member Boys Choir *(Escolania)* established in the 13th century. If you time your visit right, you can hear them sing the Salve and the Virolai (the hymn of Montserrat) at 1pm or the Montserratine Salve at 7:10pm.

About 80 Benedictine monks make the monastery, which cannot be visited, their home. What can and should be visited, however, are the basilica, the Chapel of the Virgin, and the museum. The **basilica** dates from the 16th century, although its facade, memorable for the sculptures of Jesus and the 12 Apostles, was not completed until the turn of our century. Inside, all is rather heavy and dark. The main altar is made of rock from the mountain, and suspended from a baldachin above it is a beautiful 16th-century ivory image of Christ of Italian origin mounted on a modern cross.

To see the image of the revered **La Moreneta (Black Madonna)** of Montserrat, Catalunya's patron saint, you must exit the basilica and reenter through the side door on the right. The chapel may be visited Monday through Saturday from noon to 1:30pm and 3 to 6pm, and on Sunday from noon to 6:30pm. The image, housed in a splendid chapel adorned with glittering mosaics, is of Virgin and Child.

For many the trip to Montserrat is a pious pilgrimage; for many others it's a day's diversion—especially of a Sunday when the throngs of visitors and vendors give the place the feel of a religious Disneyland.

The **museum**—admission is 225 ptas. ($2)—is made up of two parts. The old section contains religious paintings of the old Italian and modern Catalonian schools; a biblical collection containing Egyptian, Roman, and Arab archeological artifacts; and a display of Jewish liturgical items, including Torahs from the 17th and 18th centuries. The new section houses secular paintings of the 19th and 20th centuries primarily by such Catalan artists as Raurich and Urgell, although there are a Sorolla and three Picassos here as well. The museums are open July 1 to October 31 and during Holy Week daily from 10:30am to 2pm and 3 to 7pm; from November 1 to June 30 the old museum is open daily from 10:30am to 2pm and the new one daily from 3 to 6pm.

Beyond these man-made sights there is the mountain itself, crisscrossed with numerous funiculars and paths leading to some 13 uninhabited hermitages and numerous shrines—or simply to spectacular views. For a soaring vista, take the funicular up to **Sant Joan.** The round-trip fare is 510 ptas. ($4.25) for adults, 280 ptas. ($2.25) for children 3 to 9 years old, and free for those under 3.

Another interesting outing is that to the **Santa Cova (Holy Grotto).** A funicular takes you half-way down and then you walk to the chapel of the Holy Grotto, built in the 17th century on the spot where, as legend has it, the image of the Black Virgin of Montserrat was found. Along the mile-long road leading to it you will find 15 monuments recalling the Mysteries of the Rosary, some by such famous architects, artists, and artisans as Gaudí, Puig i Cadafalch, and Llimona. A round-trip ticket for both the Santa Cova and Sant Joan funiculars costs 560 ptas. ($4.75) for adults and 305 ptas. ($2.50) for children 3 to 9 (children under 3 free). The funiculars run every 15 or 20 minutes between 10am and 7pm.

Now it's time for lunch. Take the Monistrol/Manresa road back down from the monastery to see the other side of the mountain. When you get to the bottom, take the road toward Barcelona and Martorell for about 25 kilometers (15.5 miles) to the turnoff for **Can Amat,** the flagship of the Paradis group of restaurants, located at kilometer 585 on the N-11. (tel. 771-40-27 or 771-47-77). Here you'll turn into an industrial park. Go straight for about a kilometer, then follow the sign to the left for the restaurant.

Installed in a magnificent Catalan mansion dating from 1890, this restaurant exudes an atmosphere of cozy elegance. A large number of daily specials are offered, along with a fixed menu heavily weighted with seafood (including over half a dozen ways to eat bacallà, or cod). The turbot in a cava-cream sauce was sinfully tasty. But long before you have a chance to study the menu, your table will fill up with olives, bread with tomato, and snails to *abrir el apetito* (open the appetite) in case the menu itself doesn't do the trick. Then, before dessert, you will be served muscatel in a *porrón,* a flask with a pointed spout that must never touch your lips as you lift it up and pour the golden elixir down your throat. (Note: If you've never done this before, ask for a demonstration and an extra napkin to tuck under your chin.) Besides the appetizing desserts on the display cart, the house specializes in exotic ice-cream flavors. How about rice-pudding ice cream? Or chocolate ice cream with spaghetti? (The spaghetti, by the way, is sweet and served warm.) Open daily from 1 to 4pm, with extended hours on Saturday from 9pm to midnight. Meals average about 4,000 ptas. ($33.25). Reservations are urged, especially on weekends.

From Can Amat it's about 30 kilometers (19 miles) back to

Barcelona via the N-11, which leads into the A-2, which eventually becomes Barcelona's Avinguda Diagonal.

---

2. Cava Country

GETTING THERE

The Penedés wineries that produce the fine sparkling wines known as *cava* in Spain are principally found in the area of Sant Sadurní d'Anoia, about 40 kilometers (25 miles) from Barcelona via the A-2 (Exit 27).

Trains run daily to Sant Sadurní d'Anoia (the station is right next to the Freixenet bodega) from Barcelona Sants. To visit the Codorniu winery, however, you need a car, because taxis from the train station are unreliable. Round-trip train fare from Barcelona is 390 ptas. ($3.25). For departure information, call R.E.N.F.E. at 322-41-42.

EXPLORING THE WINERIES

Codorniu, 08770 Sant Sadurní d'Anoia (tel. 891-01-25), is Spain's oldest cava producer (since 1872) and proud to show visitors around its extensive and remarkably immaculate facilities, both above and below ground (down to 29 meters, 95 feet). A brief audio-visual presentation precedes a guided tour that includes the modernist, cathedral-like Hacienda Codorníu designed by Josep Piug i Cadafalch and the 16 kilometers (10 miles) of underground wine cellars where the sparkling wines are produced by the "champenoise" method. (This endless maze of multilevel cellars must really be seen to be believed.) The old pressing section has been converted into a museum, and the whole complex has been declared a national monument. Codorniu produces some 40 million bottles of cava annually, making it the world's largest cava vintner. At any one time, it has about 100 million bottles in stock. The tour concludes with a tasting.

About 160,000 visitors annually take the one- to two-hour tour, which is free and conducted in several languages Monday through Thursday between 8 and 11:30am and 3 and 5:30pm, and on Friday from 8 to 11:30am. The most interesting time to visit is during the grape harvest in September/October; the least interesting time is in August when most of the production facilities are shut down for vacation. (Codorniu now also produces Cava in California's Napa Valley.)

The **Freixenet** winery, 08770 Sant Sadurní d'Anoia (tel. 891-07-00), presents a 30-minute video followed by a one-hour tour detailing the elaboration of its wines. In business since 1889, it has recently also acquired vineyards in California's Sonoma Valley and in France. Although this is not the showpiece vineyard that Codorniu is, its free tour, including a tasting, is every bit as informative as Codorniu's and again is conducted in various languages. Tours are held Monday through Friday at 9:30am, 11am, 3:30pm, and 5pm, except holidays.

If you have a car, you can enhance your oenological knowledge still further with a visit to the **Museu del Vi (Wine Museum),** Plaça Jaume (near the cathedral), in Vilafranca del Penedés (tel. 890-05-82), about 10 kilometers (6 miles) from Sant Sadurní d'Anoia. Surprising in its scope—not only does it have exhibits relating to wine production, storage, and consumption throughout the ages, but impressive collections of art, ceramics, and geological and archeological items—this museum calls itself "the ethnological museum of Vilafranca and of the Penedés . . . the 'Musée de l'Homme' on a Penedés scale." Upon the conclusion of your visit, you are offered a sample of a local white, red, or rosé wine. The museum is open October to May Tuesday through Sunday from 10am to 2pm and 4 to 7pm and June to September Tuesday through Sunday from 10am to 2pm and 4:30 to 7:30pm; closed holidays and the Tuesday after Monday holidays. In other words, call first to make sure it's open. Admission is 200 ptas. ($1.75).

From here you can make an afternoon of it by the sea in Sitges (see Section 5, below), about 22 kilometers (14 miles) away, before returning to Barcelona.

3. North to Girona (Gerona)

GETTING THERE

Located at the confluence of the rivers Ter and Onyar some 96 kilometers (60 miles) north of Barcelona is Girona, a provincial capital with a 2,000-year pedigree.

Trains run daily between Girona and Barcelona Sants station; round-trip fare is about 1,400 ptas. ($11.75). Call R.E.N.F.E. for details at 93/322-41-42. There is also **bus service** from Barcelona's Estacion de Vilanova; call 93/232-04-59. If you're traveling **by car,** take the A-2 to A-7 north.

Tourist information in Girona is located at Plaça del Vi 1.

EXPLORING GIRONA AND ENVIRONS

A key city along the Roman Via Augusta that passed through it, Girona is still today one of Catalonia's most important cities. But it lived its most splendid moments in the Middle Ages and was a focal point for the Jews of the region. Numbering up to 300 strong in its day, Girona's Jewish community—the second largest in Catalonia after Barcelona's—established the first Cabalistic school on the Iberian Peninsula during the first half of the 12th century.

As you cross the Onyar River dividing the old and new towns, you will see its banks lined with colorful houses dating from the late Middle Ages. These border on Girona's old town, which retains its cobblestone streets (bring sensible shoes) and a network of narrow alleys and steep, staircased streets that seem immune to the passing of time. Once inside the old town, take note of the sturdy walls and tower that date from Roman times but were reconstructed during the Middle Ages.

Dominating the old town from its perch at the top of an impressive 17th-century baroque staircase (90 steps) is the city's unusual **cathedral,** on Plaça Catedral. Considered one of the most beautiful examples of Catalan baroque, it is, however, rooted in Romanesque times and really blends a variety of architectural styles. Its nave has the widest unsupported Gothic arch in the world, measuring 22.98 meters (75 feet). In fact, it is the widest nave of any style except for that of St. Peter's Basilica in Rome. The **cathedral museum** (tel. 972/21-44-26) contains two pieces of singular importance. The first is the Tapestry of the Creation, a unique piece of 11th- to 12th-century Romanesque embroidery fashioned from colored wool whose hues have remained remarkably vibrant. The second is the *Códex del Beatus,* a 10th-century illuminated manuscript of commentary on the Book of the Apocalypse, which was illustrated by a nun, Sister Eude. The cathedral's Romanesque cloisters feature well-preserved carvings representing the creation of Man and his fall from grace. The cathedral and museum are open in summer daily from 9:30am to 8pm and in winter daily from 9:30am to 7 pm. Admission to the museum is 150 ptas. ($1.25).

From 890 to 1492, Girona's Carrer de la Força was the backbone of the *Call (Jewish Quarter).* Periodic tensions between the Christian and Jewish communities caused successive modifications in the configuration of the quarter, but nevertheless it remains one of the best-preserved Jewish ghettoes in Western Europe. The tiny Carrer de Sant Llorenç and Carrer de Cúndaro are other vestigial arteries of the Call. On Sant Llorenç is a former synagogue that now houses the **Isaac el Cec Center** (tel. 972/21-67-61), dedicated to presenting exhibitions relating to the Jewish presence in Girona. Visiting hours are Tuesday through Saturday from 10am to 2pm and 4 to 7pm; closed holiday afternoons.

Of special historic interest are the 21 Jewish tombstones with Hebrew inscriptions found in the small Romanesque cloister of the 12th-century **Monestir de Sant Pere de Galligants,** Santa Llúcia 1 (tel. 972/20-26-32), home of the archeological museum. A noteworthy example of Catalan Romanesque architecture, this Benedictine monastery also contains an important collection of prehistoric objects together with items from the Greek and Roman periods, all of which were found in the province of Girona. The museum is open Tuesday through Saturday from 10am to 1pm and 4:30 to 7pm, and on Sunday and holidays from 10am to 1pm. Admission is 100 ptas. (85¢).

Al-Andalus Expreso

In July and August the *Al-Andalus Expreso,* Spain's luxury train, cruises between Barcelona and Santiago de Compostela, following in part the medieval pilgrimage route of St. James. A stunning eyeful of Lalique glass, gleaming brass, meticulous marquetry, and art deco glamour, the *Al-Andalus* actually outclasses the *Orient Express*—it's wider; has showers, a cellular phone, video entertainment, and air conditioning; and makes sightseeing stops. These include Hemingway's Pamplona, Burgos (famed for its cathedral and proximity to the birthplace of El Cid), and León (famed for the stained-glass artistry of its cathedral).

En route to Santiago the train traverses the brooding, mist-suckled landscape of Galicia. Aptly nicknamed "Green Spain," it calls to mind the countryside of Wales, Ireland, and Brittany, with which it shares a common Celtic heritage. In Santiago you'll tour the important Romanesque cathedral that is the alleged final resting place of St. James, Spain's patron saint. Those beginning the trip in Santiago and finishing in Barcelona will stop in Logroño (instead of Pamplona), in the heart of the Rioja wine region, and enjoy a private tour of a noted winery.

The three-day/two-night train journey costs $950 per person in a deluxe double cabin and $1,450 per person in a luxury suite. Prices include all guided sightseeing visits and meals on the train. Special vacation packages, including visits to Madrid or Barcelona, are also available. In the off-season, the *Al-Andalus* offers special holiday excursions and is available for charter. For information and reservations, call 203/454-8916 in Connecticut, or toll free 800/992-3976.

Another museum "must" is the **Museu d'Història de la Ciutat,** Força 13 (tel. 972/20-91-60), installed in an 18th-century convent. Tracing the city's evolution from the ancient settlers of Puig d'en Roca, Catalonia's oldest prehistoric site, to the present day, it displays the apparatus that first illuminated the streets of Girona, the first city on the Iberian Peninsula to have electric street lights. Additional displays of tools, technical materials, and the accoutrements of passing life-styles make up a kind of municipal résumé. Also on proud display are the works of the local *noucentista* sculptor, Fidel Aguilar. From the original Capuchin convent there remains the cemetery used for drying corpses before mummifying them (one of the three of this type left in the world). The museum is open Tuesday through Saturday from 10am to 2pm and 5 to 7pm, and on Sunday and holidays from 10am to 2pm. Admission is 200 ptas. ($1.75).

The **Museu d'Art de Girona,** Plaça de los Apóstoles s/n (no street number) (tel. 972/20-95-36), occupies the former episcopal palace, which preserves a number of Romanesque and Gothic features inside and a Renaissance facade and entrance courtyard outside. Outstanding among its collection of art stretching from the Romanesque period to the present day are the 15th-century altarpiece of Saint Pere of Púbol by Bernat Martorell and that of Saint Michael of Cruïlles by Lluís Borrassa, two exemplary works of Catalan Gothic painting; the 10th- to 11th-century altarstone of Saint Pere of Roda, depicting figures and legends carved of wood and stone and covered in embossed silver; the 12th-century Romanesque biga de Cruïlles (Cruïlles timber) in polychrome wood; a carved alabaster image of Our Lady of Besalú from the 15th century; and a glazier's table from the 14th century, which indicates how Gothic stained glass was prepared. The museum is open Tuesday through Saturday from 10am to 1pm and 4:30 to 7pm, and on Sunday and holidays from 10am to 1pm. Admission is 100 ptas. (85¢).

Girona's **Passeig Arqueològic** is a 20th-century walk skirting a large section of the old city ramparts. The stroll is pleasant and punctuated with scenic views of the city. Just off it near the cathedral are the **Jardins de la Francesa,** which lie within the city wall and offer a view of the impressive bulk of the cathedral and the outskirts of Girona.

The city's *banys árabs* (Arab baths) are a Romanesque copy of Moorish models and were heavily restored in 1929. In their prime they were the setting for parties and merriment just beyond the city walls, with areas for hot baths, steam baths, and cold baths. In summer you can visit the baths Tuesday through Saturday from 10am to 1pm and 4:30 to 7pm, and on Sunday and holidays from 10am to 1pm; in winter, Tuesday through Sunday (including holidays) from 10am to 1pm. Admission is 100 ptas. (85¢).

The eight pinnacles of **L'Església de Sant Feliu** distinctively mark the Girona skyline and signal a church of artistic importance. Dating from the 14th to the 17th century, its Romanesque pillars and arches support a central nave in the Gothic style surrounded by an elegant triforium. Note the 14th-century reclining Christ sculpted in alabaster by Aloi de Montbrai; it demonstrates a naturalism unusual in Catalan Gothic. Also exceptional are the eight pagan and Christian sarcophagi set in the walls of the presbytery on either side of the high altar. The two oldest are from the 2nd century and are in a late Roman style. One depicts Pluto carrying Proserpina off to the depths of the earth in a chariot; the other, a lion hunt. There is no admission charge and the church is open most of the time.

If you wish to have lunch in Girona, **Bronsoms,** Avinguda Sant Francisco 7 (tel. 972/21-24-93), serves regional specialties with home-cooked goodness. One eye-catching feature in its otherwise plain decor is a collection of menus that owner-chef Josep Bronsoms has worked hard to assemble. Try the chipirones for 785 ptas. ($6.50) or the pulpitos for 645 ptas. ($5.50) to start, and then perhaps a fish dish or a tender veal filet, at 1,150 ptas. ($9.50). Meals average under 1,500 ptas. ($12.50). Bronsoms is open Monday through Friday from 1 to 4pm and 9 to 11pm; on Saturday, Sunday, and holidays from 1 to 4pm only. It is closed the third Sunday of every month and three weeks in August.

After a morning's sightseeing in Girona, consider heading to Figueres, about 37 kilometers (23 miles) north, to see the **Teatre-Museu Dalí,** Plaça de Salvador Dalí i Gala s/n (no street number) (tel. 972/50-56-97). Installed in the former municipal theater, it is every bit as eccentric as the man who conjured it and, among Spanish museums, second only to the Prado in number of visitors. It contains paintings, sculptures, jewelry, drawings, and sketches by the artist himself; works from his private collection; and various "constructions" from different periods of his career. Dalí would permit no catalog of its contents to be prepared, however, believing his museum to be not an intellectual experience but a spiritual one.

Truly a celebration of one man's unbridled imagination, this artistic funhouse is replete with optical illusions and sleights—not of hand but of mind. Some of it is even done with mirrors. In the courtyard, drop a coin into the slot and the vintage Cadillac will drench its trailing plastic plants with water. Drop a coin into the viewer on the ground floor and a painting of Gala looking at the sea becomes a representation of Abraham Lincoln. Surprises in every nook and cranny are the order of the day here. The museum is open in summer daily from 9am to 8:15pm and in winter daily from 10:30am to 5:15pm. Admission is 300 ptas. ($2.50).

Those who want to enjoy a fine dinner and some excitement before returning to Barcelona can visit the **Casino Castell de Peralada** (tel. 972/53-81-25), less than 10 kilometers (6 miles) north of Figueres (bring your passport). Installed in a 14th-century castle built in the Majorcan Gothic style, the main gaming salons and restaurant are appropriately aristocratic, with vintage tapestries and palatial paintings.

The restaurant, offering a menu of the day for 3,500 ptas. ($29.25), is noted for its emphasis on Empordán cuisine with such specialties as goose liver with sour apples and magrêt of duck stuffed with liver and walnuts. Outstanding among its seafood selection are the filet of sole and curried saltwater prawns. The wine list is laden with regional and Spanish representatives but also offers a good selection of French wines and champagnes. The restaurant is open daily from 9pm to midnight, and meals begin at about 5,000 ptas. ($41.75).

During July and August the casino offers concerts and top entertainment under the stars; recent headliners have included Jerry Lewis, Liza Minelli and Sammy Davis, Jr., and Julio Iglesias. Depending on the entertainment, tickets run from 2,500 ptas. ($20.75) to ten times that amount. In summer you can dine in the open-air terrace restaurant from 8:30pm. From July 15 to September 3 the casino is open daily from 7pm to 5am; the rest of the year it closes at 4am. You'll need your passport to get in; admission is 550 ptas. ($4.50).

4. South to Tarragona

GETTING THERE
Heading out of town on the A-2, you will pass through cava country en route to Tarragona, some 110 kilometers (68 miles) south of Barcelona. Though it's physically longer and more costly to

go via the A-2 and then the A-7 than via the N-340 (tolls amount to over 600 ptas., or $5, by the time you get there), it's faster. Later in the day, after you've seen all the sights, take the more leisurely route back to Barcelona.

Trains run daily to Tarragona from Barcelona Sants; round-trip fare is 740 ptas. ($6.25). For detailed information, call R.E.N.F.E. at 93/322-41-42.

Just before Exit 33 into Tarragona along the A-7, you'll see on your right the **Pont del Diable,** part of the Roman aqueduct that served this city whose origins hark back to the arrival of the Romans around 218 B.C. Recognizing that the rocky bluff at the edge of the sea was a perfect natural defense for the port below, the Romans established Tarraco as a base for conquering the peninsula. Soon it blossomed into the most elegant and cultured city of the Roman Spanish provinces and became one of Rome's four Catalonian capitals. Later, the emperors Hadrian and Augustus each put their architectural stamps upon the city, which was then both an administrative center and a favored holiday resort.

Tourist information is located at Rambla Nova 46.

EXPLORING TARRAGONA AND ENVIRONS

Today Tarragona is Catalunya's second-largest city, with the attendant industrialization and ugly outskirts to prove it. The ancient and medieval walled city sits on high while the modern urban expanse radiates beyond the 19th-century town below, whose Rambla Nova is a showpiece promenade lined with fashionable shops and cafés. The Rambla Vella, running parallel to the Rambla Nova to the east, marks the limits of the old town. Vestiges of Tarragona's Roman days are scattered throughout both areas of the city.

To explore the sights of the old, upper reaches of the city, I suggest the following walking tour, which should take you right up to lunch. Try to get to Tarragona by about 10am, when things open up. Park near the cathedral or Plaça del Rei (you may have to ask directions as the signs are poor).

Begin the day's tour at the **Museu Nacional Arqueològic,** Plaça del Rei (tel. 977/23-62-06), built atop part of the ancient Roman city wall. Its attractive displays of Roman artifacts, mosaics, statuary, pottery, and architectural fragments date primarily from ancient Tarraco. From July to September the museum is open Tuesday through Saturday from 10am to 1pm and 4:30 to 8pm, and on Sunday and holidays from 10am to 2pm; from October to June it's open Tuesday through Saturday from 10am to 1:30pm and 4 to 7pm, and on Sunday and holidays from 10am to 2pm. Admission is 100 ptas. (85¢), free on Tuesday.

Next door is the **Museu d'História de Tarragona** (tel. 977/23-21-26), where you can continue to follow the history of the city through its Visigothic, Moorish, and medieval periods while exploring the Roman Praetorium in which the museum is installed. Just wandering through these impressive vaults is worth the price of admission. Ask for an English-language brochure to help explain the displays, which are labeled in Catalan. And usually you can visit the upper terrace of this structure, which provides a panoramic view of the city. A set of exterior stairs leads you back to the Plaça del Rei while giving you a good look at the 3rd-century B.C. Roman walls that circled the old city. Only about one-fourth of the original wall remains today. The hours and admission charges are the same as its neighbor, the Museu Nacional Arqueològic (see listing directly above).

Now walk down the Passeig de Sant Antoni to take in the view from the Balcó del Mediterrani above the **Roman amphitheater,** located on the beach at the foot of the beautifully terraced Miracle Park. Dating from the end of the 1st century or the first half of the 2nd century B.C., the amphitheater took advantage of the natural slope of the bedrock for part of its tiered seats. From October to March it is open Monday through Saturday from 10am to 6pm and on Sunday and holidays from 10am to 2pm; from April to September, Sunday through Friday and holidays from 10am to 2pm and on Saturday from 10am to 8pm.

Cross over the Passeig de les Palmeres and enter the Rambla Vella. On the right is the entrance to the **Voltes del Circ,** venue for the Roman chariot races. Uncovered not too long ago, these ruins are still under excavation. They are officially open to the public October to March Monday through Friday from 10am to 1pm, on Saturday from 10am to 6pm, and on Sunday from 10am to 2pm; and from April to September Monday through Friday from 10am to 2pm. The ongoing work might disrupt the viewing hours; nevertheless, even when it's closed you can see a good deal through the fence. Admission to both the amphitheater and the Voltes is free.

Now head back up to Carrer Nau leading off the Museu d'Història and take a right on Carrer Major, a pedestrian passageway, to the **cathedral** (tel. 977/23-34-12), which you enter through the cloister. The cathedral's construction spanned the 12th to 14th centuries and combines the Romanesque and Gothic vernaculars. The main doorway is pure Gothic while the doors of the lateral naves flanking it are Romanesque. Above the transept rises a notable octagonal dome flanked on either side by beautiful Gothic rose windows. Worthy of your attention are the Chapel of the Holy Sepulchre, whose sculpture of Christ lies on a 4th-century Roman sepulchre; the open choir, which is Gothic with plateresque chairs dating from the beginning of the 16th century; and the numerous items on display in the Chapel of Corpus Christi, including medieval utensils for making Communion hosts.

The cathedral's square cloister illustrates the transitional Romanesque style with six ogival arches along each side divided into three semicircular arches. Take time to observe the capitals depicting a variety of biblical and mythical scenes and a curious procession of rats.

The cathedral is open November to March daily from 10am to 1pm and 4 to 6pm, and April to October daily from 10am to 7pm. Admission is 150 ptas. ($1.25).

Now return to Carrer Nau and follow its continuation, Carrer Cavallers, to no. 14, the **Casa-Museo Castellarnau** (tel. 977/23-69-46), a noble house whose distinguished guest in 1542 was none other than the emperor, Charles I. The mezzanine floor contains archeological, ethnological, and historical objects from Tarragona, including a collection of coins dating from the time of the Roman conquest to the early 20th century, numerous Roman ceramics, and an array of Catalan tiles dating from the 17th to the 19th century. The upper floor is a veritable palace, with floors of typical geometric Catalan tiling, trompe l'oeil wall and ceiling paintings, and a remarkable assemblage of furnishings in the Elizabethan, Empire, and Louis XV and XVI styles. Over the billiard table hangs an elaborate lamp in the turn-of-the-century modernist tradition. Open Monday through Saturday from 10am to 1pm and 4 to 7pm, and on Sunday and holidays from 10am to 1pm. Admission is 100 ptas. (85¢).

Follow Carrer Cavallers to Plaça del Pallol where the structures top Roman remains with Gothic motifs. Go through the arch at the far end of the plaça to enter the **Passeig Arqueològic,** a half-mile walkway along the old Roman wall that is attractively landscaped, perfumed with cypress, and punctuated with sporadic overviews of the city. Of special note along the way are the Minerva tower and its adjacent Roman gate and the Cyclopean doors in the megalithic base of the wall, distinguished by enormous stone blocks believed to have been laid down by pre-Roman Iberian inhabitants. The walkway is open October to January Monday through Saturday from 10am to 1pm and 3 to 5pm, and on Sunday and holidays from 10am to 2pm; from February to June, daily from 10am to 1pm and 3 to 6:30pm.; and July to September, daily from 10am to 8pm. Admission is 100 ptas. (85¢).

After lunch, visit the remains of the **Roman forum** wedged between Carrer Lleida and Carrer Soler in the new town. The reconstructed columns and skeletal excavations are so attractively set off with greenery that they create a small parklike oasis in the heart of the lower town. In the 19th century that park grew beyond the old city walls and now contains numerous examples of modernist architecture. The Roman forum is open October to June Tuesday through Saturday from 10am to 1pm and 3 to 6pm; July to September, Tuesday through Saturday from 10am to 1pm and 4 to 7pm. Admission is free.

The last major sight to visit before leaving the city is the **Museu Necropolis Paleocristians,** Passeig de la Independéncia s/n (no street number) (tel. 977/21-11-75). This ancient burial ground, conserved in situ, came to light in 1923 when the new tobacco factory was built. Comprising an open-air excavation area and an indoor museum, its great importance lies in the broad historic scope of its more than 2,000 pagan and Christian tombs—they date from the late Roman period through the 5th century. Open September 16 to May 15 Monday through Saturday from 10am to 1:30pm and 4 to 7pm, and on Sunday and holidays from 10am to 2pm; May 16 to September 15, Monday through Saturday from 10am to 1pm and 4:30 to 8pm, and on Sunday and holidays from 10am to 2pm. Admission is 100 ptas. (85¢), free on Tuesday.

If you take the N-340 back to Barcelona, you will catch glimpses of the sea along the way as well as pass by the **Torre dels Escipions** on your left about six kilometers (four miles) out of town. This funerary monument possibly dates from the first half of A.D. 1. Some 20 kilometers (12.5 miles) out of town, you'll find the **Arc de Berá,** built at the beginning of the 2nd century, right in the middle of the road. As you near Barcelona, you might want to take the turn off toward Sitges to have dinner and try your luck at the Gran Casino de Barcelona (see Section 9 in Chapter V).

5. Sitges

GETTING THERE

At the end of the Garraf coast some 43 kilometers (27 miles) from Barcelona, Sitges is about a 45-minute drive away along the C-246, the coastal road leading off the Plaça d'Espanya. But by 1991 there should be a highway between Barcelona and Sitges that will cut this time in half.

Trains run daily to Sitges from Barcelona Sants for 390 ptas. ($3.25) round-trip. Call R.E.N.F.E. for details at 322-41-42.

EXPLORING SITGES AND ENVIRONS

Popular with both Barceloneses and travelers from less sunny climes, this seaside village was once an elite retreat for wealthy Catalan merchants and industrialists and such prominent artists as Dalí, Rusiñol, and Casas. Of late it has begun to swing with the young, trendy set, and has gained increasing popularity among the gay community. On a summer weekend and during the months of July and August it bursts at the seams with a polyglot population of fun-seekers from all over Europe. By mid-October it retreats into hibernation.

In the village's old quarter, perched on a promontory, are two charming museums. **Cau Ferrat,** Fonollars s/n (no street number) (tel. 93/894-03-64), is the legacy of the well-known Catalan painter Santiago Rusiñol, who lived and worked in this 19th-century house that combined two 16th-century fishermen's homes. When he died in 1931, he left his house and his choice collection of paintings (including several small Picassos, two El Grecos, and many of his own works), wrought iron, tiles, and archeological artifacts to the town.

Right next door is the **Museu Maricel de Mar,** Fonollar s/n (no street number) (tel. 93/894-03-64), the legacy of Dr. Perez Rosales, whose impressive collection of furniture, porcelain, lamps, and tapestries draws largely from the medieval, Renaissance, and baroque periods. But there are also Romanesque frescoes and an entire 14th-century chapel! One particularly impressive room contains murals by Josep M. Sert i Badía with allegorical depictions of World War I. Originally painted for this room when the house was owned by an American, these murals traveled back to the United States with the owner and went on auction after his death. A series of subsequent auctions took them to several countries before Dr. Rosales bought them at auction and installed them once again in their original spot.

Both of these museums are open Tuesday through Saturday from 9:30am to 2pm and 4 to 6pm, and on Sunday from 9:30am to 2pm. Admission to each one is 100 ptas. (85¢).

Once you've had your dose of culture, you might want to wander the town's narrow, winding streets lined with bright, whitewashed houses or just head for the beach. Of special note at the western end of town are the numerous turn-of-the-century mansions (some in modernist style) lining Passeig Marítim. Platja de St. Sebastiá, east of the old town, is among the more tranquil of the centrally located beaches. West of the old town, along Passeig de la Ribera, is a dense concentration of restaurants and bars, and in the streets behind it are numerous trendy shops.

The **Gran Casino de Barcelona,** Sant Pere de Ribes (tel. 93/893-36-66), is just five kilometers (three miles) from Sitges along the C-246 (for more information, see Section 9 in Chapter V).

PART TWO

MAJORCA, IBIZA, AND MINORCA

INTRODUCING MAJORCA, IBIZA, AND MINORCA

Majorca, Ibiza, Minorca. Ask most people where these are and they'll probably tell you somewhere off the Mediterranean coast of Spain. But ask them where the Balearic Islands are and you'll probably draw a blank. Los Baleares (in Spanish) are an uncommon set of islands stretching along the eastern coast of Spain from Valencia to Barcelona. An archipelago comprising three sizable tourist islands and several smaller islets, the Baleares allegedly derive their collective name from *balaro,* the Phoenician term given to the slingshots the aboriginal population handled so expertly—on occasion against the armies of Hannibal.

Since February 25, 1983, the Balearic Islands have been autonomously governed by the Govern Balear, headquartered in the regional capital of Palma de Majorca on the largest island of the group. Next in size is Minorca, 35 miles northeast of Majorca, and then Ibiza, 46 miles south of Majorca. There are also several smaller islands and islets—among them, Formentera (a tourist extension of Ibiza), Cabrera, and Dragonera (uninhabited).

What these islands have in common are lots of lazy, white-sand beaches; vibrant, aquamarine waters; countless coves sheltered by towering cliffs; and a history dating back thousands of years before Christ. What they don't have in common is just about everything else. Their personalities, temperaments, and touristic miens are as different from one another as they are from the Spanish mainland.

Majorca is the most touristy of the three. Jaded in part by overexploitation, it nevertheless has stashed away a goodly number of off-the-beaten-track pleasures.

Ibiza, feisty and footloose, is unabashed, uninhibited, and uncomplicatedly carefree. A passionate nonconformist, it appeals to free spirits who ask nothing more of an island than sand and sea and the opportunity to do exactly as they please.

Minorca is the shy, serene one. Prim and proper, it yields its most beguiling charms only to those willing to reach out and seize them, to travel a few rough miles for the smiles of a deserted beach or the impassioned embrace of a glorious vista.

Easily tacked onto a Barcelona holiday or undertaken as a

stand-alone, island-hopping experience in their own right, the Balearics offer something for every vacation taste.

MAJORCA

Nicknamed "La Isla de Calma" ("the tranquil island"), Majorca can be just that in its quiet coves, but it can also be quite lively in the bustling center of its capital, Palma. Long a haven for package-tour vacationers from Britain, Germany, and northern European climes, the island has grown rather tired of throwing cheap holiday bashes for the multitudes. The time has come, some local officials say, to upgrade the offering and expand with the greatest of care. The sentiment is commendable and we should wish them well, because beach resorts are a dime a dozen, and Majorca can be a good deal more.

Scattered throughout its countryside are crumbling, megalithic monuments suggesting prehistoric habitation by the Talayotic civilization existing from the 13th century B.C. until the arrival of the Romans. The island's earliest identifiable settlers were the Phoenicians, however, followed over the centuries by the Greeks, Carthaginians, Romans, Vandals, Byzantines, and Moors. In 1229, James I, King of Aragón, captured Majorca for his realm. After a brief period of independence, it returned to the crown of Aragón in 1343 and became part of Spain when the Catholic Kings unified the nation at the end of the 15th century.

Palma de Majorca and Alcudia are the island's oldest existing settlements, dating from a 123 B.C. Roman founding. Of all the subsequent conquering presences, the 327 years of Moorish rule left the most enduring mark. Although most of the monumental structures of that period have been razed by the destructive hand of conflict, the traditional green-and-blue (Islam's sacred colors) trim on the houses and the practice of keeping one's home shut to the outside world with "jalousied" shutters are quotidian vestiges of Muslim custom.

Of all the Balearic Islands, Majorca offers the greatest scenic contrast and impact. In the north, rugged mountains shield the island from cold winds and shelter valleys verdant with orange and lemon trees. In the west, dramatic cliffs embrace quiet, reclusive coves. In the center, almond blossoms color the plains pink and white in January and February, and picturesque windmills provide scenic relief from the flatness. Along the coast, olive trees, twisted and tangled with age, survey the soothing blue waters of the Mediterranean.

For want of a river, however, Majorca, like the other Balearics, suffers from a chronic scarcity of water. In centuries gone by, it was plagued by pirates, who occasioned the construction of numerous cliff-top watchtowers, some of which linger on in ominous ruin.

In the 19th century, well before tourism was an industry on the island, Majorca attracted numerous painters, writers, and other artists in search of peace and inspiration. In fact, the island is still dining out on the brief presence of George Sand and Chopin in the

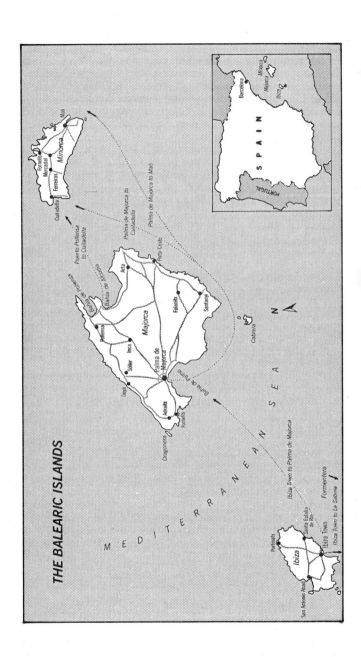

THE BALEARIC ISLANDS

winter of 1838–39. More recently, Majorca proved the muse of choice for author Robert Graves, who made his home in Deyá, and Catalan artist Joan Miró, who established his home and studio in Cala Mayor.

Among Majorca's 585,000 population are some 30,000 English-speaking residents, including many Europeans who have established second homes here. At times referred to as the "California of Europe," Majorca does bear a certain scenic and climatic resemblance to that state. No doubt native Majorcan Junípero Serra, who in the 18th century established numerous missions in California, thought so too.

Among the ranks of frequent visitors to the island are the Spanish royal family and their friends among the English royalty. But it is, of course, the "commoners" of this world who make Palma de Majorca's airport one of Europe's busiest in the summer. Annually, over four million regular folks descend upon the island for R&R.

In addition to its career as a holiday haven, Majorca engages in substantial agricultural activity, its main crops being almonds, oranges, lemons, carob, olives, pears, apples, grapes, and melons. The production of simulated pearls and the fabrication of fine leather goods are also important economic activities. Among the island's leading handcrafts are wrought-iron work, ceramics, glass, and furniture.

Its culinary accomplishments are the *calderetas* (fish stews) commonly found along the coast, the *ensaimada* (a spiral pastry), the *sopas mallorquinas* (made from a mixture of pork and vegetables whose broth is soaked up with slices of bread), *tumbet* (a vegetable dish similar to ratatouille), and *sobrasada* (a slightly piquant pork sausage).

Most visitors to Majorca come for the Mediterranean sun and sea and remain oblivious to its inland riches. If you make the trip, take some time off from tanning to dip into the till.

IBIZA

The Carthaginians called it "Ibosim"; the Greeks, "Ebysos"; the Romans, "Ebusus." Once the coin of the realm bore the name "Aivis," and the Arabs called it "Yebisah." We now call it Ibiza, and the locals increasingly insist on "Eivissa." But by any other name, it's the same enchanting holiday retreat.

A spellbinding island, Ibiza exudes an ineluctable enchantment. The tally of its myriad beaches, scores of boutiques, pine-clad hills, and remote coves is an inadequate and inappropriate measure of its mettle. For Ibiza is, above all, a celebration of individualism, a place where humankind's diversity can do, within the limits of respect for others, precisely as it pleases. "Laid back" and "mellow" may be California concepts, but they suit Ibiza to a "T." Nothing is strange or out of place here.

Basking in the Mediterranean some 280 kilometers (175 miles) from Barcelona and 137 kilometers (85 miles) from Palma de Majorca, Ibiza, with an area of 572 square kilometers (230 square miles), is the third largest of the Balearic Islands. Along with the island of Formentera, it marks the southernmost extension of the archipelago. But unlike most small islands that one exhausts quickly, Ibiza seems rather to grow as you get to know it. The more you immerse yourself in its freewheeling spirit, the richer, deeper, and more textured the place becomes. Really, it is many islands in one. Ergo, Ibiza is what you want it to be—remote and reclusive, or highly social and trendy. You define your vacation terms and the island will oblige.

Although it's been over 20 years, everyone here still talks about the halcyon "hippie" days of the '60s when Ibiza evolved its distinctive ad-lib, ad-libitum, "ad-libido" ethic. The idea remains to go with the flow. Time is unstructured, elastic; and plans are something best left to tomorrow . . . or next week . . . or next year. People still come for vacation and stay forever. Former "flower children," now often dressed to the yuppie nines, keep coming back for a dose of nostalgia, while today's New Age youth constructs its own version of Ibiza for the '90s.

Once upon a distant time the Phoenicians, the earliest-known foreigners to arrive on the scene, made Ibiza a focal point for commerce. Its strategic position along the Mediterranean's prime trade routes subsequently attracted the Carthaginians, Greeks, Romans, Vandals, Byzantines, and Moors. In the 8th century, the struggle between the Christians and the Moors began, ending in Arab victory at the beginning of the 10th century. In 1235, however, the island reverted to Christianity under the crown of Aragón. Ever since, its fate has been linked with that of the Spanish mainland.

From the 14th to mid-18th century, piracy was rampant. In the 18th and 19th centuries Ibiza's corsairs defended their home and surrounding seas against that seafaring menace. Today a monumental tribute to those swashbuckling heroes of yesteryear stands in the Port of Ibiza.

Looking inland for a moment, Ibiza's topography is irregular and varied, with many pine forests tinged a startlingly vibrant chartreuse. In fact, Ibiza and Formentera were called by the Greeks the *pitiusas,* or piny, islands, and the nickname is still bandied about today. To the Romans, Ibiza was a sacred isle because it was (and still is) devoid of any poisonous flora or fauna. In fact, many of imperial Rome's prominent citizens were brought here for burial.

One curious note of animal lore is the Ibizan hound. Most often reddish-brown and white, with a slender snout and erect pointed ears, this breed of dog, prized for its excellent hunting instincts, dates back to the time of the Pharaohs and is conserved purebred in the Ibizan countryside.

Although the juggernaut of mass tourism has considerably altered the island during the last 25 years, traditions struggle to survive, at least in the interior villages. In the 1950s the population was 30,000 and the island was very poor. Since the dawn of mass tourism, the population has more than doubled, including several thousand foreigners, among them many writers and artists. Supplementing the current population of 70,000 are well over one million tourists annually, primarily from Europe. As Ibiza's climate is somewhat warmer than Majorca's, it is a better choice for a winter escape, although many tourist facilities do shut down.

The island's second most important industry is fashion. Lagging well behind are the cultivation of olives, citrus fruit, almonds, and ground crops, and the handcrafted production of leather goods, ceramics, tapestries, jewelry, lace, and embroidery. The oldest industry on the island, however, is salt production. Started by the Romans in the 3rd century B.C., it continues in much the same way on the 400 acres known as Las Salinas.

Today some 100 Ibiza families still make their living from fishing. Red mullet, grouper, stone bass, scorpion fish, pilchard, and white bream are some of the more popular species abounding in this part of the Mediterranean. Among the island's more unusual seafood fare are *ratjada* (skate or ray) and *dentón.*

MINORCA

To poorly paraphrase Robert Frost, this is the Balearic Island less traveled—and that makes all the difference. It also makes it a little duller than its more developed siblings. But there are those among us who perhaps prefer it that way.

Minorca's most striking departure from the Balearic fold lies in its British legacy. A hundred years of British rule have left their imprint in the stone walls that crisscross the countryside and in the overall tenor of the island that tempers Spanish exuberance with British reserve. Although physically larger than Ibiza (measuring some 9 miles wide by 30 miles long), Minorca seems somehow smaller, in part because its windswept scenery stoops defensively low to the ground and in part because its limited network of roads necessarily limits the number of places one can go.

As with the other islands of the group, its history has been a collaborative effort of the Greeks, Phoenicians, Carthaginians (Mahón, the capital, owes its name to the Carthaginian general Magon), Romans, Byzantines, and Muslims—as well as the British, and, last, the Spanish. The Romans called it Menorca ("the little one") in contrast to Majorca ("the big one"). In 1287 Minorca became part of the Kingdom of Aragón and was thus inducted into the linguistic and cultural community of Catalunya, many of whose inhabitants came to repopulate the island.

In 1535 Redbeard ("Barbarossa" in Spanish) devastated Maó (Mahón), prompting the city to retreat within defensive walls whose only remnant is the Pont de Sant Roc, one of the city gates. In 1713 Spain ceded the island to England under the Treaty of Utrecht. During nearly a century of British domination, the struggle for dominion flared continuously among the English, French, and Spanish. In 1802, under the Treaty of Amiens, the Spanish got it back.

Economic activity thrived under the British, and the modern outline of the current capital began to take shape. Many important buildings, including the main barracks, the Town Hall, and the principal churches, date from this period. The British also introduced the art of distilling juniper berries into Minorcan gin (Xoriguer, Beltra, and Nelson are some local brands to look for), which advocates claim is superior to all others. You be the judge.

Somewhat surprisingly, Minorca for a long time enjoyed the highest standard of living in all of Spain, rooted not in tourism but in the shoe and costume-jewelry industries. Recently the rest of the nation has caught up, and tourism has begun to eclipse all other economic enterprises on the island—something of great concern to many locals. Tourists number slightly over half a million annually, but to date the island still retains much of its virgin beauty both along the coast and inland, and one can only hope that Minorca takes to heart the lessons harshly learned in parts of Majorca and Ibiza.

Those among the 60,000 people (many of whom speak excellent English) not engaged in tourism participate in the production of costume jewelry, leather goods, cheese and cured sausages, and assorted handcrafts.

In addition to sand, sea, sun, and virile coastal cliffs, Minorca offers many interesting archeological remains, and—though this might sound strange—an unusual moon. Somehow that earth-orbiting orb seems closer, bigger, and more commanding here. I was not alone in noting this and urge visitors to keep an eye out for this curious phenomenon.

The nice thing is that Minorca prompts such celestial observations. For those tired of life in the fast lane, Minorca's singular moon and its palette of white houses, green hills, and blue sea and sky paint a soothing portrait of escape.

PRE-TRIP PREPARATIONS

Travel Documents
See "Pre-Trip Preparations" in Chapter I.

Climate
First and foremost, the Balearic Islands tally about 300 sunny days a year. In winter, water temperatures remain moderate, and hearty souls can still enjoy a swim. The norm in summer is warm, sunny days with mild evenings; in winter, mild days with cool to chilly nights. The average maximum daily temperature is 70°F (21°C); the average minimum, 57°F (14°C). On rare occasions the mercury may approach the freezing point, but it will almost never cross that climatic threshold. The sun is spelled by brief showers now and then, mostly in autumn and early winter. April, May, September, and October are often the best months for moderate weather and moderate crowds. July and August are hot and thick with tourists. Bearing in mind that Ibiza is slightly warmer and Minorca slightly windier, the monthly averages for Palma de Majorca shown in the table serve as a barometer of the Balearic climate throughout the year.

Palma de Majorca's Average Daytime Temperatures and Days of Sunshine

	Jan	Feb	Mar	Apr	May	June	July	Aug	Sept	Oct	Nov	Dec
Temp. (°F)	50	52	54	59	63	71	76	76	73	65	58	53
Temp. (°C)	10	12	13	15	18	22	25	25	23	19	14	12
Days of Sun	23	22	23	24	26	27	30	28	25	22	22	22

What to Pack

In late spring, summer, and early fall, pack for the beach and take a light shawl or jacket for the occasional cool evening. In the winter, take clothes that can be layered at night for warmth and peeled off stratum by stratum as the sun warms the day.

Advance Tourist Information

For information to help you plan your trip, contact the **Spanish National Tourist Office** nearest you (see Chapter I for addresses and telephone numbers).

PALMA DE MAJORCA

Capital of Majorca and the Balearic Islands, Palma de Majorca is part medieval still life and part bustling, modern metropolis. Clustered around the majestic cathedral are the well-worn mementoes of centuries gone by—cobblestone streets, narrow alleys, and stoic, stone structures. Along the Paseo Marítimo are the contemporary trappings of commerce and tourism—high-rise hotels, sophisticated restaurants, and a plethora of nocturnal diversions.

Located about 80 kilometers (50 miles) from Barcelona, Palma's airport is one of the busiest in Europe, funneling over 10 million visitors to the island annually. Beginning in 1990, its capacity will be expanded to accommodate 30 million passengers annually.

Among Majorca's most prominent annual visitors is the Spanish royal family. Every Easter and summer they come to stay at the Palacio de Marivent, between Palma and Illetas, where they are often joined by Prince Charles and Lady Di.

Palma's sweeping bay, stretching 48 kilometers (30 miles) cape to cape, is one of the largest in the world. Unfortunately, haphazard construction has somewhat scarred the municipal waterfront. Still, the city is attractive. Endowed with all the cosmopolitan trappings one would expect of a city of 315,000 inhabitants, it is bustling year round and is a good base from which to enjoy the nearby beaches and explore the rest of the island.

During the Moorish domination of Majorca from the 9th through the 11th century, the old city of Palma was a walled casbah, or fortified city. After Jaime I of Aragón brought the island into the

Catalan fold in 1229, Palma steadily climbed to the pinnacle of riches and prominence it enjoyed in the 15th century as the main port of call between Europe and Africa. In 1928, with the building of Palma's first hotel, the island embarked on a new career as a purveyor of vacation pleasures. Today there are over 1,000 hotels throughout the island, most of them in Palma itself and the surrounding holiday communities strung along the island's southwestern coast.

1. Orientation

GETTING THERE

From Madrid, Barcelona, the other Balearic Islands, and many major European cities, there is frequent regular and charter air service. Barcelona is the major gateway, with several daily flights in summer. Both **Iberia** (tel. 800/SPAIN-1B) and **Aviaco** fly to Palma from Barcelona, Valencia, and Madrid, with Aviaco operating the bulk of the inter-island flights. In August the system is taxed to the limit and often breaks down, so make sure you have confirmed reservations both for transportation and accommodation during that month.

Air Europa offers charter flights from New York to Madrid and from Madrid to Palma de Majorca (with limited peak-season service from Madrid to Ibiza). For information and reservations, contact Club de Vacaciones, 775 Park Ave., Huntington, NY 11743 (tel. 516/424-9600).

Regular **ferry service** (more frequent in summer) links Majorca with the other Balearic Islands, Barcelona, and Valencia. There is also **hydrofoil service** between Barcelona and the islands of Majorca and Minorca aboard the luxury *El Leopardo*. Contact any travel agent for details.

UPON ARRIVAL

The **airport tourism office** (tel. 26-08-03) is open Monday through Saturday from 9:30am to 8pm and on Sunday from 9:30am to 2pm in winter, later in summer.

Buses from the airport to the Plaza España, in the center of Palma, run every 30 minutes and cost 120 ptas. ($1) during the day and 135 ptas. ($1.10) at night and on holidays. **Taxi** rates to various destinations throughout the island are posted by the airport taxi stand. The fare to the Paseo Marítimo is about 1,500 ptas. ($12.50).

You can **change money** 24 hours a day (except New Year's Eve and Easter) at the airport office of the Banco Exterior de España.

If you've arrived without room reservations, you can book a room at the **Ultramar Express counter** (tel. 26-62-79) at the air-

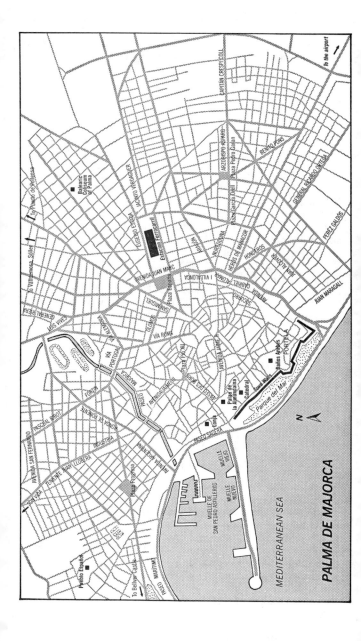

PALMA DE MAJORCA

MEDITERRANEAN SEA

To the airport

port during July, August, September, and Christmas, daily from 9am to 9pm.

If you come **by boat,** the passenger port is some 4 kilometers (2.5 miles) west of town. There is bus service into town, but to catch the bus you have to walk about half a kilometer. Buses to the Paseo de Borne run every half hour, but service may be curtailed on Sunday and late at night.

GETTING AROUND

Since tourist activity is centered in the rather compact old town or along the Paseo Marítimo, you can do a good deal of sightseeing and shopping **on foot** or by making limited use of **taxis.** Having your own car can be a hindrance because of the scarcity of parking and the stringent application of parking rules.

Municipal **buses** serve the city of Palma and full information on lines and hours is available from the tourist offices (see "Tourist Information," in Section 2, below). Since bus service to other parts of the island is offered by a variety of private companies, again contact the tourist offices for full information or call the central bus station in Plaza España (tel. 75-22-24); to find out about special service for the handicapped, call 29-57-00.

For information on **trains to Inca,** contact FEVE, Plaza España 9 (tel. 75-22-45), Monday through Friday from 8am to 5pm. For information on **trains to Sóller,** contact Train to Sóller v.v., Plaza España (tel. 75-20-28), daily from 8am to 1pm and 3 to 7:45pm. The ticket window opens half an hour before departure of trains.

Ferry information and tickets can be obtained at any travel agency or from Transmediterránea, Muelle Viejo 5 (tel. 72-67-40), Monday through Friday from 9am to 1pm and 5 to 7pm.

For **airport information,** call 26-46-24 Monday through Friday from 8am to 8pm; in summer, on Saturday and Sunday 24 hours a day; winter hours vary greatly.

The **Iberia** office, Paseo des Born 10 (tel. 46-34-00), is open Monday through Friday from 8am to 7pm and on Saturday from 8am to 3pm. For Iberia reservations, call 71-80-00; for flight information, call the airport office (tel. 26-26-00) daily 24 hours. The airport ticket office is open daily from 7am to 11pm.

CITY LAYOUT

In town, the area around the cathedral, the heart of "old" Palma, is known as the **Portela Quarter.** Beyond its cluster of alleyways the city expands into broader, more ordered avenues. Leading up from the sea beside the cathedral is the **Paseo des Born (Paseo de Borne)** a broad boulevard lined with shops and offices. At the top of the hill at the end of Calle Jaime II is **Plaza Mayor,** a focal point of tourist activity.

Along the bay west of the old town stretches the six-lane, two-mile-long **Paseo Marítimo,** lined with hotels, restaurants, discos, and souvenir shops. The streets behind it, offering more of the same, comprise the **El Terreno** district noted for its nightlife.

2. Fast Facts

AREA CODE: The area code for all the Balearic Islands when calling from other parts of Spain is 971; when calling from outside the country, dial 71.

BUSINESS HOURS: **Shop hours** are generally Monday through Friday from 9:30am to 1:30pm and 4:30 to 8pm, and on Saturday from 9:30am to 1:30pm. Department stores are open Monday through Saturday continuously from 10am to 8pm. **Restaurant hours** are generally 1:30 to 4pm and 8 to 11pm. Normal **banking hours** are Monday through Friday from 9am to 2pm.

Bear in mind, however, that hours may vary greatly throughout the year as the islands move in and out of peak and shoulder tourist seasons. Even during peak seasons, the hours and closing days of shops and restaurants often fluctuate with demand. If business is booming, they may well be open beyond their regular posted hours, but if business is lagging, you may find the doors unexpectedly closed.

CONSULATES: The **U.S. Consulate,** at Avenida Jaime III no. 26 (tel. 72-26-60), is open Monday through Friday from 4 to 7pm; if you call at other times you can leave a message on the answering machine. In the event of an emergency, contact the American Consulate General in Barcelona at 93/319-95-50. The **Consulate of the United Kingdom,** at Plaza Mayor 3 (tel. 71-24-45), is open in summer Monday through Friday from 9am to 2pm and in winter Monday through Friday from 9am to 3pm.

CURRENCY: See Section 4, "Fast Facts," in Chapter II.

ELECTRICITY: See Section 4, "Fast Facts," in Chapter II.

EMERGENCIES: For the **police,** dial 091. For an **ambulance,** call 72-22-22 or 46-62-62; in case of **fire,** 75-12-34.

HOLIDAYS: January 1 (New Year's Day); January 6 (Feast of the Three Kings); Good Friday; Easter Monday; May 1 (Labor Day); May 15 (Feast of the Pentecost); June 24 (Feast of St. John); August 15 (Assumption Day); October 12 (Columbus Day); November 1 (All Souls' Day); December 6 (Constitution Day); December 8 (Feast of the Immaculate Conception); December 25 (Christmas Day); and December 26 (Feast of St. Stephen).

Local holidays include June 29 (the Feast of St. Peter, patron saint of fishermen), when the Port of Alcudia stages a boat procession from 6 to 7pm that can be viewed from either land or sea. July 16 (the Feast of the Virgin of Carmen, patron of fishermen— apparently they need all the celestial assistance they can get!—and sailors) is celebrated in all of Majorca's port towns but especially in Puerto de Andraitx, which holds a special procession of decorated boats and a children's parade, and in Cala Ratjada and Puerto de Sóller, where the nighttime processions feature boats illuminated with torches and flares. August 2 (Feast of Our Lady of the Angels) is observed in Pollensa with a mock battle between Moors and Christians.

LANGUAGE: As in Barcelona and throughout Catalonia, Catalan is the second official language (along with Spanish) of all the Balearic Islands, so signs and streets names may appear in one or the other or both. Most newer maps will have all the names in Catalan, but you may find the actual street names and other signs still in Spanish. Although the Catalan language is common to all the islands, there are dialectical variations on each of the islands. Most different of all is the Mallorquín dialect of Majorca. While throughout this guidebook I refer to "Majorca" and "Minorca," their Spanish spellings are "Mallorca" and "Menorca."

MAIL: The central post office is at Calle Constitució 6 (tel. 72-18-67) and is open Monday through Friday from 9am to 1pm and 4 to 7pm. For postal rate information, see Section 4 "Fast Facts," in Chapter II.

NEWSPAPERS: The *Diario de Mallorca, Baleares, El Día 16 de Baleares,* and *Ultima Hora* are four Spanish-language dailies covering not only Majorca but the Balearic region. *The Daily Bulletin* is the English-language daily and *Mallorca Tourist Info* is a bimonthly English-language tourist publication available at most newsstands. Beyond that, newspapers and magazines from all over the world are ubiquitous.

PARKING: Palma has strict parking regulations that are rigorously enforced. In certain parts of the old town and along much of the Paseo Marítimo, the parking restriction plan "ORA" is in effect Monday through Friday from 9:30am to 1:30pm and 5 to 8pm. These zones are usually indicated by blue lines delineating the parking spaces. You may park here for a maximum of an hour and a half and must purchase a 30-, 60-, or 90-minute ticket in any *estanco* (tobacconist shop) and display it visibly on your dashboard.

SAFETY: Whenever you're traveling in an unfamiliar city or area, stay alert. Be aware of your immediate surroundings. Wear a moneybelt and don't sling your camera or purse over your shoulder; wear the strap diagonally across your body. This will minimize the possibility of your becoming a victim of crime. Every society has its criminals. It's your responsibility to be aware and alert even in the most heavily touristed areas.

TAXIS: For a radio taxi, call 75-54-40, 40-14-14, or 71-04-03.

TELEPHONE: There are three **central offices for international calls:** Avenida Jaime II no. 126-128, open Monday through Saturday from 9:30am to 1:30pm and 4 to 7pm, closed holidays; Avenida Jaime III no. 20, open Monday through Saturday from 9:30am to 1:30pm and 5 to 9pm; and Calle Constitució 1, open daily from 9:30am to 1:30pm, with extended hours Monday through Saturday from 4:30 to 8:30pm. For **dialing information,** see Section 4, "Barcelona Fast Facts," in Chapter II. From 8am to 10pm the base **rate** for calls to the United States and Canada is 475 ptas. ($3.95) per minute; to Great Britain, 191 ptas. ($1.60) per minute; from 10pm to 8am the rates drop to 332 ptas. ($2.75) and 137 ptas. ($1.15) per minute, respectively.

TELEVISION/RADIO: There are 30,000 English-speaking residents on Majorca served by an English-language radio station. Radiocadena Española, Radio Majorca, and Radio Popular also offer foreign-language programs. There are two national Spanish-language TV stations, a couple of regional stations broadcasting in Catalan, and via satellite hookup (which is becoming increasingly common in the hotels), multiple channels in English and various European languages.

TIPPING: See Section 4, "Fast Facts," in Chapter II.

TOURIST INFORMATION: The **airport tourist office** (tel. 26-08-03) is open Monday through Saturday from 9:30am to 8pm (a little later in summer) and on Sunday from 9:30am to 2pm. The two **municipal tourist offices** in town are located at Calle Santo Domingo 11 (tel. 72-40-90) and Plaza España s/n (no street number) (tel. 71-15-27); both are open Monday through Friday from 9am to 8pm and on Saturday from 9am to noon (closed holidays). The tourist office of the **Govern Balear,** at Avenida Jaime III no. 10 (tel. 71-22-16), dispenses information on all the Balearic Islands; it's open Monday through Friday from 9am to 2:30pm and 3 to 8pm and on Saturday from 9am to 1pm (closed holidays).

---

3. Accommodations

The bulk of Majorca's hotels are in Palma and the surrounding beach areas, where most offer your garden variety, tour-group brand of accommodation. The low-price, vacation-package business has fallen off in recent years, however, and Majorca now aspires to upgrade its overall hotel offerings to attract more upscale travelers. This is not to say that there aren't already a number of fine hotels for the independent traveler. In fact there are quite a few, and a number of them are very select indeed. You will find them below, along with the mass-market hotels that offer room, board, sand, sun, and sea at bargain-basement rates (always subject to further negotiation).

The posted rates at most lodgings are the official maximums the place can charge. Often you can negotiate at least a 10% discount—sometimes more in the off-season. For the purposes of this guide, "expensive" hotels charge 15,000 ptas. ($125) and up for a double room; "moderate" hotels, 5,000 to 15,000 ptas. ($42 to $125); and "budget" lodgings, 3,500 to 5,000 ptas. ($29 to $42). *Note:* Unless otherwise indicated, all accommodations have private bath or shower, all hotels are open year round, and all rates given include service charge but *not* IVA.

EXPENSIVE

• **Son Vida Sheraton Hotel,** Urbanización Son Vida, Palma de Majorca (tel. 971/79-00-00, toll free 800/325-3535 in the U.S.). 171 rms, 13 suites. A/C MINIBAR TV TEL

A princely haven for the well-heeled traveler looking for luxury, beauty, and tranquility, this is not your run-of-the-mill Sheraton. The list of visiting royalty, statesmen, artists, and celebrities is long and impressive, including Prince Ranier and Princess Grace, John Lennon and John Wayne. Built around the core of a castle given by King Jaime I to the Marquis de la Torre, it is a sumptuous property set in the Son Vida hills several miles outside the city and offers panoramic views of Palma and the Mediterranean. The modern extension, done in a traditional Spanish style, looks more like a noble hacienda than a hotel. The grounds include a golf course, well-manicured gardens, and several outdoor terraces. Inside, the palatial public areas are drenched in fine fabrics and sprinkled with Oriental rugs and wrought-iron chandeliers.

Although the rooms are not as palatial as the public areas, they are large and all have a private terrace or balcony.

Dining/Entertainment: The hotel restaurant has an extensive selection of international dishes and fine wines. After dinner, a glass of port or cognac in the piano bar tops off a perfect evening.

Services: Room service.

Facilities: Outdoor pool, tennis (two of the hotel's four tennis courts are illuminated), golf, health center with sauna, Turkish bath, massage, solarium, gymnasium, covered pool with whirlpool.

RATES: 11,900–21,700 ptas. ($99.25–$181) single; 15,200–26,100 ptas. ($127–$218) double; 33,000–88,000 ptas. ($275–$733) suite.

• **Valparaiso Palace/Hotel,** La Bonanova, 07015 Palma de Majorca (tel. 971/40-04-11). 150 rms (including suites). A/C MINIBAR TV

"Sybaritic" is the word that best describes the pampering pleasures of this oasis perched on a hill in a tranquil, residential area overlooking Palma Bay. From the tapestried walls and colorful wool carpets of its halls to the elegantly modern restaurant with a view of the city and sea below, it is the pride and joy of the Majorcan proprietors who live in its upper reaches. Its grounds include not only lovely gardens but also a man-made lake with a rowboat and swans.

The soundproofed rooms are refuges of comfort, all tastefully appointed and equipped with large terraces and a sea view. Decors differ from room to spacious room, but the beds in each are situated in a raised alcove. The electricity is dual voltage (125 and 200V).

Dining/Entertainment: The hotel restaurant offers Spanish and international cuisine. One of the hotel's four bars is open 24 hours and features nightly musical entertainment.

Service: 24-hour room service.

Facilities: Indoor and outdoor pools, mini-golf, tennis, sauna, hairdresser, art gallery, laundry, gymnasium, shops, solarium, garage. The hotel offers special discounts at three island golf courses.

RATES: 11,900–13,000 ptas. ($99.25–$108) single; 21,000–27,400 ptas. ($175–$228) double; 25,300–59,400 ptas. ($211–$495) suite.

- **Meliá Victoria Hotel,** Avenida Joan Miró 21, 07014 Palma de Majorca (tel. 971/23-43-42). 167 rms. A/C MINIBAR TV TEL.

This is a gracious, five-star choice smack in the center of things along the Paseo Marítimo. A member of the Sol Group of hotels, whose first-class properties carry the name "Meliá," this one dates from 1905 but was last refurbished in 1987.

The spacious, carpeted rooms all have terraces. Doubles have a sea view; singles, a castle view. The junior suites have a small sitting room and king-size bed. Each room is furnished differently, with the occasional antique piece here and there contributing a charming grace note of distinction.

Dining/Entertainment: The restaurant serves regional, national, and international dishes and a wonderful buffet breakfast (a trademark of the Sol group). Before and after dinner the piano bar attracts both guests and locals. In summer, the outdoor terrace becomes a dance floor with live music.

Services: 24-hour room service.

Facilities: Indoor and outdoor pool, sauna, hairdresser, solarium, fitness center, massage, shops.

RATES: 11,000–13,100 ptas. ($91.50–$109) single; 18,700–20,800 ptas. ($156–$173) double; 26,300–33,600 ptas. ($219–$280) suite.

- **Sol Palas Atenea,** Paseo Ingeniero Gabriel Roca 29 (next door to the Meliá Victoria), 07014 Palma de Majorca (tel. 971/28-14-00). 370 rms. A/C MINIBAR TV TEL

This four-star Sol hotel is comfortable, modern, and businesslike. The carpeted rooms all have terraces. Those facing the bay have a wonderful view but are noisier than the ones in the back overlooking Bellver Castle.

Dining/Entertainment: The restaurant serves an ample breakfast buffet and dinner. There are also an outdoor terrace bar and an indoor piano bar with live music nightly.

Facilities: Indoor and outdoor pool, sauna, solarium, Jacuzzi, beauty parlor, and shops.

RATES (INCLUDING BREAKFAST): 9,950 ptas. ($83) single; 15,675 ptas. ($131) double.

• **Bellver Sol,** Paseo Marítimo 11, 07014 Palma de Majorca (tel. 971/23-51-42). 393 rms. A/C TV TEL

Another Sol entry, the Bellver is conspicuous for its tiers of scalloped white terraces. The marble lobby and large public areas have recently been stylishly refurbished. The spacious rooms have carpeting, terraces (one-third with a view of the bay), and roomy baths.

Dining/Entertainment: In addition to a cafeteria, there is a restaurant that serves the typical Sol buffet breakfast and has a mixed buffet and à la carte service at lunch and dinner. Nightly from 9pm to midnight there is live musical entertainment in the bar, followed by dancing in the lounge.

Facilities: Pool.

RATES (INCLUDING BREAKFAST AND IVA): 11,650 ptas. ($97) single; 15,350 ptas. ($128) double.

Sol Hotels

The Sol Group, headquartered in Palma and with over 140 properties throughout Spain, is the largest hotel company in the country, the 3rd largest in Europe, and the 16th largest in the world. Its "Meliá" hotels are five-star properties, while the "Sol" line comprises over 100 three- and four-star hotels geared to mass tourism but with higher standards of quality than the usual hotels of that ilk.

The empire began modestly enough when native Majorcan Gabriel Escarrer, current president and major shareholder of the group, opened a 60-bed hotel in Palma in 1956. Today his company tallies over 150 hotels worldwide, including such far-flung corners as Bali, Venezuela, Turkey, and Iraq, with Mexico, Moscow, and the Dominican Republic projected.

All Sol beach hotels offer children's swimming pools, menus, and baby-sitting services. Sports facilities vary, but each hotel offers a wide range of activities, including gymnastics, volleyball, archery, and assorted indoor games. The Sol Group takes particular pride in its food and ample buffet spreads.

For information or reservations at any Meliá or Sol hotel, call toll free 800/336-3542, or contact Meliá Hotels at Coral Plaza Building, Suite 402, 2100 Coral Way, Miami, FL 33145 (tel. 305/854-0990).

MODERATE

- **Hotel Jaime III Sol,** Paseo Majorca 14B, 07012 Palma de Majorca (tel. 971/72-59-43). 88 double rms. TEL TV

Right at the end of Palma's main shopping street, this is a good choice for those who prefer to stay in the urban heart of things and commute to the beaches. Its recently renovated rooms are large and carpeted, with big baths. The air-conditioned restaurant serves an ample buffet-style breakfast and dinner for those on the half-board plan. The hotel's cafeteria is popular with both visitors and locals.

RATES: 6,480 ptas. ($54) single use of double room; 7,855 ptas. ($65.50) double occupancy.

- **Residencia Nacar,** Avenida Jaime II no. 21, 07012 Palma de Majorca (tel. 971/72-26-41). 60 rms. TEL

Very central and clean, the Nacar's dimly lit rooms are out of the 1950s. All are good sized and most have a terrace or balcony. Facilities include a lounge sitting area, snackbar, and cafeteria.

RATES (INCLUDING BREAKFAST): 5,040 ptas. ($42) single; 7,700 ptas. ($64.25) double; 10% less during low season.

- **Hotel Saratoga,** Paseo Majorca 6, 07012 Palma de Majorca (tel. 971/72-72-40). 189 rms. TEL

Near the medieval moat of the old city's fortifications, the Saratoga has an airy, inviting reception area and bright, modern, comfortable rooms, some with pretty balconies and some singles with a shower only.

Facilities: Two pools, one on the roof and one at lobby level.

RATES: 4,575–4,800 ptas. ($38.25–$40) single; 7,120–9,490 ptas. ($59.25–$79) double.

- **Hotel-Residencia Almudaina,** Avenida Jaime III no. 9, 07012 Palma de Majorca (tel. 971/72-73-40). 80 rms. A/C TEL TV

They don't come any more central than this. Smack in the middle of the city's central shopping street, the Almudaina nevertheless offers peace and quiet in most of its large, bright, recently renovated rooms. Some have a view of the cathedral and port. The owner, Mateo Cabrer Parera, takes good care of the place and loves to chat with guests. On-premises parking is free.

RATES (INCLUDING BREAKFAST): 4,200–4,800 ptas. ($35–$40) single; 6,400–7,400 ptas. ($53.25–$61.75) double.

- **Hotel Costa Azul,** Paseo Marítimo 7, 07014 Palma de Majorca (tel. 971/23-19-40). 130 rms. TEL

If you can't find a room elsewhere, the spacious—but a bit worn and barren—rooms here are an acceptable fall-back option. Both the lobby-level bar and restaurant, which offers buffet service at all meals, are cozy in their traditional Spanish styling.

Facilities: The very small pool on the third floor is covered and heated in winter.

RATES: 3,800 ptas. ($31.75) single; 6,100 ptas. ($50.75) double.

- **Hotel Majorica,** Calle Garita 3, 07015 Palma de Majorca (tel. 971/40-02-61). 153 rms. TEL

Located in the hills above Palma Bay at the far western end of Avenida Joan Miró, the Majorica exudes a cozy, Spanish charm and has nice, bright rooms. Off the lobby is a small, friendly bar; another bar serves sunbathers. At this writing, it is a solid choice that, after scheduled renovations, should be even better.

Facilities: Pool.

RATES: 3,700–4,600 ptas. ($30.75–$38.25) single; 5,100–8,050 ptas. ($42.50–$67) double.

- **Hotel Mirador,** Paseo Marítimo 10, 07014 Palma de Majorca (tel. 971/23-20-46). 78 rms. TEL

A charming hostelry hiding behind a very humble facade, the Mirador dates from the late 1950s and retains the gracious charm of an era when hotels were less homogeneous and more homey. Throughout the lobby, lounges, and rooms are beautiful hand-crafted furnishings made by local Majorcan artisans. The oversize rooms feature lots of fine dark wood—as do some of the vintage elevators—and the halls have parquet flooring. The baths are a bit passé in styling but not in comfort. All in all, a good value. Meals in the restaurant are buffet style; there are also a cafeteria and a bar.

Facilities: A tiny rooftop pool and token solarium.

RATES: 3,250–4,350 ptas. ($27–$36.25) single; 5,000–6,780 ptas. ($41.75–$56.50) double.

BUDGET

- **Hotel Horizonte Sol,** Vista Alegre 1, 07015 Palma de Majorca (tel. 971/40-06-01). 199 rms. TEL

A block away from the Hotel Majorica (see "Moderate," above) on a parallel street, the Horizonte is another reliable Sol property. Most of its ample rooms have a terrace and sea view. Although this is only a two-star hotel, the extensive buffets at breakfast, lunch, and dinner uphold the high standards of the Sol group.

Facilities: Pool, solariums.

RATES (INCLUDING BREAKFAST): 3,000–3,900 ptas. ($25–$32.50) single; 3,600–5,400 ptas. ($30–$45) double.

- **Hotel Borenco,** Avenida Joan Miró 61, 07015 Palma de Majorca (tel. 971/23-23-47). 65 rms. TEL

The Borenco's functionally furnished rooms have terraces with a view of either Bellver Castle or the Paseo Marítimo and the sea. The air-conditioned dining room offers Spanish and international fare. The adjoining TV room is rather shabby, but a small pool and sunbathing area on the roof that overlooks the port makes up for it.

RATES (INCLUDING BREAKFAST): 2,520–2,730 ptas. ($21–$22.75) single; 3,780–4,620 ptas. ($31.50–$38.50) double.

- **Hotel Apartamentos Bosque Sol,** Camilo José Cela 5, 07014 Palma de Majorca (tel. 971/23-44-45). 284 studio apts.

Just off Avenida Joan Miró a block behind Paseo Marítimo, this member of the Sol group offers small, carpeted studio apartments where the daytime sofas in the sitting rooms become beds at night. Each unit has a fully equipped kitchenette and terrace. Gradually, they are all being renovated. Try to get one that's been rejuvenated, but don't worry if you don't—the old ones are quite acceptable. The restaurant serves buffet breakfasts and dinners only; the bar serves snacks.

Facilities: Indoor and outdoor pool, laundry, sauna, and supermarket.

RATES (INCLUDING BREAKFAST): 3,160–3,900 ptas. ($26.25–$32.50) single; 3,590–5,100 ptas. ($30–$42.50) double.

- **Hotel Rosa Mar,** Avenida Joan Miró 74, Palma de Majorca (tel. 971/23-27-23). 40 rms.

The Rosa Mar is a clean, inexpensive option about two blocks behind the Paseo Marítimo. Half the rooms have a sea view. Downstairs you'll find a billiard table and TV room. Off to one side is the bar.

RATES (INCLUDING IVA): 2,000 ptas. ($16.75) single; 3,500 ptas. ($29.25) double; discounts offered from Oct–June and for those staying a week or more.

---

4. Dining

The cuisine of Majorca, and to a great extent that of the other Balearic Islands, relies heavily on pork products. Two of Majorca's culinary trademarks are *ensaimada* and *sobrasada*. Every morning many Majorcans enjoy the former, a type of pastry prepared with lard, with their morning coffee. Ranging from breakfast-roll size to pizza size for family celebrations, ensaimada can be plain or filled with cream, custard, or shredded pumpkin. Sobrasada is a savory sausage composed primarily of pork and red pepper.

Among the Balearic Islands, Majorca is the only one that produces a commercial quantity of wine. Of its three wine-producing areas—Binissalem, Porreres, and Felanitx—the first produces the best wines (most notable are the reds). The local *Palo* is an apéritif composed of sweet wine enriched with iodine, sugar, and herbs. A rather thick, dense drink, it is usually served cold with a dash of soda.

The rustic *celleres* of Majorca, found mostly in the countryside, are traditional eateries located in vaulted, cavelike confines. They typically feature traditional dishes such as *lechona* (roast suckling pig), *frit* (a mixture of all sorts of animal innards fried together with herbs and hot peppers), *sopas mallorquines* (a hearty bread-and-vegetable soup), pork tenderloin in cabbage leaves, or, in winter, thrush wrapped in cabbage. All the meals are accompanied by a wine likely to come from the barrels flanking the walls.

In Palma, Paseo Marítimo and Avenida Joan Miró are lined with all types of snackbars, restaurants, countless pizzerias, and bars. The Spanish eat later than Americans and other Europeans.

Typical restaurant hours are 1 to 4pm and 8pm to midnight. Where prices below are indicated for "meals," they refer to an average three-course meal without wine. As with the hotels, service is usually included in the prices, but IVA is *not*. Many restaurants offer very economical three-course luncheon menus, including bread and house wine. At cafeterias, tapas bars, and other informal eating establishments, it often costs less to eat at the bar than at a table.

EXPENSIVE

• **Tristan,** Puerto Portals, Portals Nous (tel. 68-25-00). *Prices:* Meals average 5,000 ptas. ($41.75); seven-course degustation menu 8,500 ptas. ($70.75).

Perhaps the island's priciest restaurant, Tristan hosts the yachting crowd whose boats are docked in the swanky marina of Puerto Portals. Just inside the restaurant entrance is a purple-topped circular bar surrounded by purple wicker chairs. Elsewhere all is white-linen elegance.

Chef Heinz Winkler, born in Italy but of German descent, varies his menu markedly from day to day depending on what's best in the market. The selection is largely international nouvelle cuisine, with some dishes reflecting Spanish and Majorcan influences. The day I was there he offered smoked salmon with caviar, tuna tartare, lamb's kidneys in red wine, and a plethora of fish dishes.

Open: Tues–Sun 1–2:30pm and 8:30–11pm. *Closed:* Mid-Nov to mid-Dec. *Reservations:* Imperative for dinner. NOUVELLE CUISINE

• **Restaurante Zarzagan,** Paseo Marítimo 13 (tel. 23-74-47). *Prices:* Meals average 4,500 ptas. ($37.50).

This modern, sophisticated eatery has large picture windows overlooking the port and has an ambience of casual elegance.

The specialty of the house, as evidenced by the tank full of live specimens, is lobster. But among the numerous outstanding seafood dishes on the menu, perhaps the most innovative is the centro de merluza al estilo waleska (hake topped with lobster medallions and a white cream sauce). Another fine selection is the parrillada, an abundant array of grilled seafood. There is also a fine choice of meat dishes, including suckling lamb Segovia style and filet mignon prepared half a dozen different ways.

Open: Sun–Fri 1–3:30pm and 8–11:30pm. *Closed:* Usually in July. *Reservations:* Recommended at dinner. SEAFOOD

• **Porto Pi,** Calle Joan Miró 174 or Calle Garita 25 (tel. 40-00-87). *Prices:* Meals average 4,500 ptas. ($37.50).

Installed in a turn-of-the-century house, Porto Pi's dining rooms and outdoor terrace are intimate and elegantly simple. The restaurant has two entrances—the one on Garita is the main one and offers the best possibilities for parking.

Porto Pi's menu varies greatly with the season and is studded with unusual dishes like pigeon salad, kokotxas de merluza (the gills of the hake), and lubina (sea bass) with a green pepper and tequila sauce. Another house specialty is grilled magret fileted and draped appetizingly over puff pastry filled with spinach and pears. In winter, game is the culinary gambit.

Open: Mon–Fri 1:30–3:30pm and 8:30–11:30pm, Sat 8:30–11:30pm. *Closed:* Holidays. GAME

• **Mediterraneo 1930,** Paseo Marítimo 33 (tel. 45-88-77). *Prices:* Meals average 3,500 ptas. ($29.25).

As its name suggests, Mediterraneo 1930 is a chic art-deco dining experience with a Mediterranean flair. Specializing in seafood, it prominently displays the catches of the day. Owners Juan and Mary Martí offer more than two dozen seafood dishes and a dozen or so meat entrées.

Open: Daily 1–4pm and 8pm–1am; nightly live piano music beginning 9pm. *Reservations:* Recommended. SEAFOOD

• **Es Recó d'en Xesc,** Paseo Marítimo 17, next to the auditorium (tel. 45-21-12). *Prices:* Meals average 3,500 ptas. ($29.25), unless you go for the pricey caldereta (fish or soup) or shellfish dishes.

Situated in a small, indented plaza along the waterfront, Es Recó d'en Xesc offers both indoor and outdoor dining amid splashes of greenery.

Seafood is the house specialty. Some outstanding selections include pescado mallorquín prepared with spinach, potatoes, and tomatoes, and caldereta de mero y langosta, which comprises the soup broth, then the fish and lobster that was cooked in it. An unusual house offering is gambas al "Xesc," shrimp in a spicy sauce prepared according to an old recipe that owner-chef Xesc (Francisco) Bonnin found in a book given him by Rafael Pomar, the artist who did most of the paintings covering the restaurant's walls. Among the meat dishes, solomillo al rey (filet mignon with an almond sauce served with mashed potatoes and mushrooms) is recommended.

Open: Six days a week (at presstime, the day off had not yet been determined) 1–4:30pm and 8pm–12:30am. *Closed:* Jan. SEAFOOD

MODERATE

• **Diplomatic,** Calle Palau Reial 5 (tel. 72-64-82). *Prices:* Meals average 3,000 ptas. ($25); three-course menu of the day 1,000 ptas. ($8.25).

Located near the cathedral in the center of Palma, this is an excellent choice for anything from a sandwich or tapas at the bar to a full-fledged meal. As you penetrate from the outdoor terrace to the inner recesses of this medieval structure with beamed ceilings and white stucco walls, the atmosphere becomes increasingly formal and intimate. Similarly, the wall decor runs from rustic knickknacks to sophisticated artwork.

The menu is a compendium of international dishes. Some house specialties are pâté with green peppercorns, sole with almonds, filet mignon in port wine, and steak tartare. Wine connoisseurs should note that owner Juan Contesti is particularly proud of his wine cellar and will happily show it to any interested parties.

Open: Mon–Fri 1–4pm and 8–11pm, Sat 8–11pm. CONTINENTAL

• **Restaurante Caballito de Mar,** Paseo Sagrera 5 (tel. 72-10-74). *Prices:* Appetizers 350–1,450 ptas. ($3–$12); main dishes 600–2,300 ptas. ($5–19.25).

The emphasis at this indoor/outdoor restaurant near the water is on food, not frills. To start, try the datiles (thin, long, mussel-like creatures that are sweetly succulent) and shrimp. For a main course, the lubina (sea bass) baked in sea salt is a tender, juicy, and very traditional selection. Other house specialties include bouillabaisse and sea bass with fennel. Some nonfish dishes complete the offering. Leave room for the almond ice cream or cake, both typical Majorcan desserts.

Open: Mon–Sat noon–3:45pm and 8–11:30pm. SEAFOOD

• **Restaurante Xoriguer,** Calle Fábrica 60 (tel. 28-82-32). *Prices:* Meals average 3,500 ptas. ($29.25).

Located in a quiet corner of Palma between the El Terreno area and the old town, Xoriguer offers indoor dining in a cheerful, homey setting. Chef Juan Romero's menu shifts with the season and is spiced with half a dozen daily specials based on the freshest fish in the market. During my last visit there were also such unusual dishes as prawns in whiskey sauce, lentil beans with quail, and suckling lamb.

Open: Mon–Sat 1:30–3:45pm and 8:30–11:30pm. *Closed:* Aug. INTERNATIONAL

• **Restaurante La Lubina,** Muelle Viejo, across from the Transmediterránea offices (tel. 72-33-50). *Prices:* Meals average 3,000 ptas. ($25).

La Lubina greets you with a pretty tiled bar surrounded by a few tables and chairs for sipping apéritifs before dinner. For dining there are two informal terraces (one enclosed) that look out on the sea, the source of most of what you'll find on the menu. They have, however, some unique ways of preparing their marine goods. The caldereta, for example, is lobster (fresh from their tanks) prepared in a broth flavored with almonds. The arroz a banda is rice cooked with fish in a broth—then the fileted fish and rice are served separately. Likewise with the bullavesa—the fish is first cooked in the broth and then the two are served separately.

The menu also includes fish prepared the traditional Majorcan way, en papillote (encrusted with salt—the end result is in no way salty, however), or served with allioli (garlic mayonnaise).

Open: Daily 12:30–3:30pm and 8–11:30pm. SEAFOOD

• **Lonja del Pescado** (commonly known as **Casa Eduardo**), Muelle Viejo s/n (no street number) (tel. 72-11-82). *Prices:* Meals average 2,500 ptas. ($20.75).

At this no-frills wharfside restaurant, the fish pass directly from the fishermen's boats at the front door to the kitchen. Don't be put off by the warehouselike entrance—the restaurant is one flight up. High-ceilinged and of modest decor, it is utterly devoid of pretensions, preferring to put its stock in the day's catch.

The house specials include zarzuela (a local interpretation of bouillabaisse), a delicious seafood paella, and lobster. Beyond this, there is an extensive menu with a heavy Majorcan accent. If you don't want fish, though, go elsewhere.

Open: Tues–Sat 1–3:30pm and 8–11pm. *Closed:* Last two weeks in Dec. SEAFOOD

- **Restaurante Eboli,** Calle Joan Miró 17, near the Hotel Meliá Victoria (tel. 28-59-38). *Prices:* Meals average 2,000 ptas. ($16.75).

Eboli projects a slightly rustic image with lots of wood and checkered tablecloths. If you're eating inside you can watch the tropical fish in the aquarium as you savor the pizza or flambéed meat dishes that are the house specials. Unusual among the latter is the filet mignon with almond-and-banana sauce. Meat fondue is on the menu too. All flambés are prepared tableside.

Open: Thurs–Tues 12:30–4pm and 7:30pm–midnight. PIZZA/FLAMBÉS

- **Mesón Los Rafaeles,** Paseo Majorca 28 (tel. 71-77-96). *Prices:* Meals start at 1,500 ptas. ($12.50).

This small, family-style place is popular with locals, who come for the handful of quality meat entrées and the varied selection of fresh seafood on appetizing display behind the bar and priced according to the day's market.

Open: Mon–Sat 1–4pm and 8pm–midnight. SPANISH

BUDGET

- **C'an Pelut,** Paseo Marítimo 30 (tel. 23-26-00). *Prices:* 400–1,500 ptas. ($3.25–$12.50).

One of the seemingly thousands of places in Palma offering pizza and pasta. The advantage here is that you can sit at a sidewalk table on a sunny day and watch the passing parade along the paseo.

Open: Winter, Wed–Mon 1–4pm and 8pm–12:30am; summer, Wed–Mon 1–4pm and daily 8pm–12:30am. *Closed:* Dec. ITALIAN

- **Celler Sa Prensa,** Avenida Joan Miró 35 (tel. 23-17-39). *Prices:* 500–1,200 ptas. ($4.25–$10).

A favorite among toreros during the summer bullfight season, Celler Sa Prensa serves Majorcan cuisine in a dark, high-ceilinged space filled with wine casks, garlic braids, wooden tables, beamed ceilings, and dangling gourds. Among the mostly meat dishes on the menu, the suckling pig and frito mallorquín (medallions of fried lamb) stand out.

Open: Summer, Wed 8pm–midnight, Thurs–Mon 1–4pm and 8pm–midnight; winter, Fri–Sun 1–4pm and 8pm–midnight. SPANISH/MAJORCAN

- **C'an Salvador,** Federico García Lorca 21 (tel. 28-60-41). *Prices:* Daily three-course menu 750 ptas. ($6.25).

At the top of Calle 297 behind the Sol Palas Atenea, this is the place to come when you're not sure what you want or if you just want to pick. Either indoors amid hints of art-deco styling or outdoors on the terrace, it offers everything from a refreshing glass of horchata (a national drink made from the earth almond) to a limited à la carte menu whose most expensive entrée is the 1,500-pta. ($12.50) steak. In addition, you can choose among a small selection of fine tapas, assorted sandwiches made with crusty French bread or croissants, pastas, and pizzas. It's hard to beat the price/quality ratio here.

Open: Daily 8:30am–1:30am, with meals served 1–4pm and 8pm–midnight.

- **La Casita,** Avenida Joan Miró 68 (tel. 23-75-57). *Prices:* Meals average 1,000 ptas ($8.25); three-course daily menu 850 ptas. ($7).

La Casita advertises French and American specialties, but the American accent is barely discernible. What *is* accented, however, is economy. The price here is reasonably right, and the half a dozen dowdy tables are rescued from seediness by the country-print wallpaper, lazy ceiling fans, and a soupçon of artwork. Owner Denyse Mangin, a native of Marseilles, came to Majorca 21 years ago with her American husband. Her roots are reflected in the numerous French specialties such as onion soup, pepper steak, and trout almondine.

Open: Daily 1–4pm and Wed–Sun 7:30pm–midnight. *Closed:* Six weeks beginning the end of July. FRENCH

- **Restaurante Mario's,** Calle Bellver (tel. 28-18-14). *Prices:* 300–1,200 ptas. ($2.50–$10).

A block off the bustling Avenida Joan Miró, Mario's offers peaceful outdoor dining on an ivy-rimmed terrace amid all the trappings of a trattoria—white stucco, lots of wrought iron, and checkered curtains and tablecloths. Pasta is the main attraction.

Open: Thurs–Mon 1–3:30pm and daily 8pm–midnight. ITALIAN

- **La Trattoria,** Calle Robert Graves 10 (tel. 23-79-86). *Prices:* Meals under 1,500 ptas. ($12.50).

This is a modest eatery with an extensive and inexpensive selection of pastas and above-average pizzas.

Open: Fri–Wed 1–4pm and 8pm–midnight. ITALIAN

- **Bon Lloc,** San Felio 7 (tel. 71-86-17). *Prices:* Main dishes under 750 ptas. ($6.25); four-course luncheon menu 750 ptas. ($6.25).

Bon Lloc is a commendable vegetarian restaurant near Paseo des Born. Installed in a noble house where Carlos V is said to have spent some time, its decor is simple. The menu, which varies every three months with seasonal offerings, includes cereals, rice dishes, tofu, and pastas. Drinks include exotic milkshakes made with almonds, dates, or carob, and lassi made with kefir and spices. Also has a dozen exotic teas.

Open: Tues–Sat 1–4pm, and Fri–Sat 8:30–11pm. VEGETARIAN

- **McDonald's,** Plaza Pio XII 7.

Yes, Virginia, there is a McDonald's in Majorca, smack in the center of Palma.

Open: Mon–Sat 10am–midnight, Sun and holidays 11am–midnight. FAST-FOOD

SPECIALTY DINING

For Tapas

- **Mesón Las Tinajas,** Berengario de Tornamira 13, behind Galerias Preciados (tel. 71-87-86). *Prices:* Meals average 2,300 ptas. ($19.25).

Both a tapas bar and restaurant, Las Tinajas specializes in several varieties of paella, duck drumsticks in champagne sauce, and seafood. The selection of tapas is ample and tasty and runs about 300 pesetas ($2.50) per plate. If you're in the mood for a sweet snack, the cakes and pies here are homemade (try the lemon meringue pie).

Open: Mon–Fri 10:30am–12:30am, Sat 10:30am–5pm; kitchen open for meals 12:30–10:30pm. *Closed:* Holidays. TAPAS

- **Alborada Restaurant** (also known as Casa Gallega), Plaza Weyler 2 (tel. 72-46-20). *Prices:* Meals average 2,300 ptas. ($19.25).

Just off Plaza Mayor in the heart of Palma, Alborada is a local favorite for tapas at the bar beneath dangling beer mugs, garlic strands, and gourds or full-fledged meals at one of a handful of simple tables. Its more than two dozen tapa selections, many flown in from Galicia, range from 450 to 2,000 ptas. ($3.75 to $16.75). The traditional empanada gallega is a good choice.

Just last year the owners opened a second restaurant, the Alborada Mar at Paseo Marítimo 25 (tel. 28-49-74), which offers the same menu in a fancier setting.

Open: Daily 1–4pm and 8:30pm–midnight (Alborada Mar, 8pm–midnight).

- **Bodega La Rambla,** Rambla 15 (tel. 21-61-06). *Prices:* Tapas under 400 ptas. ($3.25) a plate.

This is a 50-year-old fixture in central Palma devoted strictly to tapas—you can get a small or large plate of mixed tapas too. The place is small and you'll have to eat standing at the bar—there aren't even any bar stools. Overhead hangs an eccentric assortment of shells, pine cones, hooks, gourds, and more. The very friendly owner, Roberto, has been in charge for the last 40 years.

Open: Thurs–Tues 9:30am–3pm and 6:30–10pm. *Closed:* Aug. TAPAS

For Dessert

- **Ca'n Juan de S'aigo,** Calle Sans 10 (tel. 71-07-59). *Prices:* A cup of ice cream 110 ptas. (90¢).

Dating from 1700, this is the oldest ice-cream parlor on the island. Correspondingly elegant and old world, it serves its homemade ice creams—try the almond—pastries, cakes, ensaimadas, fine coffee, and several kinds of hot chocolate amid marble-top tables, lots of wood, beautiful tile floors, and an indoor garden with a fountain.

Open: Wed–Mon 8am–9pm.

---

5. Things to See and Do

Cathedral, Calle Palau Reial 29 (tel. 72-31-30).

Dominating the heart of Palma, this intricate limestone construction known locally as "La Seo" evolved in a largely Renaissance style from the 13th to the 16th century and was built in gratitude for James I of Aragón's victory over the Moors on December 31, 1229. Noteworthy are the Gaudí reformations within—moving the choir behind the altar and adding a baldachin over it. The window over the altar is one of the largest in the world.

As you exit the cathedral, a glass floor reveals three subterranean Roman columns discovered during a recent renovation.

The cathedral's museum and treasury contain many silver and gem-encrusted religious objects and reliquaries, some 15th- and 16th-century Gothic paintings, the tomb of the 14th-century antipope (who, curiously enough, was demoted to bishop by the real pope), and two human-size baroque silver candelabra (500 lbs. each) of the 18th century depicting mythical figures supporting a world of gambolling cherubs.

Open: Cathedral, daily; museum and treasury, Mon–Fri 10am–12:30pm and 4–6:30pm, Sat 10am–2pm. *Admission:* Cathedral, free; museum and treasury, 200 ptas. ($1.75).

Pueblo Español, Capitán Mezquida Veny 39 (tel. 23-70-75).

Like Barcelona's, this is an assemblage of scaled-down replicas of Spain's important architectural highlights. Unlike Barcelona's, it is not a focal point for nightlife.

Open: Winter, daily 9am–8pm; summer, daily 9am–8:30pm. *Admission:* 250 ptas. ($2) for adults, 175 ptas. ($1.50) children under 12.

Bellver Castle, between Palma and Illetas.

Built in 1309, Bellver ("beautiful view") Castle is the former summer palace of Majorca's King James II. After his death it was turned into a fortress with the addition of a double moat. It is Europe's only round castle; its sandstone construction looks eternally new. During the Civil War it served as a prison; now it houses the Municipal Museum, containing archeological relics and old coins. Its chief attraction, however, is the 360° panorama of Palma, the sea, and the distant mountains from its upper terrace.

Open: Daily 8am–8pm (Good Friday, Easter Sunday and Monday 8am–2pm). *Closed:* Jan 1. *Admission:* 110 ptas. (90¢).

Baños Arabes (Moorish Baths), Calle Serra 7 (tel. 72-15-49).

These baths in the narrow streets of the old quarter east of the cathedral are the only completely Moorish construction remaining in Palma. Although it is impossible to determine when they were built, most experts agree that it was probably the 10th century.

While they are less impressive than the Arab baths of Granada or Girona, they have an interesting room whose dome is supported by 12 columns with diverse capitals. The tables and chairs in the garden area outside urge you to linger.

Open: Daily 8am–8pm. *Admission:* 75 ptas. (65¢).

Palau de la Almudaina, Calle Palau Reial (tel. 71-43-68).

Another structure with Moorish roots, the Palau de la Almudaina is opposite the cathedral. Originally a fortress, it contains the trademark gardens and fountains of the Moors and was converted into a royal residence during the brief reign of the Majorcan kings. Now one of the most popular attractions of Palma, its museum gathers together antiques, arts, suits of armor, and several Gobelin tapestries.

Open: Summer, Tues–Sat 9:30am–1:30pm and 4–6:30pm, Sun and holidays 10am–2pm; winter hours may vary so check with the tourist office. *Admission:* 150 ptas. ($1.25).

La Lonja, Paseo Sagrera s/n (no street number) (tel. 71-17-05).

This former commodities exchange of the 15th century is a strikingly innovative rendition of the Gothic.

Open: Only during exhibitions (check the local papers) Tues–Sun 11am–2pm and 5–9pm.

Bullfights, Balearic Coliseum of Palma (tel. 25-16-34).

Held Sunday afternoons during July and August. Though not of the caliber you'll find on the Peninsula, go see one if this is your only opportunity.

---

6. Shopping

Palma's prime shopping streets are **San Miguel, Calle Sindicato** (the street of bargains in shoes, clothing, and spices such as saffron), **Avenida Jaime III** (the poshest shopping street), **Calle Jaime II** (for modern boutiques), **Calle Platería** (for jewelry), **Vía Roma, La Rambla, Paseo des Born,** and the streets radiating out from this paseo to the Plaza Cort with its handsome city hall.

Palma's lone department store is **Galerías Preciados,** Avenida Jaime III no. 15 (tel. 29-42-00). It's open Monday through Friday from 10am to 8pm and on Saturday from 10am to 9pm.

One of Majorca's main industries is leather; another is simulated pearls. Both are quite visible in Palma's shops.

Pink, Plaza Pio XII no. 3 (tel. 22-73-51) and Avenida Jaime III no. 3 (tel. 22-23-33).

These two luxury leather-goods stores offer exclusive designs that can be custom-made.

Open: Mon–Fri 10am–1:30pm and 4–8pm, Sat 10:30am–1:30pm.

Passy, Avenida Jaime III no. 6 (tel. 71-33-38), San Miguel 53 (tel. 72-56-86), and Tous y Ferrer 8 (tel. 71-73-38).

These three shops offer locally made quality shoes and handbags.

Open: Mon–Fri 10am–1:45pm and 4:45–8:15pm, Sat 10am–1:45pm.

Perlas Majorica, Avenida Jaime III no. 11 (tel. 72-52-68).

This factory store (see Section 4, Chapter IX) offers a wide selection of Majorica pearl rings, necklaces, bracelets, and brooches produced on the island at Manacor. Authorized Majorica retailers display the sign "Majorica Simulated Pearls Official Agent." The authenticity of the product is signaled by a red label with the gold inscription "Perlas Majorica," on the back of which you'll find a quality-control number. An international certificate of guarantee is also attached ensuring free replacement of any pearl showing a defect within 10 years of the date of purchase; simply take the certificate and faulty pearl to an official agent anywhere in the world. In addition to pearl creations, this store offers some fine gold and silver jewelry.

Open: Mon–Fri 9:30am–1:30pm and 4:30–8pm, Sat 9:30am–1:30pm.

Adolfo Dominguez, Calle Bonaire 2 (tel. 71-23-83).

The shop features the oversize angular fashions for both men and women of this trendy Spanish designer, who outfitted Don Johnson during the second season of "Miami Vice." He also has shops in Madrid and Barcelona.

Open: Mon–Fri 10am–1:30pm and 4:30–8:15pm, Sat 10am–1:30pm and 5–8pm. *Closed:* Sat evenings in summer.

Yanko, Calle Unión 3 (tel. 22-27-88).

A classic, high-fashion, high-quality leather-goods store for both men and women. You get your money's worth here.

Open: Mon–Sat 9:45am–1:30pm and 4:30–8pm.

La Casa del Hierro, Calle Victoria 6 (tel. 71-16-21).

This pretty shop sells a wide variety of wrought-iron decorative items made on the island. Be it a door knocker, andiron, wall sconce, or fanciful iron hoop for mounting a flowerpot, the work is graceful, tasteful, and delicate. Many of the items aren't as heavy as they look, so don't worry about weighing yourself down.

Open: Mon–Fri 9:30am–1:30pm and 4:30–8pm, Sat 9:30am–1:30pm.

---

7. Nightlife

Palma is the focal point for island nightlife. Most of the bars, cabarets, topless clubs, and discos are in the El Terreno district stretching along Avenida Joan Miró behind Paseo Marítimo.

Abaco, San Juan 1 (tel. 21-49-39).

Installed in a 17th-century house in the vicinity of the cathedral, this place for exotic drinks is a bacchanalian feast for the eyes, with decadent displays of fruits and flowers by the bushel and heaps of candles dripping wax wantonly. It is said that the florist's bill alone runs $500 a day! Dozens of tables share an inner courtyard with exotic caged birds, fountains, sculptures, and more flowers, fruits, and candles. Upstairs are several small rooms with antique furnishings and an old-fashioned kitchen. The long bar downstairs is made of stone; cocktails as overpowering as the decor (one combines whiskey, rum, Grand Marnier, and fruit juice) are served.

Open: Daily 9pm–3am. *Prices:* Drinks run about $10.

Tito's Palace, Plaza Gomila 3 (tel. 23-58-84).

One of the shopping-mall breed of discos spreading across many floors and offering numerous bars. There is also an entrance via elevator from Paseo Marítimo.

Open: Daily 10:30pm–5am. *Prices:* Cover charge 1,500 ptas. ($12.50), includes one drink.

Broadway Night Club, Avenida Joan Miró 36 (tel. 28-52-73).

Appeals to the prurient interest with a series of shows that get increasingly risqué as the night grinds on. The last show of the night is quite explicit and not recommended for demure viewers.

Open: Daily 10pm–4 or 5am; first of two or three shows starts at 11pm. *Prices:* Admission of 2,000 ptas. ($16.75), includes one drink.

Zhivago, Robert Graves 18 (tel. 23-15-82).

A dark dance hall with fringed lamps over the bar acknowledging the Russian theme. Two orchestras play a selection of music of all eras, including tangoes, salsas, waltzes, and rock. This is the place for those who like to hold their partners while dancing.

Open: Mar–Nov, daily 10pm–4:30am; the rest of the year, Fri and Sat 10pm–4:30am. *Prices:* Cover charge 800 ptas. ($6.75), includes one drink.

Bar Mam's, Avenida Joan Miró 39 (tel. 23-04-91).

This hole-in-the-wall watering hole is popular with English-speaking tourists from many nations. Posters of Marilyn Monroe, Humphrey Bogart, and James Dean keep company with the stand-up drinkers. Chicken curry, chili con carne, spaghetti, and other inexpensive fare are served in a small courtyard with close-set tables.

Open: May–Oct, daily 6:30pm–5am; Oct–May, daily 1pm–3am. *Prices:* Beer 125 ptas. ($1).

Azzurro, Paseo Marítimo 30, near the Sol Palas Atenea (no phone).

This sophisticated piano bar draws an older crowd appreciative of its more sedate musical offerings.

Open: Daily 7:30pm–4:30am; the live music begins about 10pm. No cover.

Casino Mallorca, Urbanización Sol de Mallorca, Costa de Calvía (tel. 68-00-00, or 71-26-76 Mon–Sat 9am–1:30pm and 4–7:30pm for show information and reservations).

Casino Mallorca offers both gambling and a Las Vegas–style nightclub show complete with sexy ladies in sequins and feathers, dance numbers, singers, and so on.

Open: Mon–Sat 7pm–5am, Sun 7pm–4am; show given Mon–Sat in summer, several times a week in winter. *Prices:* Admission 550 ptas. ($4.50), and you must have your passport to get in; show 3,335 ptas. ($27.75); show and dinner 4,735 ptas. ($39.50) or 5,475 ptas. ($45.50) including wine, champagne, casino admission, and IVA. *Directions:* Take the Cala Figuera exit off the autopista to Andraitx.

---

8. The Greater Palma Area

PLAYA DE PALMA, C'AN PASTILLA, AND ARENAL

On either side of Palma along Majorca's southwestern coast are popular beach resorts. The largest and best known is Playa de Palma, a 7-kilometer-long (4¼-mile) uninterrupted flow of fine, white sand and crystalline blue water skirting the "hotel forests" of C'an Pastilla and Arenal, about 12 kilometers (7½ miles) east of Palma.

In recent years the place has grown to the point where sometimes you can't see the beach for the people. In July and August this group-tour resort area is packed with young people. In winter it's a haven for senior citizens. Just before and after the peak summer season it seems to appeal primarily to families. The crowd is mostly European.

Unfortunately, the hotel offering is not on par with the natural beauty of the setting. The hotel, restaurant, and nightlife offerings are more or less homogeneous all along the beach without great fluctuations in quality or price. All the hotels are close to, if not on, the beach, and their facilities are geared to mass tourism, with half- and full-board buffet meals and organized sports activities and entertainment daily. For a better grade of restaurant and nightlife, one must go to Palma. Nevertheless, some popular names to remember for an evening of disco dancing are Grand Joy, Riu Center, Zorba, and Kiss.

Accommodations

Here is a handful of suggestions. Remember to ask for a discount, especially off-season.

▪ **Hotel Rio Bravo,** Calle Misión de San Diego s/n (no street number), 07620 Playa de Palma, Majorca (tel. 971/26-63-00). 199 rms. A/C TEL

The Rio Bravo, set several blocks back from the beach, has a distinctive facade with round balconies. Within are luxuriously appointed public areas studded with marble. Although the rooms are not on a par with the public areas, they are pleasant enough, with tile floors, country print wallpaper, and dark-wood furnishings from a few decades ago.

Facilities: Pool.

RATES (INCLUDING BREAKFAST AND IVA): 6,450–8,800 ptas. ($53.75–$73.25) single; 10,000–14,900 ptas. ($83.25–$124) double.

- **Hotel Java Sol,** Calle Goleta s/n (no street number), 07610 C'an Pastilla (tel. 971/26-27-76). 250 rms. TEL

Yet another Sol entry a block from the beach with simply furnished rooms with terraces and sea views.

Facilities: Pool.

RATES (INCLUDING BREAKFAST): 4,300–5,700 ptas. ($35.75–$47.50) single; 5,750–8,550 ptas. ($48–$71.25) double. Open May–Oct.

- **Hotel Alexandra Sol,** Calle Pineda 15, 07610 C'an Pastilla, Majorca (tel. 971/26-23-50). 164 rms. TV

A cut above the largely homogenized hotel offerings in this area, this Sol hotel has carpeted rooms with terraces. The large pool on the lobby level features a bar and sea view; a set of stairs takes you across the street to the beach. A second small pool is on the fifth floor by the solarium. The restaurant here serves the ample buffets the Sol group is famous for.

Facilities: Barbershop, beauty parlor, two pools.

RATES (INCLUDING BREAKFAST): 4,200–5,300 ptas. ($35–$44.25) single; 4,850–7,100 ptas. ($40.50–$59.25) double.

- **Ayron Park,** 07620 Playa de Palma, Majorca (tel. 971/26-06-50). 103 rms. TEL

The rooms here are large but basic.

Facilities: Pool, tennis court.

RATES (INCLUDING BREAKFAST AND IVA): 2,850–3,450 ptas. ($23.75–$28.75) single; 4,950–7,100 ptas. ($41.25–$59.25) double. Closed Nov.

- **Hotel Oasis,** Bartolomé Riutort 25, 07610 C'an Pastilla, Majorca (tel. 971/26-10-50). 110 rms. TEL

This was one of the first hotels on the Playa de Palma and sits just across the street from the beach. That it has survived the rampant construction boom says a lot for it. The atmosphere is quiet and subdued.

Facilities: Small pool.

RATES (INCLUDING BREAKFAST AND IVA): 2,800–5,300 ptas. ($23.25–$44.25) single; 4,550–9,550 ptas. ($38–$79.50) double. Closed Nov and part of Dec.

- **Hotel Royal Cupido,** Calle Marbella 32, 07620 Playa de Palma, Majorca (tel. 971/26-43-00). 197 rms. TEL

Another good choice awaits here behind a rather uninviting blank white facade. All rooms have a terrace with sea view.

Facilities: Pool.

RATES (INCLUDING BREAKFAST AND IVA): 2,700–6,000 ptas. ($22.50–$50) single; 3,900–9,900 ptas. ($32.50–$82.50) double.

- **Hotel Neptuno,** Laud 34, 07620 Playa de Palma, Majorca (tel. 971/26-00-00). 103 rms. TEL

Right across the street from the beach, the Neptuno's public areas are more antiquated than its comfortable rooms with terraces.

Facilities: Pool, solarium, tennis, mini-golf.

RATES (INCLUDING BREAKFAST AND IVA): 3,100–5,200 ptas. ($25.75–$43.25) single; 3,550–6,624 ptas. ($29.50–$55.25) double. Closed Nov and Dec.

- **Hotel Niagara,** Padre Bartolomé Salvá, 07620 Playa de Palma, Majorca (tel. 971/26-09-00). 140 rms. TEL

This gleaming white hotel has recently refurbished its facade, pool, and public areas with lots of marble. The rooms were left untouched, but are clean and comfortable and furnished in a Spanish style of yesteryear.

Facilities: Pool.

RATES (INCLUDING BREAKFAST AND IVA): 1,950–3,600 ptas. ($16.25–$30) single; 2,950–6,300 ptas. ($24.50–$52.50) double. Closed Nov and Dec.

ILLETAS, PALMA, NOVA, AND MAGALLUF

To the west of Palma is a series of small, sandy coves—Illetas, Palma Nova, and Magalluf. Frequent in-season bus service runs from the center of Palma to both Illetas and Arenal. At Palma Nova there is almost no beach to speak of—just a thin strip of sand. Magalluf has a curving bay with a respectable beach and offers glass-bottom-boat rides, waterskiing, and parasailing.

Accommodations

- **Antillas Sol,** Calle Violeta 1, 07182 Magalluf, Majorca (tel. 971/68-15-00). 332 rms. TEL

At a slight remove from the in-town sprawl, it offers newly renovated rooms with marble baths, carpeting, telephone, and terrace. Just beyond the large pool is a solarium on the sand, and beyond that, access to the beach. In conjunction with the hotel Barbados Sol next door, it offers tennis, mini-golf, and, in winter, an indoor pool.

RATES (INCLUDING BREAKFAST): 4,400–7,400 ptas. ($36.75–$61.75) single; 5,350–11,275 ptas. ($44.50–$94) double.

- **Hotel Meliá de Mar,** Carretera de Illetas 7, 07015 Illetas, Majorca (tel. 971/40-25-11). 133 rms, 11 suites.

A prime choice in Illetas, its rooms are well appointed and its suites have a terrace with a sea view, complete bath, air conditioning, and 24-hour room service. The hotel has a tennis court, facilities for water sports, and indoor and outdoor pools.

RATES: 14,950–17,000 ptas. ($125–$142) single (really, a double for individual use); 18,700–20,800 ptas. ($156–$173) double.

THINGS TO SEE AND DO

Between Palma Nova and Illetas is **Puerto Portals,** where the jet set park their major-league yachts. Along the marina are some fancy shops and restaurants and some pleasant places to enjoy an al fresco drink or ice cream while contemplating the flotilla of pleasure craft harbored nearby.

For children, **Aquapark,** near Magalluf on the road toward

Cala Figuera (tel. 68-08-11), offers swimming pools and water slides and rides. Open May to October daily from 10am to 6:30pm. Admission is 1,250 ptas. ($10.50) for adults and 650 ptas. ($5.50) for children. From Palma's Plaza de España there is half-hourly bus service on Playasol buses 2 and 3.

About 40 kilometers (25 miles) southeast of Palma near La Rapita is **Es Trenc,** a beauty of a beach. To get there you'll drive through the flat, cultivated Majorcan plains studded with working windmills. After La Rapita, follow the signs for "Ses Covetes." From where you park the car it's a short walk to a beach almost as long and broad as the one at Playa de Palma but without a single hotel. At one end there are thatched beach umbrellas and lounge chairs; at the other end it's just you and your towel. And along the entire beach there is, blessedly, just one snackbar. The sand is fine, soft, and white and the water is clear and clean. Fringed by a pine forest and sand dunes, this beach is so secluded that people have long favored it for nude bathing, although its status as a nudist beach remains unofficial (unlike Ibiza, Majorca has always been more conservative in matters of public undress).

The **Playa del Mago,** a tiny beach in the Bay of Portals Vells not far from Magalluf, has been given the official nod for nude bathing nevertheless. To get there, leave the Palma–Andraitx road at Cala Figuera and follow the pine-tree forest road. About 6.5 kilometers (4 miles) on you will see a sign for Playa del Mago. There is no bus service to either of these two "nude" beaches. The latter, being quite small, gets crowded on weekends with less-conservative locals.

For a complete change of pace, consider the 30-kilometer (18-mile) trip to **Sóller** in a vintage wooden train operated by Ferrocarriles Sóller (tel. 75-20-28). En route it passes through the fruit-growing Sóller Valley, famous for its oranges. Of interest in Sóller are the cathedral and the bank building next door, designed by a pupil of Gaudí.

AROUND MAJORCA

1. GETTING AROUND
2. DEIA (DEYÁ) AND THE WESTERN COAST
3. PUERTO DE POLLENSA AND THE NORTH
4. THE EASTERN COAST

From the rugged drama of its wild west coast to the level serenity of its central plains, Majorca packs a wide variety of scenery into 3,640 square kilometers (1,405 square miles). Inland are the virile vistas of the Sierra de Tramontana, where the island reaches its highest peak at Puig Mayor (1,445m, 4,750 ft.), the bucolic orange- and lemon-grove valleys of the Sóller region, and the mountainside artists' refuge at Deyá. Similarly varied is the 400-kilometer-long (250-mile) coastline that runs from the tame, white-sand beaches of the north and south to the jagged, cliff-tucked coves of the west.

Overland, the longest distance from one point to another on the island is a little over 80 kilometers (50 miles) north to south and slightly more than that east to west.

The island's cleanest and most peaceful seaside havens are outside the Palma Bay area. In the southwestern corner of the island, try the beaches of Camp de Mar and the port of Andraitx. Also in the vicinity is the beautiful beach at San Telmo, opposite the uninhabited island of Dragonera.

Southeast of Palma are a number of wonderful beaches with crystal-clear water beginning at Cala Blava in the eastern corner of Palm Bay and continuing along the Platja d'es Trenc (see Section 8, "The Greater Palma Area," in Chapter VIII) to Sant Jordi.

The eastern coast from Cala Santanyi north to Cala Ratjada is notched with charming, lagoon-type *calas* (coves), often with sandy beaches and stands of pines. At Porto Cristo, 60 kilometers (37.5 miles) east of Palma, there is a lovely beach on a beautiful horseshoe-shaped bay. Also over here are several impressive caves whose illuminated stalactites and stalagmites conjure some melodramatic optical illusions.

In the north, a chain of beaches stretches for miles and miles along the bays of Alcudia and Port de Pollença (Puerto de Pollensa).

Here the sand is whiter than anywhere else on Majorca and the pines provide not only shade but a pretty scenic accent. The water is generally shallow, warm, and clean, and the beaches are long enough to offer some privacy even when the area hotels are fully occupied.

To the north of Puerto de Pollensa, the virtually virgin Formentor Peninsula combines all of Majorca's best features — pine forests, plunging cliffs, silken sand, and water so turquoise it must be painted fresh daily.

1. Getting Around

From Palma there are numerous half- and full-day **bus tours** to all corners of the island for under 3,600 ptas. ($30). Contact any travel agency or your hotel reception desk for details. In addition, there is regularly scheduled **bus and train service** to some of the interior cities (see Section 1, "Orientation," in Chapter VIII for details).

From Puerto de Pollensa there is frequent bus service to Pollença, Inca, Palma, and Alcudia in the summer. Details are available at the tourist office.

However, **renting a car** is by far the best way to explore the island, as many of Majorca's special treats lie off the beaten path of mass tourism. Rates begin at about 3,200 ptas. ($26.50). Atesa, Avis, BC Betacar, and Hertz all have offices at the airport, in Palma, and elsewhere on the island, as follows:

Atesa: At the airport (tel. 26-61-00), open daily from 7:30am to 11:30pm; Tous y Maroto 6, Palma (tel. 71-38-81), open Monday through Friday from 9am to 1pm and 4 to 7pm.

Avis: At the airport (tel. 26-09-20), open in summer 24 hours daily, in winter daily from 7:30am to midnight; Paseo Marítimo 16, Palma (tel. 23-07-20), open Monday through Saturday from 8:30am to 1pm and 4 to 7:30pm, and on Sunday from 8:30am to 1pm.

BC Betacar: At the airport (tel. 26-38-11), open in summer 24 hours daily, in winter 7:30am to midnight; Paseo Marítimo 19, Palma (tel. 45-48-00), open Monday through Saturday from 8am to 1pm and 4 to 8pm, and on Sunday from 8am to noon and 6 to 8pm.

Hertz: At the airport (tel. 26-08-09), open in summer 24 hours daily, in winter daily from 7am to midnight; Paseo Marítimo 13, Palma (tel. 23-47-37), open Monday through Saturday from 8:30am to 1pm and 4 to 7pm, and on Sunday from 9am to 1pm.

2. Deia (Deyá) and the Western Coast

Majorca's most imposing mountains run along the western coast, where from time to time the road zigzags narrowly through sloping pine forests. Although distances arc short, the time required to cover them is considerably more than the mileage suggests, so leave yourself enough time to explore at leisure and savor the scenery.

The route indicated under "Things to See and Do," below, can be covered in one day if you get an early start. Or spend a night in Deyá and take the extra time to take photos at each of the numerous *miradores* (overlooks) along the way (marked with a roadside sign depicting a camera) and to travel some of the rugged, tertiary roads down to the private pleasures of remote, rocky coves.

ACCOMMODATIONS

The following hotels in and around Deyá, some 30 kilometers (19 miles) from Palma, are tranquil bases from which to explore the western coast. They are also very popular, so reserve well in advance.

- **Hotel La Residencia,** Son Moragues, 07179 Deyá, Majorca (tel. 971/63-90-11). 49 rms and suites. TEL

This charming four-star hotel created from two old manor houses of the 14th and 16th centuries attracts such five-star guests as Michael Douglas and Peter Bogdanovich. In 1988, *Architectural Digest* saw fit to feature its stylish accommodations in one of its issues.

The rooms have tile floors, area rugs, canopy beds, antique and reproduction furnishings from the mainland and Majorca, marble baths, and beamed ceilings, and a TV is available on request. The artwork throughout is by natives or longtime island residents.

Dining/Entertainment: The hotel's elegant gourmet El Olivo restaurant, serving "nouvelle Mediterranean" cuisine, is popular with both guests and the public at large and is open for lunch and dinner in winter and for dinner only in summer.

Facilities: Tennis court, pool, private access to the sea.

RATES (INCLUDING BREAKFAST): 8,400–12,600 ptas. ($70–$105) single; 14,700–21,000 ptas. ($123–$175) double; 24,200–26,300 ptas. ($202–$219) suite. Generally closed Jan 7–Easter, depending on demand.

- **Hotel Es Moli,** Carretera Valldemosa, 07179 Deyá, Majorca (tel. 971/63-90-00), 70 rms. A/C TEL

At the other end of diminutive Deyá, Es Moli is built into the slope of a hill. Though less opulent than La Residencia, it exudes a comparable sense of refuge amid its beautiful gardens. Most of Es Moli's spacious, carpeted rooms have terraces from which to contemplate the surrounding scenic beauty, and their attractive furnishings are mainly Majorcan.

Dining/Entertainment: Weather permitting, guests can dine poolside beneath a grape arbor or in the simple, elegant dining room serving international cuisine with local accents.

Facilities: Heated, spring-water swimming pool; tennis court; free transport to a secluded beach nearby.

RATES (INCLUDING BREAKFAST AND IVA): 9,750–10,850 ptas. ($81.25–$90.50) single; 15,700–17,900 ptas. ($131–$149) double; 31,300–33,600 ptas. ($261–$280) suite. Closed Nov–Mar.

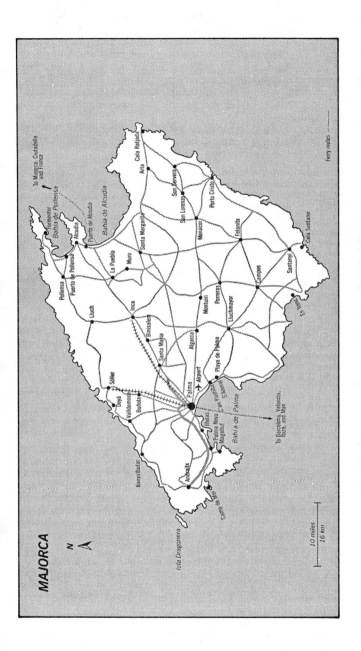

- **Pension Miramar,** Ca'n Oliver s/n (no street number), 07179 Deyá, Majorca (tel. 971/63-90-84). 9 rms (with sinks only).

To get to this economical, hilltop outpost, take the road leading up between Bar Las Palmeras and Christian's Bar along the main road. The Miramar's rooms are very basic but clean, and guests share two modern baths. At least a century old, this former village house has a cozy dining room, beamed ceilings, a lounge with wicker rockers, and Majorcan furnishings throughout. From the outdoor terrace you can glimpse the sea in the distance (hence the name Miramar).

RATES (INCLUDING BREAKFAST AND DINNER): 2,800 ptas. ($23) single; 4,950 ptas. ($41) double; 7,000 ptas. ($58) triple. Closed Dec–mid-May.

- **Monastery de Lluch,** Plaza de los Peregrinos, 07315 Lluch, Majorca, about five kilometers (three miles) from Escorca (tel. 971/51-70-25 or 51-70-50). 108 rms (half with bath, some with kitchen).

Near Puig Major north of Deyá, this monastery offers inexpensive, year-round accommodations with a humble charm for those who don't mind being at an isolated remove from tourist life (see "Things to See and Do" below for details on the monastery). Bear in mind that this is a functioning monastery with nine priests in residence—guests are expected to maintain a certain respect and quiet decorum. Units with a kitchen can accommodate up to six. For the kitchenless, there are two restaurants.

RATES (INCLUDING IVA): 1,515 ptas. ($13) single with bath; 1,515 ptas. ($13) double with bath for one night, 1,155 ptas. ($10) per night for two or more nights; 1,815 ptas. ($15) quad with bath for one night, 1,465 ptas. ($12) per night for two or more nights.

DINING

According to the mistress of Son Marroig, the two best restaurants in Deyá are Restaurante Suizo and Restaurante Jaime.

- **Restaurante Suizo,** Calle Archiduque Luis Salvador (tel. 63-91-39). *Prices:* Meals average 3,000 ptas. ($25).

Located on the main road in town and occupying a house that is over 100 years old, Restaurante Suizo is actually two restaurants in one. The upstairs Bodega La Ticinesa, where guests often play the piano after dinner, is intimate and informal and has an outdoor terrace. In winter its fireplace and candles create a very special ambience. Among the specialties are cabrito al horno (roast baby lamb) and jamón serrano (cured ham) from Granada.

The larger, more formal dining area downstairs features ceiling fans, wrought-iron chandeliers, and cushioned benches. A full-fledged menu is offered here, including at least half a dozen fondues and grilled meats. Seafood is not a fixed feature on chef-owner Pedro Ferrer's menu because he insists on freshness—fish is served only when the market has the best. Ferrer studied cooking in Switzerland and lived there for 27 years, hence the name of his restaurant. His pastas are homemade daily, and he has come up with some signature dishes, among them rabbit with prawns and leg of baby lamb with fresh mushrooms and garlic.

Open: Fri–Wed 12:30–3:30pm and 7:30pm–midnight.
Closed: Downstairs in Jan and Feb. *Reservations:* Recommended in
summer and on weekend evenings all year. INTERNATIONAL

■ **Restaurante Jaime,** Calle Archiduque Luis Salvador 13 (tel.
63-90-29). *Prices:* Meals average under 2,000 ptas. ($16.50); three-
course menu of the day 1,000 ptas. ($8.25).

Just a few doors down from the Restaurante Suizo and one
flight up, this family-style place serves mostly grilled meats and fish
and features daily Majorcan specialties. Though the service is rough
around the edges, the food is good and the price is right. A fine winter dish is the pork loin rolled in cabbage leaves and stuffed with
sausage and raisins. A must for dessert is the almond cake served
with almond ice cream.

Open: Winter, Tues–Sun 12:30–3pm and 7:30–10pm; summer, Tues–Sun 12:30–3pm and 7:30–10:30pm. *Closed:* Two
weeks in Nov and two weeks in May. MAJORCAN/SPANISH

THINGS TO SEE AND DO

After heading west out of Palma on the coastal highway, take
the C-710 along the western coast. At kilometer 103 you'll come
across the first in a series of **miradores,** this one looking down on a
rocky cove at the juncture of two coastal mountains. Several kilometers farther along at Es Grau, where there is a restaurant/bar, some
stairs lead up to a plunging panorama of tree-crowned cliffs. As you
continue on past Estallench toward Banyalbufar, look back at the
former to fully appreciate its picturesque cascade of orange-roofed,
dun-colored houses. Between Estallench and Banyalbufar there is a
mirador with a ruined tower (don't bother to climb the ladder inside as there is no view from the top—the best view of the coast here
is from the road). Banyalbufar is also best appreciated once you have
passed it and can look back on its terraced splendor.

At Valldemossa, visit the **Real Cartuja** (tel. 61-21-06), the Car-
thusian monastery where Chopin and George Sand spent two
months in the winter of 1838–39. Formerly the palace of King Martin I, it was given to the monks in the 14th century and expropriated
by the government in 1835. The church itself is an 18th-century neoclassical structure. Cells nos. 2 and 4 were inhabited by Chopin
and Sand, but only a few items (a high-back chair, a small painting,
and a French piano) remain here from their time; most of what they
left behind was burned by the locals out of fear of contagion by the
tubercular Chopin. Also remaining is the Majorcan piano he used to
compose several preludes. Several of Chopin's original scores and
some original manuscript pages of Sand's *A Winter in Majorca,* a
biting account of their time on the island, are on display. In another
part of the monastery is a pharmacy dating from the end of the 17th
century.

Real Cartuja is open Monday through Saturday from 9:30am
to 1:30pm and 3 to 7pm. Admission is 450 ptas. ($3.75) and tickets
are sold until 1pm and 6:30pm.

Just shortly before you reach Deyá, you'll come to **Son
Marroig** (tel. 63-91-58), the Majorcan refuge of Archduke Luis Sal-

vador. Born in 1847, he fled from life at court in Tuscany and wandered throughout the Mediterranean on his yacht, writing numerous books about the area. In 1870 he bought the Son Marroig estate, whose tower dates from the 16th century. The highlights of this beautiful stone house today are the fully furnished salon with a coffered ceiling and the dining room filled with drawings, photographs of the archduke, a notable assemblage of Majorcan furniture and paintings, and a collection of ceramics from around the world. The views are the house's greatest asset, however, especially from the Carrara marble pavilion set in the gardens. The estate now belongs to the grandchildren of the archduke's private secretary, who inherited the mansion. Part of the estate is Sa Foradada, a small peninsula with a spectacular view that is three kilometers (two miles) from the house and accessible only on foot. You must ask permission at the house to go there, and it will require not only climbing over a fence that keeps in the family sheep, but a somewhat strenuous hike sprinkled with steep inclines.

Son Marroig is open Monday through Saturday from 9:30am to 1:30pm and 3 to 6pm (to 8pm in summer). Admission is 175 ptas. ($1.45).

Deyá, dramatically sheltered in a fertile valley on the slopes of a 4,000-foot mountain, is primarily an artists' and writers' hangout. It has two museums, a historic church, and several cafés, bars, restaurants, boutiques, and art galleries. Noted writer Robert Graves lived here for 45 years and is buried in the village church cemetery. Mike Oldfield, when he comes, has been known to play for hours in the local bars. Many other prominent people are also attracted by its beauty and upscale, bohemian atmosphere.

En route from Deyá to Cala de Sa Calobra, you will pass through the dramatic northern reaches of the **Sierra de Tramontana,** whose white-rock peaks above the tree line suggest a Mediterranean rendition of the Alps. **Cala de Sa Calobra** itself is the king of Majorcan coves, embracing waters of fierce turquoise. From here a foot path partially tunneled through the face of the cliff leads to the Torrent de Pareis, where people splash in the surf that washes up on the small, pebble beach.

Inland from here is the **Monastery de Lluch,** about 44 kilometers (27.5 miles) from Palma. Originally a 17th-century hostel for pilgrims, it is now the sanctuary of the Virgin of Lluch, the island's patron saint, known as "La Moreneta," because, like Catalonia's Virgin of Montserrat, she is black. In the chapel behind the church altar stands a 13th-century statue of La Moreneta topped with a halo and crown rimmed with emeralds. The altar lighting for the statue is the work of Gaudí.

The church is open daily from 8am to 8pm; admission is free. Daily at noon and sunset the famed boys' choir sings. The monastery's museum, containing a collection of fans, vestments, traditional costumes, ceramics, glass, Nativity scenes, instruments, paintings, and traditional Majorcan furnishings and jewelry, is open daily from 10am to 6pm; admission is 160 ptas. ($1.35) for adults, free for children under 12.

3. Puerto de Pollensa and the North

The bay at Puerto de Pollensa is large, graceful, and rimmed with mountains. In short, it's a knockout, especially at sunset. Pleasure boats are anchored everywhere, and for the moment it is a high-rise–free haven. Let's hope it stays that way.

If you don't need hundreds of souvenir shops and dozens of clubs and discos within a five-block radius, you'll like it here, some 65 kilometers (40 miles) from the perpetual motion of Palma and its nearby beaches. A series of low-rise hotels, private homes, restaurants, and snackbars line the very attractive beach, which is somewhat narrow at its northwestern end but has some of the island's finest, whitest sand and warmest, clearest water. There is only one luxury hotel in the area, however, and that is out on the Formentor Peninsula.

Recently, additional tons of fine, white sand have been imported to the beach at the southeastern end of Pollensa Bay to create a broad ribbon of sun- and sea-bathing space stretching for a kilometer along the bay's beautiful, clear waters. Windsurfing, waterskiing, and scuba diving are among the water sports offered in the area.

Puerto de Pollensa's **tourist office** is located at Plaça Miquel Capllonch 2 (tel. 53-46-66) and is open May to October Monday through Friday from 9:30am to 1pm and 4 to 7pm, and Saturday from 9:30am to 1pm; closed holidays. In an **emergency,** if you need an ambulance, a policeman, or the fire brigade call 53-04-37.

ACCOMMODATIONS

The hotels in the Puerto de Pollensa area are mostly small and happily lacking in the mass-tourism sameness that prevails on the island's southern coast.

- **Hotel Formentor,** Formentor Peninsula (postal address: 07470 Puerto de Pollensa, Majorca) (tel. 971/53-13-00). 127 rms and suites. A/C MINIBAR TV TEL

Set on 15 square kilometers (5.5 square miles) of grounds, this is one of Europe's most exclusive hotels. At once elegant and unpretentious, it is an oasis of peace and quiet, a paradise for sun-lazing. When it was built in the late 1920s, all construction materials had to be transported to the site by sea as the road was not built until the next decade.

The rooms are tastefully appointed in a country style with area rugs and gracious furnishings.

Dining/Entertainment: The Grill Room, which features in the hotel's full-board plan, is open to the public at night for informal dining, but in the more elegant upstairs dining room a jacket and tie are required. On the upper terrace there is live music nightly, making it a most pleasant place for pre- and post-dinner sipping.

Facilities: Pool, tennis, horseback riding, and a well-tended beach.

RATES (INCLUDING BREAKFAST): 9,800–16,500 ptas. ($82–

$138) single; 14,900–26,250 ptas. ($124–$219) double; 24,300–35,450 ptas. ($203–$295) junior suite. Closed Nov–Mar.

• **Hotel Illa D'Or,** Paseo Colón 265, 07470 Puerto de Pollensa, Majorca (tel. 971/53-11-00). 120 rms. TEL

To paraphrase Conrad Hilton, the three most important things about a hotel are location, location, and location, and few hotels can beat the Illa D'Or on that score. Ensconced at the quiet northwestern end of Pollensa Bay, it is a vivid white presence with a certain colonial charm. Its terrace bar, where the Mediterranean waters lap gently as you sip your drink, is the best seaside bar in all of Majorca. At sunset you can sit here and watch the mountains behind the bay fade to purple against the pink-orange sky. Another nice thing about staying here is that you can walk the kilometer or so into town along a stone path at the very water's edge. Location aside, however, its combination of comfort, meticulous housekeeping, and warm, friendly service make it one of the best choices in town.

Dating from 1929, the 80 rooms in the Illa D'Or's original structure contain some beautiful vintage Majorcan furniture. The furnishings in the newer wing are mundanely modern. Many of the rooms have terraces and a sea view, and a third are air-conditioned. Although the shower behaved erratically during my last visit, rumor has it that the plumbing has been overhauled by now.

Dining/Entertainment: All meals are served in the friendly, airy dining room. Half and full board are available.

RATES (INCLUDING BREAKFAST AND IVA): 3,900–5,050 ptas. ($33–$42) single; 7,000–9,700 ptas. ($58–$81) double.

• **Hotel Capri,** Anglada Camarasa 69, 07470 Puerto de Pollensa, Majorca (tel. 971/53-16-00). 33 rms. TEL

This is another bright, white entry on the water near the town center. The furnishings in its pleasant rooms (about half with terrace) have a certain passé charm about them. If you're more interested in space than a sea view, the interior rooms are larger. The first-floor bar has a great view from its outdoor terrace.

RATES (INCLUDING BREAKFAST AND IVA): 4,195–6,745 ptas. ($35–$56) single; 7,550–12,030 ptas. ($63–$100) double. Closed Nov–Mar.

• **Hotel Daina,** Atilio Boveri 2, 07470 Puerto de Pollensa, Majorca (tel. 971/53-12-50). 60 rms. TEL

Right in the heart of town, this is one of three hotels in Puerto de Pollensa with a pool. The one here is unique, however, in that it juts out into the sea and has a sandy beach on either side.

The Daina's rooms are attractively furnished in a Spanish style and have equally attractive baths. About a quarter of them have a sea view.

RATES (INCLUDING BREAKFAST AND IVA): 4,280–5,040 ptas. ($36–$42) single; 8,050–9,390 ptas. ($67–$78) double. Closed Nov–Mar.

• **Hotel Residencia Sis Pins,** Anglada Camarasa 77, 07470 Puerto de Pollensa, Majorca (tel. 971/53-10-50). 50 rms. TEL

A hacienda-style facade with flower-bedecked arches marks the entrance to the Sis Pins, which sits along the water close to the town center. Some of its rather functional rooms have a terrace. The lounge in the lobby is quite comfortable and feels much like someone's living room.

RATES: 1,700–4,200 ptas. ($14–$35) single; 3,200–10,050 ptas. ($27–$84) double. Closed Nov–Mar.

• **Hotel Raf,** Paseo Coronel Llorente 28, 07470 Puerto de Pollensa, Marjorca (tel. 971/53-11-95). 40 rms.

This is a central choice across the street from the newly enhanced southwestern stretch of beach. The large, rather charming rooms are colorfully decorated and feature simple wood furnishings.

RATES (INCLUDING BREAKFAST AND IVA): 2,100–3,045 ptas. ($18–$25) single; 4,200–6,090 ptas. ($35–$51) double. Closed Nov–Mar.

• **Hotel Residencia Eolo,** Carretera Pollensa 10, 07470 Puerto de Pollensa, Majorca (tel. 971/53-15-50). 52 rms. (with showers only, no tubs). TEL

Right in the middle of town and a stone's throw from the beach, the Eolo is nicely furnished and comfortable. Some of the rooms have ample terraces.

RATES (INCLUDING BREAKFAST): 1,640–3,120 ptas. ($14–$26) single; 2,990–4,620 ptas. ($25–$37) double.

• **Hostal Galeón,** Berlín s/n (no street number) (Apartado de Correos 18), 07470 Puerto de Pollensa, Majorca (tel. 971/53-16-50). 43 rms.

If you're having trouble finding something in town, this is a fall-back. Located at the southwestern end of Puerto de Pollensa along the road to Alcudia, the Galeón's rooms are lackluster and a bit worn here and there, but the rates are very reasonable.

RATES (INCLUDING BREAKFAST AND IVA): 1,155–1,785 ptas. ($10–$15) per person per day. Closed Nov 26–Mar.

DINING

The numerous quality restaurants in Puerto de Pollensa and the surrounding area offer both traditional island dishes and culinary accents from abroad.

• **Stay Restaurant,** Muelle Nuevo s/n (no street number), Puerto de Pollensa (tel. 53-00-13). *Prices:* Entrées 1,350–5,000 ptas. ($11.25–$41.75).

One of the priciest restaurants in town, Stay offers an international menu with a nouvelle bent. The selection of appetizers is ample and includes such unique pasta offerings as seafood ravioli stuffed with shrimp and crab and topped with a savory seafood sauce. Among entrées, the house specialties include a grilled, marinated chicken; grilled or broiled lobster; caldereta de langosta (lobster soup); arroz marinera, a fish soup with rice; and parrillada de mariscos, a platter of grilled prawns, shrimp, crab, and more. The menu changes substantially about every two months, however, so surprises are always in store. The luscious desserts are all homemade.

Open: May–Oct daily 12:30–4pm and 7:30–11pm. *Closed:* Mon in winter, and Feb. NOUVELLE/INTERNATIONAL

• **Bec Fi Restaurante,** Avenida Anglada Camarasa 91, Puerto de Pollensa (tel. 53-10-40). *Prices:* Meals average 3,500 ptas. ($29).

This is one of Puerto de Pollensa's best restaurants, with a simple dining area indoors and a small outdoor patio sheltered with palm trees. The specialty is meat and fish prepared on a grill fueled by local encina (holm oak) wood.

Open: Tues–Sun 1–3:30pm and 7–10:30pm. *Closed:* Dec and Jan. MAJORCAN/SPANISH

• **Daus,** Escalonada Calvari 10, Pollença (tel. 53-28-67). *Prices:* Entrées up to 5,500 ptas. ($45.75).

Located in the town of Pollença several kilometers from Puerto de Pollensa, Daus sits at the bottom end of the 365 steps of Pollença's Monte Calvario (see "Things to See and Do," below). If you're in the mood for a romantic meal, this is the place to come. The entranceway, adorned with a white drape and a large urn with a candle, sets the tone. Inside, the stone ceilings of its two dining areas attest to its former function as the *bodega* (wine cellar) of the Jesuits. Soft, classical music accompanies the meal, along with a very sophisticated level of service.

All this and good food too. The menu, which changes every several months, is rich in Majorcan specialties such as lamb, rabbit, suckling pig, and caldereta de langosta. Some fixed offerings include arroz negro (rice with shrimp and cuttlefish in its own ink); lubina (sea bass) stuffed with monkfish and shrimp; a cazuela (casserole) that combines monkfish, lobster, and baby eels; and roast baby lamb. Outstanding among the homemade desserts is the crema catalana.

Open: Wed–Mon 12:30–3:30pm and 7:45–11:30pm (later in summer). *Closed:* 40 days in winter (they vary from year to year). MAJORCAN/SPANISH

• **Restaurante La Lonja del Pescado,** Muelle Viejo s/n (no street number), Puerto de Pollensa (tel. 53-00-23). *Prices:* Meals begin at 2,500 ptas. ($20.75).

Another top Puerto de Pollensa restaurant, La Lonja serves top-flight seafood flown in fresh daily from Galicia. The upstairs dining room, where lunch is served, overlooks the port. The menu selection is small but select, and stars the caldereta de langosta.

Open: Daily 12:30–3:30pm and 7:30–10:30pm (closing hours a little later in summer). *Closed:* Wed mid-Dec through Jan. SEAFOOD

• **American Dream Restaurant,** Virgen del Carmen 14, Puerto de Pollensa (tel. 53-45-66). *Prices:* Meals average 2,500 ptas. ($20.75); children's menu 700 ptas. ($5.75).

As its name suggests, American Dream offers a few things to remind you of home. One of them is the unlimited salad bar included with every main course. Some others are barbecued ribs and deep-fried chicken wings. Although steak is a specialty here, the fisherman's platter with lobster, avocado, smoked fish, and melon is also a good bet. A somewhat unusual but very popular dish is the chicken curry served with mango chutney and Indian bread.

Another thing that sets this restaurant apart is its glitzy decor. Hanging on the walls are portraits of James Dean, Judy Garland, and Humphrey Bogart. Gracing the placemats and menu is Marilyn Monroe. Since this street is closed to traffic at night, outdoor dining here is peacefully pleasant.

Vegetarians, note that you can come here and have a large salad plus potatoes or fruit for a minimum of 1,000 pesetas ($8.25).

Open: Easter–Oct, Mon–Sat 7pm–whenever. AMERICAN

• **Ca Vostra,** Carretera Puerto de Pollensa–Alcudia, Puerto de Pollensa (tel. 53-15-46). *Prices:* Entrées 500–3,500 ptas. ($4–$29); three-course menu of the day 1,150 ptas. ($9.50).

One of the celler genre of restaurants, Ca Vostra has a beamed ceiling and wine barrels along the walls. According to the locals, it is the most traditionally Majorcan of Puerto de Pollensa restaurants. The hearty, unpretentious food is in keeping with the rustic, red-and-white-checked tablecloth ambience. The frito mallorquín, a conglomeration of lamb innards sautéed with potatoes, peppers, garlic, and bay leaves, is not for everyone, but those who enjoy liver and such might want to give this traditional dish a try. Also good is the tumbet, a local-style ratatouille. Other house specialties include caldereta de rape (angler fish soup), caldereta de langosta (quite economical here), paella with lobster, and civet de conejo (rabbit marinated in red wine).

Open: Daily noon–4pm and 7pm–midnight. *Closed:* Wed in winter. MAJORCAN

• **Bar/Restaurante La Victoria,** Ermita de la Victoria, Alcudia (no phone). *Prices:* Meals average 2,500 ptas. ($20.75).

At lunch La Victoria offers both scenic food for the soul and tasty fare for the palate. Perched high up on the Alcudia Peninsula, its outdoor terrace surveys all of Pollensa Bay and the Formentor Peninsula. Inside is a two-tiered dining room.

The menu is weighted with grilled meat and fish dishes, but there are a number of Majorcan specialties such as sopa mallorquina, frito mallorquín, pork with cabbage, and pescado a la mallorquina (fish with potatoes topped with vegetables). My lechona (suckling pig) was excellent—crispy on the outside; sweet, tender, and succulent on the inside.

Note: You can combine a luncheon visit to La Victoria with bathing at one of the two pretty sand beaches at Mal Pas. The water is marvelous. Also, as you drive up to La Victoria, you'll pass a series of rocky coves. If you don't mind parking your towel on a rock, these are fine for sunbathing too, and command wonderful views of the deep turquoise waters of Pollensa Bay.

Open: Daily 12:30–4pm and 6:30–10:30pm. *Closed:* Mon in winter, and Nov. MAJORCAN/SPANISH

• **Cafeteria Neptuno,** Carretera de Formentor 13, Puerto de Pollensa (tel. 53-29-54). *Prices:* Tapas from 225 ptas. ($1.75).

This economical eatery a block from the beach specializes in tapas. Small plates are 225 ptas. ($1.75); large plates, 400 ptas. ($3.25). Or you can order mixed tapas plates for 500 ptas. ($4) or 650 ptas. ($5.50) respectively. If your appetite calls for something more, there are sandwiches, platos combinados for 850 to 1,100 ptas. ($7 to $9), and a full menu.

Open: Daily 9:30am–midnight. *Closed:* Thurs in Nov and Jan, and from mid-Dec to mid-Jan. SPANISH

THINGS TO SEE AND DO

The plunging cliffs and rocky coves of Majorca's northwestern coast are a stunning prelude to Puerto de Pollensa. From the **Mirador des (del) Colomer** there is an expansive view of the striking Californialike coast that stretches from Punta de la Nau to Punta de la Troneta and includes El Colomer, or Pigeon's Rock, named for the nests in its cave.

But it is the 20-kilometer (12.5-mile) stretch of winding, at times vertiginous, road leading from Puerto de Pollensa to the tip of the Formentor Peninsula that delivers the island's most intoxicating scenic visions. The cliffs over 200 meters (650 ft.) high and spectacular rock-rimmed coves embrace intense turquoise waters. About halfway along this road is the **Cala del Pi de la Posada,** where you will find the Hotel Formentor and a lovely bathing beach. Continuing on to the end you'll come to the lighthouse at **Cabo Formentor.**

For those who prefer the perspective from the sea, various **boat excursions,** including glass-bottom-boat outings, are offered in Pollensa Bay. Boats to Formentor leave from Puerto de Pollensa's Estación Marítima several times daily in summer and on a limited basis in winter. Ask at your hotel or the marina itself for the latest schedule. **Calipso Tours,** Gommar 43, Puerto de Pollensa (tel. 53-05-70), offers fishing and sport excursions. To rent a windsurfer, catamaran, or light sailing boat, or to take instruction in their use, contact **Bellini,** Paseo Anglada Camarasa 47, Puerto de Pollensa (tel. 53-11-56), from April to October. For information on the **waterskiing** school, check at the Hotel Illa D'Or or the Bar Katy along the water between the Hotel Illa D'Or and town. Organized excursions on **horseback** are available at Rancho Grande, Pollença Road (tel. 53-14-80).

Wednesday is **market day** in Puerto de Pollensa, so head for the town square (there's only one) from 8am to 1pm and browse through the fresh produce, leather goods, embroidered tablecloths, ceramics, and more. Bargaining is part of the fun. Sunday is market day in the town of Pollença.

Alcudia Bay is a long stretch of narrow, sandy beach with beautiful water backed by countless hotels whose hordes rather overwhelm the beach in peak season. The nightlife is more abundant and varied here than in Puerto de Pollensa, and for those who care to partake, the disco of the moment is Menta—the usual multibar, multi-dance floor mecca of modern youth.

Between Puerto de Alcudia and Ca'n Picafort is the **Parc Natural de S'Albufera,** Carretera Alcudia-Artá, Km. 27, 07458 C'an Picafort (no phone). A wetlands area of lagoons, dunes, and canals covering some 800 hectares (1,975 acres), it attracts birdwatchers and other assorted nature enthusiasts. To date, more than 200 species of birds have been sighted here, among them heron and owl, osprey, and, in the warbler family, the moustached, willow, and fan-tailed varieties. The best times to visit are spring and fall when migratory birds abound. Spring, too, offers a marvelous display of flora. The park is open daily, except Christmas, from 9am to 5pm in winter, to 7pm in summer. Visits are free, but you must get a permit at the reception center, where all motorized vehicles must be left. From there you can proceed on foot, horseback, or bicycle. At press-time, plans were to offer bike rentals on the site. Binoculars are available for the token fee of 200 ptas. ($1.65) (no time limit). Detailed information and itineraries are provided at the reception center.

In the town of Pollensa, about six kilometers (four miles) from Puerto Pollensa, is an 18th-century stairway leading up to an *ermita* (hermitage). Consisting of 365 stairs, it is known as the **Monte Calvario** (Calvary); but you can also reach the top by car via Calle de las Cruces, which is lined with three-meter-high (10-ft.) concrete crosses.

At **Cala San Vicente,** between Pollensa and Puerto de Pollensa, is a pleasant, small sandy cove with some notable surf. Several small hotels and restaurants provide the necessary amenities.

Although the nightlife offering in Puerto de Pollensa is rather meager—most people make the 10-kilometer (6.5-mile) trip to Alcudia—there are a few places in town with lots of atmosphere both in and out of tourist season. One is **Añoranza,** Calle Juan XXIII no. 22 (tel. 53-10-52), which is both a bar and restaurant. Day and night the crowd here is lively, and after 10pm, when all the dinner dishes have been cleared, owners Juan and Manolo break out their guitars and start to sing. From time to time patrons, too, get up and entertain. It's all very informal and lots of fun. Open in summer daily from noon to 3:30pm and 7pm to 3:30am; closed Sunday and holidays in winter.

Just around the corner is **New Aniara,** Formentor 6 (no phone), owned by brothers of Juan and Manolo. One of the new breed of bars with a billiard table, sofa seating, and taped rock music, it attracts a somewhat younger crowd. In summer it is definitely the bar *con más marcha* ("with the most action") in town and is renowned for its special theme parties—hat night, costume parties, and the like. Open daily from 9pm until. . . .

For dancing there is **Discotheque Chivas,** Calle Médico Llopis 5 (tel. 53-15-29), a modern, smallish place with the standard flashing colored lights and loud music. Though the crowd is predominantly young, those in their 30s, 40s, and even 50s do put in an appearance, especially in the wee hours. Open in summer daily from 11pm to 5am; in winter, on Friday, Saturday, and Sunday. Cover, including one drink, is 600 ptas. ($5).

In addition, there are numerous bars, pubs, and assorted watering holes along the waterfront and in some of the small streets in the center of town.

4. The Eastern Coast

Less majestic than Majorca's western coast, the eastern coast is mostly rolling hills and farmland that meet the sea in a series of rocky coves, many now overpowered by high-rise construction. The upper portion of the east coast is easily explored from a base in Puerto de Pollensa, and the lower portion from a base in Palma.

THINGS TO SEE AND DO

In Manacor you can visit the 100-year-old Majorica pearl factory and store, Calle B-2 s/n (no street number) (tel. 55-02-00), whose selection of simulated pearl jewelry is the largest on the island. The handmade Majorica pearls are formed around a natural mineral core that is coated with layers of a secret mixture of fish scales that simulates the sheen of real pearls. Over 300 artisans work diligently to shape, polish, string, and inspect the pearls one by one. Their production consumes the scales of more than 100 million fish annually. Beware the sly fakes sold under such similar names as "Majorca," "Mallorca," or "Majorque," however; the genuine article, guaranteed for 10 years, carries a red tag with "Perlas Majorica" inscribed in gold lettering and a quality-control number. Sold in *agencias oficiales* (official agencies) in some 45 countries and hundreds of airport shops around the world, Majórica pearls are, of course, more attractively priced here at the source.

The factory is open Monday through Friday from 9am to 12:30pm and 3 to 6:30pm, and on Saturday and Sunday from 10am to 1pm. The store is open Monday through Friday from 9am to 7pm, on Saturday and Sunday from 10am to 1pm, and on holidays from 10am to 6pm. Both the factory and store are closed on Christmas Day.

The **Cuevas del Drach** (Caverns of the Dragon) (tel. 57-00-02), 60 kilometers (37.5 miles) from Palma near Porto Cristo on the east coast, are one of Majorca's best-known attractions. A series of spectacular "gothic" grottoes with amazing stalactite and stalagmite formations, they are a truly memorable experience, especially when teamed with a floating classical-music concert. While visitors sit in the cavernous darkness, three boats trimmed with lights—one carrying the musicians—cross one of the world's largest underground lakes. In all, the visit covers about half a mile of strikingly illuminated subterranean splendor and lasts one hour. From November to March daily visits with concert are conducted on the hour from 11am to 3pm; without concert, at 4 and 5pm. From April to October there are daily visits on the hour from 10am to 5pm, all with concert. Admission is 500 ptas. ($4).

You may think that when you've seen one cave you've seen them all. But the **Cuevas de Artá** (tel. 56-32-93), near the Platja de Canyamel (Playa de Cañamel), while similar to the Cuevas de Drach, offer a more intimate and, in some ways, more impressive display. During the 45-minute visit, you meander among cavernous rooms reaching 45 meters (145 ft.) in height, while formations variously resembling a virgin with child and a pipe organ suggest that you have strayed into some surrealistic, underground cathedral. These caves are open in summer daily from 9:30am to 7pm, in winter daily from 9:30am to 5pm, with guided visits every 20 minutes, on average, or whenever a sizable group forms. Admission is 450 ptas. ($3.75).

You can combine a visit to the Cuevas de Artá with a swim at the adjacent **Platja de Canyamel,** one of the nicest beaches along the eastern coast.

Inca, in the center of the island, is Majorca's leather-manufacturing center. You may or may not find a bargain at its factory outlets, which primarily offer seconds, so check prices in Palma before coming. Most of the outlets are open Monday through Friday from 9:30am to 7pm and on Saturday from 9:30am to noon. FEVE, Plaza España 9, Palma (tel. 75-22-45), operates the "Leather Express" train service between Palma and Inca.

IBIZA TOWN

A party town extraordinaire, Ibiza annually stages a dazzling summer spectacle that truly lights up the night. By day, the all-night clubbers rest up on the island's beaches. At night, they don their provocative fashions and outrageous coifs and strut their freewheeling stuff through the Ibiza Town alleys lined with the come-ons of trendy tourism—bars, boutiques, sidewalk cafés, and stylish restaurants where you might spot such vacationing celebs as Roman Polanski, Goldie Hawn, and Julio Iglesias.

Though Ibiza Town is the island's capital and only true urban entity, it's not a resort town but a tourist port. There is no beach here, just a marina brimming with yachts and other pleasure boats. Visitors typically stay at the nearby beach resorts of Figueretas and Playa d'en Bossa and come into town primarily to shop and play the night away. These two resorts are of the concrete-jungle, tour-group ilk, with little to recommend them except the beaches that they now overwhelm. If you want to avoid the overcrowded sensation of their too-many hotels, consider staying in town and commuting out to the sand and the sea. It's merely a matter of a mile or two.

Founded by the Carthaginians 645 years before Christ, the city rises vertically from the port and forms a romantic mound of twinkling lights at night. The old barrios of the city's upper reaches contain the cathedral, city hall, and numerous noble mansions of earlier eras. In the small, interior villages (and occasionally in town) you'll see the grandmothers of the island draped in the traditional long dresses and scarfs of another time.

Every year the island's local population of 70,000 plays host to a contingent of tourists numbering over one million, most of whom pour in between June 15 and September 15. Because Ibiza is tolerant of mankind's myriad eccentricities and can cater to them all, you never know just what awaits around the corner—but you can bet it won't be boring!

1. Orientation

GETTING THERE

A mere 35-minute flight from Barcelona, Ibiza is accessible by air and sea from Palma de Majorca (35 miles), Valencia (105 miles), Barcelona (175 miles), and many European cities. From New York, **Air Europa** offers charter flights to Madrid and limited service from Madrid to Ibiza in peak season. **Iberia** and **Aviaco** offer both domestic and international flights to the island, and several European carriers provide direct service from London, Paris, Marseilles, Lyon, Zurich, Frankfurt, Brussels, Nice, Geneva, Athens, Rome, and Milan.

Trasmediterránea, Avenida Bartolomé Vicente Ramón s/n (no street number) (tel. 971/31-50-11), offers hydrofoil service in August between Ibiza and Alicante and Ibiza and Palma de Majorca. The three-hour trip from Alicante is 5,650 ptas. ($47); the two-hour trip from Palma is 3,850 ptas. ($32). Trasmediterránea runs regular ferries between Barcelona and Ibiza Monday through Saturday in high season (several times a week throughout the rest of the year), and generally twice weekly service from Palma de Mallorca and Valencia. Fares from both Barcelona and Valencia are 4,690 ptas. ($39) for a seat, 7,590 ptas. ($63.25) per person in a quad cabin, 10,320 ptas. ($86) per person in a double cabin, and 11,900 ptas. ($99.25) for a single. If the crossing is direct, the ferry from Barcelona takes 9 hours; from Valencia, 6½ hours. For the four-hour trip from Palma the respective fares are 3,410 ptas. ($28.50), 6,260 ptas. ($52.25), 7,530 ptas. ($62.75), and 9,070 ptas. ($75.50). Tickets are available at Trasmediterránea or any travel agency. The Trasmediterránea office in Ibiza Town is open all year Monday through Friday from 9am to 1pm and 5 to 7pm, and on Saturday from 9am to 12:30pm; it is closed holidays.

Flebasa Lines, Estación Marítima (tel. 971/31-09-27), offers hydrofoil service between Denia and Ibiza several times a week in the summer.

As all ferry and hydrofoil services tend to change annually, check current schedules before planning your itinerary.

Note: Space on ferries and planes is extremely tight in July and August. If you're planning to come during these months, book everything well in advance.

UPON ARRIVAL

Every hour on the half hour there is daily **bus service** from Es Codolar airport into Ibiza Town. (Buses depart *for* the airport from the ticket kiosk at Avenida Isidor Macabich 24, daily every hour on the hour from 7am to 10pm.) The fare for the 9-kilometer (5½-mile) ride to or from the airport is 60 ptas. (50¢).

A **taxi** from the airport to the center of town is 950 ptas. ($8), plus 50 ptas. (40¢) for each suitcase.

At the airport, you can **change money** at the Banco Exterior de España daily from April 1 to October 31 from about 8:30am to 10pm; in winter, hours revert to normal banking hours (see Section 2, "Fast Facts," below).

For **airport information,** call 30-03-00. For **Iberia Airlines** reservations, call 30-09-54. Iberia's in-town office at Avenida de España 34 (tel. 31-13-54) is open Monday through Friday from 9:30am to 1:15pm and 5 to 7:45pm, and on Saturday from 8:30am to 1:15pm; closed holidays.

GETTING AROUND

Ibiza Town is small enough that you can get around easily on foot.

For information on the comings and goings of boats, airplanes, and buses, check the daily listings in *La Prensa de Ibiza* and *Diario de Ibiza.*

CITY LAYOUT

"D'Alt Vila" (Upper Town) is sheltered within the old city walls that date from five different eras: Phoenician in the area of Carrer Major near the cathedral; Byzantine on Carrer de Joan Roman; Roman here and there; Arab along Carrer de Sant Josep; and Christian, from the time of Felipe II, in the newer sections. Visually and architecturally—not to mention panoramically—D'Alt Vila is the most interesting area of Ibiza Town and houses numerous pensions, shops, and restaurants. At the end of Calle Conquista is the house of the last Arab king of Ibiza (look through the gate of house no. 8). Also in D'Alt Vila are the Ayuntamiento (Town Hall), whose magnificent belvedere looks out over the sea; the archeological museum; and the cathedral (see Section 5, "Things to See and Do," below).

If you exit D'Alt Vila through the Portal Nou, you will see the graceful silhouette of **Puig des Molins,** site of the Carthaginian and Roman necropolis dating back to the beginning of the 7th century B.C. More than 4,000 hypogeum-type tombs were carved into the rock of this hill, and many of the world's leading archeologists have come here to study them. Most of the treasures on display in the archeological museum were unearthed here.

At the eastern end of Ibiza Town by the marina is **Sa Penya,** the former seafaring district that was long home to local fishermen and sailors. Nowadays their dwindling ranks share the quarter's labyrinth of alleys with artists, designers, and astute businesspeople who have installed shops, bars, and restaurants in the picturesque, whitewashed structures huddled between the D'Alt Vila and the harbor.

Near the western end of the marina is the **Paseo Vara de Rey,** the town's brief, central boulevard that, along with its extension, Avenida de España, comprises what might loosely be termed Ibiza's business district.

2. Fast Facts

BUSINESS HOURS: Time in Ibiza bends to humans rather than the other way around, so hours are erratic, subject to weather, whim, tourist demand, whatever. Generally speaking, however, **stores** are open Monday through Friday from 10am to 1:30 or 2pm and from 4:30 to 8:30pm (though in the peak summer months hours extend well beyond this). On Saturday most are open in the morning only.

Banks are generally open Monday through Friday from 9am to 2pm and on Saturday from 9am to noon, but there are numerous *oficinas de cambio* (exchange offices) open all day.

Office hours are typically Monday through Friday from 9am to 1:30pm and 4:30 to 6 or 7pm.

Restaurant hours are generally 1 to 5pm and 8 to 11pm, but patrons are often allowed to linger well past midnight.

CONSULATES: The **Consulate of the U.K.,** Avenida Isidor Macabich 45, 1st Floor (tel. 30-18-18), is open Monday through Friday from 9am to 2pm and on Saturday from 9:30am to noon. The nearest **U.S. Consulate** is in Barcelona (tel. 93/319-95-50) (see Section 4, "Fast Facts," in Chapter II for hours) and has a 24-hour emergency answering service.

CURRENCY EXCHANGE: In addition to banks, there are several oficinas de cambio (exchange offices) in town. A central one is at Vara de Rey 19 (tel. 30-18-96), open in summer Monday through Friday from 8:30am to 1:30pm and 4 to 7pm, and on Saturday from 8:30am to 1pm; in winter, Monday through Saturday from 8:30am to 2pm.

ELECTRICITY: Most tourist lodgings have 220V electricity, but you will still find some 125V outlets, so check first.

EMERGENCIES: For **medical emergencies,** call 30-02-00 or 31-16-71. For the **Red Cross ambulance,** call 30-12-14. A complete, **24-hour medical service** operating out of San Antonio Abad and serving the whole island can be reached at 34-00-00 or 34-11-34. In case of **fire,** call 31-30-30. For the **police,** dial 091.

HOLIDAYS: In addition to all Spanish national holidays (see Section 4, "Fast Facts," in Chapter II), Ibiza Town observes the following local holidays: the Focs de San Joan from June 21 to 24 and town fairs from August 2 to 8.

LANGUAGE: Ibicenco, the island's subdialect of Catalan, shares official status with Spanish (see Section 2, "Fast Facts," in Chapter VIII). The local name for Ibiza is "Eivissa."

LOST AND FOUND: There is a Lost and Found Office at the Municipal Police headquarters at Calle Vicente Serra 25 (tel. 31-58-61).

MAIL: The central post office is located at Calle Madrid 21, Ibiza Town (tel. 31-13-80), and is open Monday through Friday from 9am to 2pm and 3 to 8pm, and on Saturday from 9am to 1pm and 2 to 6pm. Other post offices around the island are open Monday through Friday from 9am to 2pm and on Saturday from 9am to noon. You can also buy stamps at any *estanco* (tobacconist).

NEWSPAPERS: *La Prensa de Ibiza* and *Diario de Ibiza* are the leading Spanish-language dailies. *Ibiza Now,* the island's English-language newspaper, is published fortnightly.

PHARMACIES: Any closed pharmacy displays in its window the location of the nearest open one. *La Prensa de Ibiza* and *Diario de Ibiza* also list the pharmacies open around-the-clock that day.

SAFETY: Whenever you're traveling in an unfamiliar city or area, stay alert. Be aware of your immediate surroundings. Wear a moneybelt and don't sling your camera or purse over your shoulder; wear the strap diagonally across your body. This will minimize the possibility of your becoming a victim of crime. Every society has its criminals. It's your responsibility to be aware and alert even in the most heavily touristed areas.

TAXIS: There are **taxi stands** at the bus terminal, at the port terminal, and at the end of the Paseo Vara de Rey. For a **radio cab** in Ibiza Town, call 30-70-00 or 30-66-02.

Ibiza taxis do not have meters, but a list of official prices for specific routes is available from every driver. To give you some idea, the ride from Ibiza to San Antonio Abad (about 15km, 9 miles) is 1,400 ptas. ($11.75) and from the airport to the Hotel Hacienda in Na Xamena (about 30km, 19 miles) is about 2,000 ptas. ($16.75). Between 11pm and 6am, a 50-pta. (40¢) supplement is charged, and suitcases are 50 ptas. (40¢) additional apiece.

TELEPHONE: The local area code is 971 (do not dial the 9 when calling from outside Spain). You can make international calls from most public phones but you'll need a heavy supply of coins. Since hotels often tack a surcharge of 25% or more onto long-distance calls, it is best to go to one of the numerous telephone centers around the island for your international conversations. Rates are substantially lower at night and on holidays.

From May to the end of October you can make **international calls or change money** daily from 11am to 1am (to 3am in summer) behind the Bar/Restaurante El Puerto, Plaza Sa Riba 4, El Puerto, Ibiza Town.

Eivissol, Avenida Bartomeu Vicent Ramon 1 (tel. 31-06-49), is another private international telephone service open in summer,

Monday through Saturday from 9:30am to 1:30pm and 5 to 10pm, and on Sunday and holidays from 5 to 10pm; closed Sunday in October. From November to May the hours are Monday through Friday from 9:30am to 1:30pm and 5 to 8pm, and on Saturday from 9:30am to 1:30pm; closed holidays. Collect calls carry a charge of 280 ptas. ($2.25) if accepted and 785 ptas. ($6.50) if not.

The national telephone company (**CTNE** or **Compañía Telefónica Nacional de España**) offers service from its kiosk on Avenida Santa Eulalia by the marina daily in summer from 10am to 1pm and 5:30 to 11pm; in winter, daily from 10am to 1pm and 5 to 8:30pm; closed the first two weeks of January. Collect calls require a deposit of 168 ptas. ($1.50) for national calls and 784 ptas. ($6.50) for international calls, which is refunded if the charges are accepted.

To make an international call, first dial 07, wait for the tone, then dial the country code, city (or area) code, and phone number. For local **information,** dial 003. If you need to get an area code, want to make a collect call (other than at a telefónica), or have any other queries that require the assistance of an operator, dial 9198 for Europe and 9191 for the rest of the world.

TELEVISION/RADIO: There are three Spanish-language radio stations on Ibiza—Radio Popular (AM 837), Popular FM Ibiza (FM 89.1), and Radio Ibiza-SER (FM 98.1). There are two Spanish-language TV stations (Channels 1 and 2) and one Catalan (Channel 3). TVs with satellite hookups are becoming increasingly common throughout the island and offer a variety of global programming in many languages. Check *La Prensa de Ibiza* for daily listings.

TIPPING: See Section 4, "Fast Facts," in Chapter II.

TOURIST INFORMATION: The **tourist office,** Vara de Rey 13 (tel. 30-19-00), is open May to September Monday through Saturday from 9:30am to 1:30pm and 5 to 9pm, and on Sunday and holidays from 10am to 12:30pm. In winter, it is open Monday through Saturday from 9am to 1:30pm (more or less).

Two handy publications that provide detailed information on all aspects of island life are **"Welcome Ibiza Spotlight"** and **"Your Master Guide to Ibiza,"** both available at bookstores, newsstands, and hotels.

---

3. Accommodations

Most visitors staying in town opt for rented apartments or small pensions, so there are no mass-tourism monstrosities to impinge on the intimate charm of the island's capital. On the other hand, there are also none of the select, stellar hostelries that stud the inland hilltops and the coast.

The posted rates at most lodgings are the official maximums the place can charge. Often you can negotiate at least a 10% discount—sometimes more in the off-season. For the purposes of this guide, "expensive" hotels charge 8,500 ptas. ($71) and up for a double room; "moderate" hotels, 6,000 to 8,500 ptas. ($50 to $71); and "budget" lodgings, 1,600 to 6,000 ptas. ($13 to $50). *Note:* Unless otherwise indicated, all accommodations have private bath or shower, all hotels are open year round, and all rates given include service charge but *not* IVA.

EXPENSIVE

In Ibiza Town

- **Hotel Royal Plaza,** Calle Pedro Francés 27-29, 07800 Ibiza (tel. 971/31-00-00). 117 rms. A/C MINIBAR TV TEL

Located three blocks from the port, this is a comfortable, modern, businesslike hotel from the sleek, clean lines of its marble lobby to the brown-and-beige decor of its rooms, most of which have a terrace.

Dining/Entertainment: The Plaza Snack Bar/Restaurant serves snacks from 11:30am to midnight, lunch from 1:30 to 4pm, and dinner from 7 to 11:30pm. The breakfast buffet is served in Le Relais from 8 to 11am. The adjoining bar is open from 8am to 11pm.

Facilities: A small, L-shaped pool with a view of the old city.

RATES: 5,395–10,650 ptas. ($45–$88.75) single; 8,640–15,660 ptas. ($72–$131) double; 16,575–30,250 ptas. ($138–$252) suite.

- **La Torre del Canónigo,** Calle Mayor 8, D'Alt Vila, 07800 Ibiza (tel. 971/30-38-84). 7 apts. For reservations, contact Marketing Ahead, 433 Fifth Ave., New York, NY 10016 (tel. 212/686-9213).

This former 15th-century bishop's mansion sits on a hilltop in the D'Alt Vila about 50 meters (160 ft.) from the cathedral. Now magnificently restored, it has been divided into attractive apartments with modern conveniences, fine works of art, and antique accent pieces. It is accessible by car and there is ample parking available in the plaza.

Five apartments have spectacular views, and the deluxe units are duplexes. The top choice is A6, which has its own small pool. Other guests may use the lap pool at the owner's house nearby.

RATES: 5,000–21,750 ptas. ($41.75–$181) per day, although minimum one-week reservations are requested, especially in high season. Weekly rates for one-bath studios for two are 32,500–70,000 ptas. ($271–$583); a two-bath apartment for four, 63,200–139,000 ptas. ($527–$1,158). Closed Nov–Holy Week.

In Figueretas and Playa d'en Bossa

Figueretas and Playa d'en Bossa, the beaches closest to Ibiza Town, are virtually a continuation of the capital and bursting at their overexploited seams with lackluster hotels. A notable cut above the throng of package-tour institutions are the two seaside hostelries below.

■ **Hotel Los Molinos,** Ramón Muntaner 60 (Apartado 504), 07800 Figueretas (tel. 971/30-22-50). 147 rms. A/C MINIBAR TV TEL

Among the waterfront properties of Figueretas, Los Molinos gets high marks for its beautifully landscaped setting and lovely pool area with access to a small beach. Two-thirds of the rooms have a terrace and sea view, but the singles, which are somewhat cramped, mostly face the street.

Facilities: Pool, beauty parlor, water sports from the hotel jetty (you can even fish from the rocks surrounding the garden).

RATES: 4,600–8,000 ptas. ($38.25–$66.75) single; 7,400–13,350 ptas. ($61.75–$111) double.

■ **Hotel Torre del Mar** (Apartado 564), Playa d'en Bossa, 07800 Ibiza (tel. 971/30-30-50). 219 Rms. A/C TV TEL

A little farther out but still only 1½ kilometers (1 mile) from Ibiza Town, the Torre del Mar is the top hotel on the Playa d'en Bossa. Its lobby lounges and bar studded with baroque and brocade accents are quite elegant. The cheery rooms here are well appointed and have terraces; half have a sea view.

Facilities: Outdoor and indoor pool, sauna, tennis court, playground, a small beach nearby.

RATES: 6,500–9,850 ptas. ($54.25–$82) single; 9,400–16,800 ptas. ($78.25–$140) double.

MODERATE

■ **La Ventana Hotel,** Sa Carrossa 13 (Apartado 1360), 07800 Ibiza (tel. 971/30-15-48). 13 double rms.

Located in D'Alt Vila, this charming hostelry occupies a traditional *ibicenco* house that was stylishly restored in 1984. The rooms are bright and cheerful, and owner Catherine Bagnis-Vogel makes guests feel like they're staying in someone's home rather than in a hotel. The lobby bar, which feels more like a living room than a hotel lounge, works on the honor system—take what you want and pay later. The third-floor rooms have the best views; six of the seven largest rooms have balconies. Air conditioning is available on an optional basis for an additional charge. The fine view of the port from the large outdoor terrace is shared by everyone.

RATES: 6,500–7,500 ptas. ($54.25–$62.50) small double; 7,500–9,500 ptas. ($62.50–$79.25) large double. Closed Nov-Holy Week.

■ **Hostal Residencia El Corsario,** Calle Poniente 5 or Santa María 12, 07800 Ibiza (tel. 971/30-12-48). 14 rms (most with bath).

This quaint inn shares an old corsair's residence with its restaurant (see Section 4, "Dining," below). Located within the old city walls, it has lovely arbored courtyards with olive trees and a good deal of antiquated charm. Some of the rooms feature antique furnishings.

Room 13 has three beds, beamed ceilings, arched doorways, and a wonderful view of the harbor. Rooms 1 and 2 share an outdoor terrace. Room 15 is in a newer part of the building and has the best view of all. Room 10 is a single with the same great view. One room, known as the "estudio," has four beds. Try to avoid Room 5—it's the hottest and has no view. Reservations are a must in the summer.

RATES: 5,500–6,500 ptas. ($45.75–$54.25) single with sink only, 7,000–8,000 ptas. ($58.25–$66.75) double with bath.

BUDGET

- **Hostal Residencia Aragón,** Calle Aragón 54, 07800 Ibiza (tel. 971/30-60-60). 10 rms (with sinks only).

Within easy walking distance of the town center and Figueretas beach, the Aragón is the best low-priced pension in town. Its entrance is one flight up and its atmosphere is very homey. Triples and quads are available; some rooms have TVs.

RATES (INCLUDING IVA): 2,000 ptas. ($16.75) single; 4,000 ptas. ($33.25) double; 5,600 ptas. ($46.75) triple; 6,600 ptas. ($55) quad.

- **Hostal Residencia Montesol,** Paseo Vara de Rey 2, 07800 Ibiza (tel. 971/31-01-61). 55 rms (with toilet). TEL

Adjacent to the popular café of the same name (see Section 4, "Dining," below), the Montesol's rooms are right on the marina and have white tile flooring throughout. Although all are clean and comfortable, there is a dearth of charm.

RATES: 2,950–3,675 ptas. ($24.50–$30.50) single; 4,350–5,500 ptas. ($36.25–$45.75) double with shower, 4,900–6,500 ptas. ($40.75–$54.25) with bath.

- **Hostal/Apartamentos El Puerto,** Calle Carlos III no. 22, 07800 Ibiza (tel. 971/31-38-27). 96 rms (including 12 singles) and 70 apts. (including 10 studios). TEL

Just a few blocks from the port, El Puerto's rooms and apartments all have simple wood furnishings. Half the rooms and all the apartments have terraces. The apartments also have fully equipped kitchenettes. There is lots of sunbathing space around the pool.

RATES: 2,575–4,275 ptas. ($21.50–$35.75) single; 3,100–6,750 ptas. ($25.75–$56.25) double; 2,750–7,200 ptas. ($23–$60) studio apartment; 3,350–9,200 ptas. ($28–$76.75) one-bedroom apartment, double occupancy; 300–650 ptas. ($2.50–$5.50) third-person supplement. Closed mid-Dec to end of Jan.

- **Hostal Residencia Parque,** Calle Vicente Cuervo s/n (no street number), 07800 Ibiza (tel. 971/30-13-58). 39 rms.

Located in the center of town near the old city walls, the Parque's rooms are small and friendly but largely functional. The seven corner rooms have terraces, but this means added noise at night. The doubles all have bath, and the singles, sink only.

RATES: 2,100 ptas. ($17.50) single; 5,100 ptas. ($42.50) double; 6,875 ptas. ($57.25) triple. Closed Dec.

• **Hostal Residencia Apartamentos Ripoll,** Calle Vicente Cuervo 10-14, 07800 Ibiza (tel. 971/31-42-75). 15 rms (10 doubles and several triples, without bath but with sink) and 16 one-bedroom apts.

The reception desk is one flight up. While the rooms are merely adequate, the apartments are very comfortable and all have terraces, modern kitchens, complete bath, and sofa-beds in the sitting room.

RATES: 1,100–1,525 ptas. ($9.25–$12.75) single; 1,600–2,570 ptas. ($13.25–$21.50) double; 300 ptas. ($2.50) per shower; 3,150–6,350 ptas. ($26.25–$53) per apartment per day, whether occupied by two or three people.

• **Hostal Residencia Sol y Brisa,** Avenida Bartolomé Vicente Ramón 15, 07800 Ibiza (tel. 971/31-08-18). 19 rms (with sinks only).

The Sol y Brisa offers very basic accommodation just a few blocks from the port. Here, too, the reception area is one flight up. The rooms are small, clean, and thanks to the tiled flooring, surprisingly friendly.

RATES (INCLUDING IVA): 900–1,200 ptas. ($7.50–$10) single; 1,600–2,200 ptas. ($13.25–$18.25) double.

---

4. Dining

Although similar dishes turn up on menus throughout the Balearic Islands, they are often rendered with distinctive local twists—except, of course, the *ensaimada,* the pastry of choice on each island. My favorite Ibizan confection, however, is *flao,* a kind of cheesecake made with herbs, a hint of mint, and honey.

In most Ibiza restaurants, coarse, peasant bread, olives, and *ali oli* (garlic mayonnaise) are an automatic prelude to meals. One distinctive local dish you should try is *sofrit pages*—sautéed pork, lamb, and chicken simmered with potatoes, peppers, and whole garlic cloves. But seafood is clearly the island's culinary forte, and though many of the fish may be unfamiliar to you—such as denton, rape, besugo, dorada, and emperador—they are as commonplace here as sole, cod, and halibut are in the United States.

Among the island's home-brewed spirits are *frígola,* a sweet, aromatic liqueur made with wild thyme; *palo,* a somewhat bitter apéritif made from carob; and *hierbas ibicencas,* a liqueur combining anis and numerous herbs.

Most of Ibiza's restaurants fall into a narrow price range, with meals running from 2,500 ptas. ($20.75) to 5,000 ptas. ($41.75). Bargain eating amounts to having a sandwich in a bar or a quick bite in the cafeterias and at the food stands that abound in the tourist centers. Where prices below are indicated for "meals," they refer to an average three-course meal without wine. Service is usually included in the prices, but IVA is *not.* Many restaurants offer economical three-course luncheon menus, including bread and house wine. At cafeterías, tapas bars, and other informal eating establishments, it often costs less to eat at the bar than at a table

EXPENSIVE

- **Sausalito,** Plaza Sa Riba (at the eastern end of the port) (tel. 31-01-66). *Prices:* Meals average 4,000 ptas. ($33.25).

An Ibiza institution run by emigré Frenchman (via Algeria) Alain Mion, Sausalito serves international food to an international clientele in a bistro setting. On the walls are photos of famous stars (not the usual celebrity-poses-with-restaurant-owner shots, but actual movie stills). Daily meat and fish specials complement a well-rounded standard menu.

Open: April–Oct, daily 8pm–midnight. CONTINENTAL

- **El Brasero,** Calle Barcelona 4 (tel. 31-14-69). *Prices:* Meals average 3,500 ptas. ($29.25).

This romantic, bistro-type restaurant with ornamental wrought-iron railings offers both indoor and outdoor dining. Most patrons opt for the former to view the funky nightlife pageant as it parades by.

The Brasero's menu is a mixture of Spanish and international fare. The tomato-and-goat-cheese salad is delicious; likewise the breast of duck with Armagnac sauce. Also good is the "Formenterafish," prepared in a variety of ways.

Open: Mid-April–Oct, daily 8pm–12:30am. SPANISH/ CONTINENTAL

- **El Portalón,** Plaça dels Desamparats 1 & 2 (tel. 30-39-01). *Prices:* Meals run up to 3,500 ptas. ($29.25).

El Portalón offers romantic patio dining in D'Alt Vila as well as indoor intimacy in a rustic, old-world setting. The menu is a mixture of Spanish and international dishes. At lunch, it offers a lighter, more moderately priced menu with most dishes costing under 1,000 ptas. ($8.25).

Open: Mon–Sat 12:30–3:30pm and 8pm–12:30am, Sun 8pm–12:30am. *Closed:* Mid-Jan–mid-Feb. SPANISH/INTERNA-TIONAL

MODERATE

- **El Corsario,** Calle Poniente 5 or Santa María 12 (tel. 30-12-48). *Prices:* Main dishes 900–2,300 ptas. ($7.50–$19.25).

Installed in the former home of a corsair built at the turn of the 16th century, El Corsario specializes in all manner of fresh fish from the market. Apéritifs on the outdoor terrace are accompanied by a splendid harbor view.

Open: Holy Week–Oct, Mon–Sat 1–3:30pm and 7:30pm–midnight. SEAFOOD/SPANISH

- **Restaurant Bar Can'Alfredo,** Paseo Vara de Rey 16 (tel. 31-12-74). *Prices:* Meals average 2,000 ptas. ($16.75); daily lunch menu 900 ptas. ($7.50).

Right in the heart of town, this small, simple, unpretentious place with only a dozen tables is very popular with locals and visiting celebrities (note photos of them with owner Alfredo Riera). The ibicenco specialties here include burrida de ratjada (a skate stew with almonds, garlic, and potatoes) and bullit de peix (fish and potato stew).

Open: June–Sept, Mon–Sat 1pm–midnight, Sun 1–5pm; Sept–June, Mon–Sat 1–5pm and 8pm–midnight, Sun 1–5pm. SPANISH/IBIZENCAN

■ **Pomelo,** Calle La Virgen 53 (tel. 31-31-22). *Prices:* Meals average 2,300 ptas. ($19.25).

This bright, friendly place on a fashionable street serves manta ray, steak tartare, and a large selection of seafood dishes. Specialties of the house are roast lamb and escalopines. Grab an outdoor table for people-watching.

Open: April–Nov, daily 7:30pm–1:30am. SPANISH

BUDGET

■ **Phyllis Ibiza,** Paseo Marítimo s/n (no street number), opposite Ibiza Casino (no phone). *Prices:* Meals average less than 2,000 ptas. ($16.75).

Billed as an "American Bar Restaurant," Phyllis Ibiza specializes in spareribs. But the menu goes on to offer Mexican fare (rather mediocre) as well as "Thanksgiving turkey." The funky, colorful ambience here is more Caribbean than Mediterranean, with Japanese lanterns, thatched fronds protruding from the ceiling, and a large outdoor terrace with a twinkling view of Ibiza Town by night. The bar is usually buzzing, and on weekends there is live music starting around midnight.

Most Americans make their way here at some point during their stay and meet Phyllis, formerly of Chicago and New York, who came to Ibiza over 20 years ago. Proud of her pool table, she proclaims it one of the island's best.

Open: Daily 6pm–3am. AMERICAN/MEXICAN

■ **Cap des Falco,** Las Salinas (no phone). *Prices:* Up to 550 ptas. ($4.50) for a salad and 2,500 ptas. ($20.75) for filet mignon.

Although this seaside entry has a hint of the hippy era about it, it has only been around a few years. All is very lazy and laid back here amid the salt flats. It is, however, a bit hard to find. As you head south out of Ibiza Town, there is a barely discernible dirt road off to the right just before the turnoff to the left for Escavallet Beach. Follow it as it winds through the salt flats and at the end you'll find Cap des Falco.

If you stick to the tuna, avocado, or tomato and mozzarella salads, you can eat cheaply. Among the entrées, try the grilled rabbit.

Open: Summer Tues–Sun 1:30–5pm and 8:30–11pm for dining (open continuously for drinks); winter, Tues–Sun 1–5pm and Tues 8:30–11pm for special couscous dinners. *Closed:* Jan, Feb, and 10 days in Nov. INTERNATIONAL

FOR SNACKS AND TAPAS

- **Cafeteria Montesol,** Paseo Vara de Rey 2 (tel. 31-01-61).

At the western end of the marina, the Montesol is a 30-year-old Ibiza tradition where tourists come to people-watch and locals to gossip and gab. In fact, the patrons at its sidewalk tables usually make up a spectacle in their own right. Both indoors and out, the Montesol serves snacks and sandwiches from 30 to 400 ptas. (25¢ to $3.25) as well as platos combinados for 550 to 1,400 ptas. ($4.50 to $11.75). Next door is the Hostal Residencia Montesol (see Section 3, "Accommodations," above).

Open: Daily 8am–2am.

- **Café Mar y Sol,** Calle Aragón 78, at the edge of the port (tel. 31-07-71). *Prices:* About 400–1,400 ptas. ($3.25–$11.75).

In the trendy scheme of things the Mar y Sol has in recent years upstaged the Montesol, just across the street. The people-watching from the outdoor terrace is equally fine here, but indoors the winsome wrought-iron tables, tapestry seat cushions, and decorative wooden accents make it more pleasant than the Montesol.

Snacks and sandwiches are served, and there is a small bakery next door where you can buy pastries to accompany your afternoon coffee or tea. As with most Spanish cafés, prices vary slightly depending on whether you do your consuming at the bar, at an indoor table, or at an outdoor table.

Open: Daily 8am–2am. *Closed:* Jan.

- **Bar Ses Botes,** Calle Isidoro Macabich 16 (tel. 31-27-66). *Prices:* Tapas from 200–275 ptas. ($1.75–$2.25) per plate.

At this traditional Spanish tapas bar, each plate of nibbles costs a maximum of 275 ptas. ($2.25) and several of them make a meal. Choose among squid, mushroom, kidney, pork, potato salad, and gambas al ajillo (shrimp in garlic and olive oil).

Open: Mon–Sat 6am–2am, Sun 6pm–2am. *Closed:* Three weeks in Jan.

---

5. Things to See and Do

Museo Arqueológico de Ibiza (Archeological Museum), Plaza Catedral s/n (no street number) and Vía Romana s/n (no street number) (tel. 30-12-31 or 30-17-71).

Installed in the former arsenal of the city fortress, this museum's collection (including the most important assemblage of Punic remains in the world) chronicles Ibiza's ancient days rather comprehensively. Artifacts include Phoenician tombstones and bronze dolls from 1,000 to 800 B.C.; clay figurines of Tanit (the Phoenician fertility goddess) and Best (god of fertility); and assorted jewelry, pottery, beads, and amphorae. Upstairs are Roman artifacts and a smattering of Muslim and Christian objects, including a 13th-century wooden Christ figure and some corsair cannons. Explanations and identifications, when given, are in Spanish or Catalan, so pick up an English-language brochure for 50 ptas. (40¢) to get the most out of your visit.

Open: Mon–Sat 10am–1pm and 4–7pm. *Closed:* Holidays. *Admission:* 200 ptas. ($1.75), which also includes entry to Museo Puig des Molins (see listing, below).

Museo Puig des Molins, Vía Romana s/n (no street number) (tel. 30-12-31 or 30-17-71).

The Museo Puig des Molins was built on the site of the necropolis that was the city's cemetery from about 654 B.C. (the accepted date for Ibiza's founding) to the 1st century A.D. Objects found on the site are displayed here, including many figurines, amphorae, and other assorted artifacts.

Open: Museum, Mon–Sat 4–7pm; necropolis, Mon–Sat 4:30–5:15pm and 6–6:45pm. *Closed:* Holidays. *Admission:* 200 ptas. ($1.75), which also includes entry to the Museo Arqueológico (see listing, above).

Santa María de las Nieves (Saint Mary of the Snows) Catedral, Plaza Catedral (no phone).

This cathedral's glaringly inappropriate name was bestowed by the general who ordered its construction in gratitude for his successful bid to wrest Ibiza from the Arabs. When he prayed for victory, he vowed to name the church in honor of the virgin whose feast day followed most closely upon the heels of his triumph. Saint Mary of the Snows was the one.

The cathedral's original Gothic beauty, hidden beneath a series of baroque embellishments, is now being painstakingly unmasked. Exhibited in the sacristía and museo are gold and silver cermonial objects and religious vestments.

As you leave the cathedral, follow Calle Universidad de Ibiza past a hole in the wall on the right (the remains of a Phoenician cistern) and beyond the city walls to a terrace that will afford an expansive view of the harbor and the island.

Open: Summer, Sun–Fri 10:30am–1pm and 4–5:30pm, Sat 10:30am–1pm; winter, daily 11am–2pm. *Closed:* Holidays. *Admission:* Catedral, free; sacristía and museo, 50 ptas. (40¢).

---

6. Shopping

Shopping is just one of the many vacation indulgences that make Ibiza famous. From the stands that spring up nightly at the edge of the marina to the trendy boutiques of Calle de la Virgen, you can indulge your consumer vices in everything from cheap costume jewelry to fancy clothes and fine handcrafts.

Paula's, Calle de la Virgen 4 (tel. 31-12-23).

At the pinnacle of the Ibizan fashion industry is Armin Heinemann, who designs not only the fashions at Paula's but the fabrics, prints, and perfumes as well. His clothing and hats are of a dramatic crepe de chine that he developed himself, and the styling and workmanship throughout are strictly haute couture. The prices are up there, too. Paula's carries some men's fashions as well and displays all in a richly elegant Victorian setting. Stateside, look for Paula's fashions at Ibiza, 46 University Place, in New York (tel. 212/533-4614), and Paula's Maria, 8840 Beverly Boulevard, in Beverly Hills (tel. 213/273-2600).

Open: Easter–mid-Oct, Mon–Fri 11am–1pm and 7–10pm. *Closed:* Mid-Oct–Easter.

Ibiza Fashion

Fashion is Ibiza's second most important industry (tourism, of course, is first). Since the late 1960s, a nonconformist fashion philosophy known as "ad lib" has evolved here, rooted in the first Ibizan creations combining elements of the traditional *pitiusa* attire of the natives and the natural, free-flowing garments of the hippies who flocked here in the '60s. In recent years Ibizan designs have become much more sophisticated and complex, but the nonconformist spirit has not wavered.

Indifferent to the fashion fads of the moment, Ibiza markets its distinctive designs abroad under the rubric "Adlib" or "Ibiza" fashions. "Adlib" refers to an independent, improvisational way of dressing that encourages you to be your own fashion designer in the sense that you mix and match fashion concepts to create a look that is distinctly *you*. "Dress as you like, but show good taste" is the motto coined by the founder of Adlib fashion, Smilja Mikhailovitch, a Yugoslavian princess.

"Fashion in the trendy, fad sense of the word," she says, "is made for people who have no taste. We came up with the concept of wearing minis, midis, and maxis as we liked long before the established world of fashion took up the idea. Today we have some 50 active designers on the island, about 20% of whom are very good."

Some of the leading names you will spot in Ibiza Town are Tip Top, María M, Cantonada, Paula's, Elena Deudero, John Charlie, Caty Mari, Lipstick, and Bianca.

Joaquín Berao, Antoni Mari Ribas 6 (tel. 31-05-74).

The unique jewelry designs here in bronze, titanium, silver, gold, and other precious metals are the work of innovative designer Joaquín Berao from Madrid. Besides the stunning wares in the display cases, ask to see the additional pieces kept discreetly out of sight.

Open: May–Oct, Mon–Sat 10:30am–1:30pm and 6–10pm. *Closed:* Some holidays and Nov–Apr.

Joy Borne, Calle del Mar 27 (tel. 31-25-58).

This is fashion central for the outrageous clothes and accessories that have come to be associated with this sybaritic island. The flowing, froufrou designs here are adorned with feathers, sequins, and beads, and are priced in accordance with their fancifulness.

Open: May–Oct 10am–1:30pm and 5–10pm (to midnight in high season). *Closed:* Nov–Apr.

Mango, Riambau 2 and Luis Tur Palau 20 (tel. 31-64-20).

Part of a nationwide chain of stores offering casual but stylish fashions at affordable (albeit not bargain) prices.

Open: Mon–Sat 10:30am–1:30pm and 5:30–10pm.

Tipo Ibiza, Antoni Mari Ribas 13 (tel. 31-75-31).

A small shop offering more of Ibiza's colorful and innovative fashions.

Open: Mon–Sat 10:30am–1:30pm and 5:30–10pm. *Closed:* Dec and Jan.

Cerámicas "Es Test," Calle de Mar 15 (no phone).

This shop carries a limited, but high-quality selection of Ibizan ceramics, including reproductions of some of the Punic statues in the archeological museum. But the main attraction here are the traditional black-and-white Ibizan figures by Luis Amor that are far superior to the standard, mass-produced variety sold in most other shops. Also outstanding are the beautiful plates by Gabrielet, an Ibizan artist now living in Formentera, and his pupil, Toniet.

Open: Mon–Sat 10am–1pm and 5–7pm.

Lucky Lizard, Mestre Joan Mayans 2 (tel. 31-47-06).

Connoisseurs of chic, fun footwear and bold accessories will love Beverly Feldman's original Ibiza Town store (see Section 8, "Shopping," in Chapter V as well).

Open: Mon–Sat 10am–1:30pm and 6–10pm.

S'espardenya, Ignacio Riquer 29, D'Alt Vila (tel. 30-54-16).

The Ibiza branch of Barcelona's La Manual Alpargatera (see Section 8, "Shopping," in Chapter V), S'espardenya features handmade espadrilles ranging from the simple to the glitteringly stunning.

Open: Holy Week–Oct, Mon–Sat 10:30am–2:30pm and 6–11pm in peak season and 11:15am–2:30pm and 5:30–10:30pm off-peak.

Tyke, Calle José Verdera 10 and 12 (tel. 31-02-26).

Showcases women's fashions by Tyke, an American designer, at no. 10 and men's fashions from Barcelona in no. 12.

Open: Apr–Nov, Mon–Sat 10:30am–2pm and 5–10:30pm (7pm–midnight in high season). *Closed:* Dec–Mar.

Sandal Shop, Plaça De Vila 2 (tel. 30-54-75).

Just inside the walled city, this shop purveys fine leather goods made by its own artisans. The selection of belts, some with semiprecious-stone buckles, is beautiful; the leather bags and briefcases are attractive and durable; and the sandals can be custom-made.

Open: Summer Mon–Fri 10:30am–2pm and 5:30–11:30pm, Sat 10:30am–2pm and 6–11:30pm; winter, Mon–Sat 11am–1:30pm and 5:30–7pm. *Closed:* Jan and Feb.

7. Nightlife

In summer, Ibiza swings around the clock. To keep pace with the all-night clubbers, all you need is money and transportation, for most begin their evening in Ibiza Town and then later head out to the discos of the moment elsewhere on the island.

At dusk, the marina area blossoms with vendors selling jewelry, scarves, and assorted handcrafts. Nearby, the string of bars lines up stool to stool. Just stroll along and pick one, two, three, or more from which to watch the world at play.

Ibiza Nights

Two of the brightest stars in the Ibiza night in recent years have been Ku and Amnesia, trendy discos near the town of San Rafael along the main road from Ibiza Town to San Antonio Abad.

Ku, near San Rafael (tel. 31-44-74 or 31-24-60), is a monumental disco that kicks off each summer season with a televised bash at the end of May. Every night is Halloween as the very mixed bag of uninhibited clientele dress as formally, informally, and fancifully as they see fit to dance to the droning beat of rap and disco music beneath tin-foiled trees. Numerous bars, diverse ambiences, and even a pool round out the nightly fun May to October from 11pm to 6am (its restaurant is open from 9pm to 4am). Admission runs 2,500 to 4,000 ptas. ($20.75 to $33.25), depending on the month and the particular party or festivity going on (sometimes this price includes one drink; sometimes it doesn't). Much more than a disco, Ku is an audience-participation spectacle.

Amnesia, Carretera San Antonio–Ibiza, Km. 2.5, about 300 meters (1,000 ft.) down the road from Ku (tel. 31-41-33), attracts a predominantly younger crowd with a similar musical offering and similarly spacious, multilevel dance floors, but a generally less outlandish appearance (though the parties and patrons can get wild here, too). Much of the space is open air, with canopies and awnings spread out here and there and mirrored pyramids in the small, scattered pools. Open June 15 to early October, nightly from midnight to 6am. Admission, including one drink, is 2,500 ptas. ($20.75). Snacks are served.

La Cantina, Conde Rosellón 3 (tel. 30-10-04).

A few blocks from the marina, this reincarnation of the Teatro Pereyra is now a lively music bar with a Bourbon Street feel about it. The visiting bands play soul, funk, jazz, and rock, and owner Eric Harmsen, who plays a mean piano, joins in most nights. The crowd is often moved to dancing in the aisles. La Cantina also serves snacks, breakfast, and dinner.

Open: Daily 10am–5am; music begins at 10pm. *Prices:* No cover, just a 350-pta. ($3) minimum.

Casino de Ibiza, Paseo Marítimo s/n (no street number) (tel. 31-33-12).

Here gamblers will find the usual gaming tables and slot machines in a quiet, modern setting. You need your passport to get in.

Open: Summer, daily 10pm–5am; winter, daily 10pm–4am. The adjoining nightclub offers live cabaret entertainment; May–Oct, Mon–Sat it opens at 9:30pm, and the show begins at 10 or 10:30pm. *Admission:* 500 ptas. ($4.25); 3,400 ptas. ($28.25), including show, one drink, and casino admission.

Pacha, Paseo Marítimo s/n (no street number) (tel. 31-36-12 or 31-09-59).

Frequented by the beautiful people of all ages in their beautiful clothes and kinky coifs, this spacious, split-level disco near the casino (see above) has several dance floors and numerous bars. In summer, overheated dancers cool off in the swimming pool. Unfortunately, the music is primarily of the droning disco and rap variety reminiscent of the pounding cadences of jackhammers.

Open: Apr–Oct, daily midnight–6am. *Closed:* Nov–Mar. *Admission:* Cover is 2,000 ptas. ($16.75) and includes one drink. There is also a restaurant here open 10pm to 3am with entrées ranging from 600 to 2,100 ptas. ($5 to $17.50).

AROUND IBIZA

Many different Ibizas await beyond the trademark trendiness of Ibiza Town. Some are trendy in other ways, others are very traditional, some are enticingly secluded, and still others are so overrun with bargain-basement tour groups that you'll want to avoid them. Whatever your pleasure, though, you're bound to find it somewhere.

Except, of course, mountains. Ibiza has no mountain ranges, just large lumps in the landscape. A petite 475 meters (1,550 ft.) at its highest point, its finest contours are those of its craggy, cliff-rimmed coasts sheltering a wealth of inviting coves and bays often graced with fine sand, pine trees, and Spanish cedars. Ibiza also has the only river in the Balearics.

Its total area is 572 square kilometers (230 square miles), and it measures 41 kilometers (25 miles) long and 20 kilometers (12.5 miles) wide.

Along its 600-kilometer-long (375-mile) coast are over 100 beaches of varying sizes, shapes, and sexual persuasions. Salinas, because of its large expanse and proximity to Ibiza Town, is the most popular. Nearby Es Cavallet is a nude beach. Popular in the north is the beach at Portinatx; in the south, that at Cala d'Hort. The island's longest beach is Playa d'en Bossa. Its most dangerous that at Cala Nova, where the undertow is fierce when the sea simmers with whitecaps. Almost every tourist beach offers the full array of amenities—bars, restaurants, pedalboats, lounge chairs, umbrellas, and windsurfers and other assorted water sports.

Inland, the island scenery tends to pine-clad hills, valleys of almond trees (attractively abloom in February), fig trees, orange and lemon groves, carob trees, wild herbs and flowers, and many memorable vistas across the hills to the sea. Scattered here and there are palm trees, Arab waterwheels, and charming windmills.

At Roca Llisa, the posh community where Roman Polanski has his house, is the island's sole golf course with 27 holes.

---

1. Getting Around

Viajes Ebusus, Calle Conde Rosellón 10, Ibiza Town (tel. 31-01-11), and **Viajes Meliá,** Paseo Vara de Rey 7, Ibiza Town (tel. 30-39-00), both offer bus and boat tours around Ibiza and to Formentera. Among them is an all-day bus tour of the island taking in the major points of interest and including a swim at one of the beaches. The cost is 1,900 ptas. ($15.75) without lunch. A day's tour by boat and bus of Formentera costs 3,600 ptas. ($30), without lunch. Tours are offered from May to October; hotel pickups can be arranged.

The **bus station** in Ibiza Town is at Avenida Isidoro Macabich 42 (tel. 31-56-11). Buses depart from two locations along this street—in front of the main terminal at no. 42 and in front of the ticket kiosk at no. 24. In summer there is frequent and extensive **bus service** throughout the island with fares reaching a maximum of 150 ptas. ($1.25). Schedules and routes are available at the main terminal and at bus stations around the island. You must buy your tickets before boarding, except when journeying from Ibiza Town to Playa d'en Bossa/Cala Llonga.

La Prensa de Ibiza, Diario de Ibiza, and *Ibiza Now* publish comprehensive, up-to-the-minute information on bus and ferry services.

Driving around the island is easy and pleasant, and lets you explore the many different faces of Ibiza to decide which one suits you best. Three main roads radiate from Ibiza Town and then branch out to the island's northern, southern, and western extremes. The network of secondary and tertiary roads is most developed in the south and west, making the picturesque coves here readily accessible. The splendid coves and beaches of the north and east are often accessible only by boat.

If you're interested in **renting a car** (which I strongly recommend), Avis, BC Betacar/Europcar, and Hertz have offices at the airport and elsewhere on the island, as follows:

Avis: At the airport (tel. 30-29-49), open daily 24 hours; Avenida Santa Eulalia del Rio 17, Ibiza Town (tel. 31-31-63), open Monday through Saturday from 9am to 1pm and 5 to 8pm, and on Sunday from 9am to 1pm.

BC Betacar: At the airport (tel. 30-31-84), open May to October daily 24 hours, November to April Monday through Friday from 7:30am to 11:30pm; Calle Vicente Serra 10, Ibiza Town (tel. 31-35-11), open Sunday through Friday from 9am to 1:30pm and 4

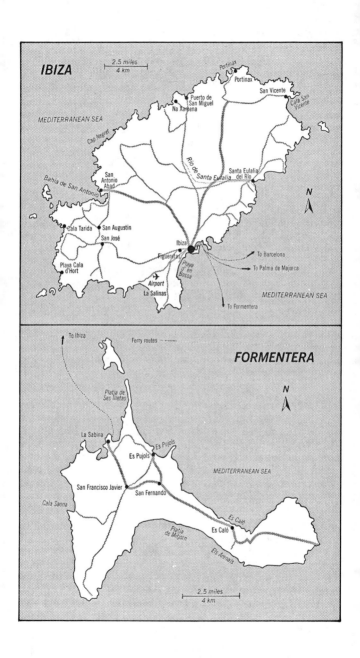

to 7:30pm, and on Saturday from 10am to noon (closed Saturday and Sunday in winter).

Hertz: At the airport (tel. 30-05-42), open Wednesday through Monday 24 hours, and on Tuesday until midnight; Calle Marina Botafoch, Botafoch Services, Puerto Deportiva (tel. 31-53-04), open summer only daily from 9:30am to 1:30pm and 5 to 8pm.

At presstime, Avis offered the lowest base rate of 2,580 ptas. ($21.50) a day.

2. San Antonio Abad and the Southwestern Coast

In the western part of Ibiza, about 15 kilometers (9 miles) from the capital, the innate beauty of San Antonio Bay has been much sinned against by the crimes of construction committed in the name of mass tourism. Known to the Romans as "Portus Magnus," the town of San Antonio Abad has been packaged for tourism since the 1950s and has recently become Ibiza's "hooligan headquarters" ("hooligans" are primarily working-class Brits on package holidays who turn into the hard-drinking, sex-crazed, vandalizing vacationers dreaded by civilized tourists and local hotel and bar owners). The fact that the local population of several thousand swells to some 45,000 in the summer months gives some indication of the abuse the town suffers annually.

Things improve as you follow the coast around to the east and south, where a number of the coves have not yet been as ravaged and many hotels cater to families.

ACCOMMODATIONS

Besides Ibiza Town, Figueretas, and Playa d'en Bossa, this is the most developed part of the island, with hordes of mediocre, tour-group hotels crowding San Antonio Abad and scarring parts of the coast to the southwest. A recent downturn in mass-tourism traffic has prompted their prices to plummet and, along with them, their standards, so if you plan to stay in package-tour digs, pick and choose with care. On the other hand, there are also a handful of choice, little hotels inland that are absolute heaven.

• **Pikes,** 07820 San Antonio Abad, Ibiza (tel. 971/34-22-22). 20 rms. A/C MINIBAR TEL

A series of signs guides you through the maze of dirt roads leading to this luxurious refuge. Forged from a complex of 600-year-old farm buildings, it has combined all manner of 20th-century creature comforts with a good many of the farm's original charms. Celebrities such as Sade, George Michael, Julio Iglesias, Joan Baez, and Grace Jones, and noncelebrities such as you and me receive the same VIP treatment in this setting of sophisticated informality.

The rooms are all different—but all very stylishly, and in some cases, sensually decorated. One room, for example, is lined with mirrors. All but two twin-bedded rooms feature queen- or king-size beds. Your room key (an antique original) will also get you into all of the island's trendy clubs.

Dining/Entertainment: The hotel's restaurant is a series of small, intimate rooms offering sedate, cushioned comfort. There is a breakfast nook outside.

Facilities: Pool, cruiser to take guests to deserted beaches nearby.

RATES (INCLUDING CONTINENTAL BREAKFAST): 15,000–40,000 ptas. ($125–$334) per room, single or double occupancy; children under 12 accepted only if accompanied by a nanny. Closed Nov–Apr, although it will open for groups requiring 10 or more rooms.

- **Apart.Hotel Victoria,** off the road toward Cala Tarida (Apartado 304), 07820 San Antonio Abad, Ibiza (tel. 971/34-09-00). 30 suites, 6 apts. A/C TV TEL

This peaceful, secluded, hacienda-style retreat some two kilometers (one mile) from Port des Torrent is perched on a hilltop overlooking the bay of San Antonio. The modern units are luxuriously appointed and all have at least one terrace. The rooms are categorized as mini-suites, suites, and luxury suites; the first have showers only (no tubs). Five of the six apartments are large enough to accommodate up to six people; all of them have large kitchens.

Dining/Entertainment: The very pretty restaurant here serves a fine view with its French cuisine.

Facilities: Indoor pool; fitness room; sauna; beauty center offering massages, facials, and other beauty treatments; private helipad.

RATES: 8,700–34,000 ptas. ($72.50–$283) suite, double occupancy; 11,400–17,900 ptas. ($95–$149) apartment, double occupancy.

- **Les Jardins de Palerm** (Apartado 62), 07830 San José, Ibiza (tel. 971/34-22-93). 10 rms, 1 suite. TV TEL

Located along a side road leading up from the village of San José, Les Jardins de Palerm is a charmingly intimate hotel conjured from a 17th-century hacienda-style *finca* (farm). Staying here is rather like being a guest at someone's country home. Scattered patios and garden terraces harbor cozy nooks for curling up with a book or just daydreaming.

The rooms, all decorated differently, are comfortably rustic and charmingly romantic with terraces, ceiling fans, mosquito netting, beamed ceilings, and the occasional antique.

Dining/Entertainment: The celebrated French restaurant here is a favorite among locals and reservations are imperative, especially in the summer when it functions outdoors. In winter, the seating moves indoors to a series of diminutive rooms, one of which has a delightful fireplace capped with a log mantle.

Facilities: Pool.

RATES (INCLUDING BREAKFAST): 6,800–22,600 ptas. ($56.75–$188) per room, double occupancy; 25,200–35,700 ptas. ($210–$298) suite. Closed Jan and Feb.

- **Hotel Village,** Urbanización Caló den Real (along the road toward Cala Tarida), 07830 San José, Ibiza (tel. 971/34-45-61). 20 rms, 3 suites. MINIBAR TV TEL

Another of the island's small, select hotels, the Village is 24 kilometers (15 miles) west of Ibiza Town. Just beyond the elegant white-marble entrance is an inviting bar/lounge whose tables are adorned with lace. From the hotel's elevated perch, a walkway leads down to a rocky beach by the sea where there are platforms equipped with lounge chairs and a small bar.

The white marble extends throughout the property and into the luxurious rooms, with a touch of gray marble added in the baths. All the accommodations have large beds, area rugs, and terraces. Six rooms face the mountains rather than the sea. Room no. 40 has an especially large terrace with a sea view.

Dining/Entertainment: The very stylish restaurant offers international fare with a Spanish accent.

Facilities: Two hard and two clay tennis courts, sauna and whirlpool, fitness room, beauty salon.

RATES (INCLUDING BREAKFAST AND IVA): 8,550–10,400 ptas. ($71.25–$86.75) double used as a single; 12,500–16,000 ptas. ($104–$133) double. Half board available.

- **Club Hotel Tarida Beach,** Playa Cala Tarida, 07830 San José, Ibiza (tel. 971/34-43-85); reservations can be made through the central Insotel office at Avenida España 20, 07800 Ibiza Town (tel. 971/30-01-00). 402 studios. KITCHEN TEL

A member of the Insotel Hotel Group, which offers a series of well-planned and well-maintained package-tour hostelries throughout the Balearic Islands, the Club Hotel Tarida Beach makes up a small, comfortable community unto itself. The transient population spans the generations, including young people, families, and elderly couples from the Continent.

The very clean and comfortable accommodations have dual living and sleeping areas (with double sofa-beds) that can be separated by means of a folding door; additional beds can also be added.

Dining/Entertainment: Several restaurants, a snackbar, TV rooms with satellite hookups, nightly poolside entertainment, and a disco.

Facilities: Two swimming pools, two tennis courts, two squash courts, saunas, a very clean 300-meter-long (1,000-ft.) beach with facilities for waterskiing, sailing, and diving. Boats also sail from here to San Antonio, Formentera, and Ibiza. Other amenities include a supermarket, laundry, on-premises clinic, beauty parlor, and multilingual day-care center with classes for children offered daily except Sunday from 10am to 1pm and 4 to 6:30pm.

RATES (INCLUDING BREAKFAST): 3,475–4,960 ptas. ($29–$41.25) per person double occupancy; children in the room cost an additional 30%–50% of the normal per-person rate. Cribs are an additional 700 ptas. ($5.75) per day. Half and full board available. Closed Oct–Apr.

- **Hotel Apolo,** 07820 San Antonio Abad, Ibiza (tel. 971/34-12-00); reservations can be made through the central Insotel office at Avenida España 20, 07800 Ibiza Town (tel. 971/30-01-00). 99 rms.

Another Insotel hostelry, this is a good in-town budget bet about a 10-minute walk from the beach. The clean rooms offer the bare essentials—two beds, a table, chair, stool, bath (some with shower only), and patio flooring. On the premises are a pool, restaurant, snackbar, and TV room.

RATES (INCLUDING BREAKFAST AND IVA): 1,960–2,065 ptas. ($16.25–$17.25) single with complete bath, 1,790–1,960 ptas. ($15–$16.25) with shower; 3,100–3,365 ptas. ($25.75–$28) double with bath, 3,000–3,300 ptas. ($25–$27.50) with shower; 3,600–3,900 ptas. ($30–$32.50) triple with bath. Closed Nov–Apr.

■ **Aparthotel Nereida,** 07829 Cala de Bou, Ibiza (tel. 971/34-33-62); reservations can be made through the central Insotel office at Avenida España 20, 07800 Ibiza Town (tel. 971/30-01-00). 72 apts., 64 studios. TEL

On San Antonio Bay, this Insotel complex offers apartments with two terraces, a bedroom with twin beds, a sitting room with sofa bed, and a sink and stove with dishes and cooking utensils. The studios have a terrace, bed-sitting room with two beds and convertible sofa, and stove. The furnishings are of plain but pleasant pine.

Facilities: Seaside pool, children's playground, restaurant, bar, cafeteria, and snackbar.

RATES (INCLUDING BREAKFAST AND IVA): 2,880–4,320 ptas. ($24–$36) per person in a double; 2,520–3,600 ptas. ($21–$30) per person in a triple; 1,920–3,000 ptas. ($16–$25) per person in a quad. Children 2–11 in the same unit with their parents get a 50%–100% discount. Half board also available. Closed Nov–Apr.

■ **Hotel/Restaurant del Carmen,** José Marí Tur (Apartado 180), 07830 San José, Playa Cala d'Hort, Ibiza (tel. 971/34-18-23). 9 rms.

On the quiet, remote Cala d'Hort at the western end of the island opposite Es Vedra rock, this simple hostelry offers clean, comfortable rooms, most with terraces. All have twin beds and a small sofa bed suitable for a child.

RATES: 3,500–4,000 ptas. ($29.25–$33.25) per room. Call Feb or Mar for May bookings and as early as possible for July, Aug, and Sept. Closed Nov–Holy Week.

DINING

Many of Ibiza's finest restaurants are tucked away in quiet coves or in the countryside, so you really need a car to sample the full range of the island's culinary savoir-faire.

■ **Sa Tasca,** San Agustín, off to the right along the road from San José to San Agustín (tel. 34-16-23). *Prices:* Meals average 3,500 ptas. ($29.25).

The very inviting Sa Tasca has a large open-air dining area and several small, interior dining rooms (some with a fireplace) that are used in the winter and retain all the old-world character of this 200-year-old Ibizan house.

The extensive international menu is sprinkled with such ibicenco specialties as sofrito pagés (some say it's the best on the island) and a special market menu that changes every two or three months. Flambés prepared tableside are also a house specialty.

Open: Tues–Sun 1–4pm and 7:30–11:30pm. *Reservations:* Imperative in summer at dinner. CONTINENTAL/IBICENCO

• **Es Cavallet El Restaurante,** Playa Es Cavallet (tel. 30-71-70). *Prices:* Meals average 2,500 ptas. ($20.75).

On a clear day you can see Formentera from the veranda of this romantic seaside restaurant. But at the very least the vista will include cactus plants, a beautiful beach, and the multi-colored Mediterranean. Although Es Cavallet is a nude beach, the bathing beach itself is far enough away so as not to offend any restaurant patrons. The Spanish and Continental cuisine changes seasonally.

Open: May–Sept, daily 1–5pm and 9pm–midnight; Sept–May Thurs–Tues 1–5pm. CONTINENTAL/SPANISH

• **El Rincón de Pepe,** San Mateo 6, San Antonio Abad (tel. 34-06-97). *Prices:* Meals average 1,000 ptas. ($8.25).

This is a great place for tapas (mostly seafood), but you can also choose among hamburgers, hot dogs, salads, and hearty entrées. The food is simple and good, the atmosphere pleasant, and the bar an attractive arrangement of tile and wood.

Open: Holy Week–Oct, daily 11am–3am. SPANISH/SNACKS

THINGS TO SEE AND DO

From San Antonio's marina **boats** depart for Formentera and Ibiza and various island tours, including glass-bottom-boat excursions. The offerings change from year to year, so check at the marina or contact **Cruceros San Antonio, S.A.,** Calle Progreso 6, 1st Floor, San Antonio Abad (tel. 34-34-71).

On the town's outskirts are the **underground Chapel of Santa Inés,** a national monument, and the **"Seis Fontanelles"** caves with interesting wall paintings.

San José is an inland town of about 1,000 inhabitants some 15 kilometers (9 miles) from the capital and gives its name to an administrative district containing one of the most ruggedly beautiful stretches of Ibizan coastline (from Cala Bassa to Cala Vadella), the famous Es Vedrá rock, the island's highest peak at Atalayassa (475m, 1,550 ft.), and the salt flats.

Offshore at the popular southern beach of Cala d'Hort is the intriguing **Es Vedrá rock** where, in times of hardship and hunger, the Ibicencos would go, at great personal risk, to gather seagull eggs for survival. Photographers and romantics take note—after June 15 the sunrise here is especially dramatic, illuminating Es Vedrá while the surrounding hills remain in darkness.

3. The Northern Coast

The north remains largely untainted by the scourge of mass tourism except for a handful of coves. Here you'll find some of the island's prettiest countryside, with fields of olive, almond, and carob trees, and the occasional *finca* raising melons or grapes.

ACCOMMODATIONS

The hotel offering is much more limited in the north than in the traditional pockets of tourism in the south and west. Nevertheless, the island's finest hotel, the Hacienda, is perched here above Na Xamena Bay. Puerto de San Miguel, Cala San Vicente, and Portinatx, former tranquil, seaside havens, in recent years have become increasingly pockmarked with package-tour hotels.

■ **Hotel Hacienda,** Na Xamena, 07815 San Miguel, Ibiza (Apartado 423, Ibiza) (tel. 971/33-30-46); to make reservations Stateside, contact Marketing Ahead, 433 Fifth Ave., New York, NY 10016 (tel. 212/686-9213). 43 rms and suites. A/C TEL

Set in a dense pine grove atop a promontory on Na Xamena Bay, this sybaritic retreat in the Moorish style is favored by such personalities as Goldie Hawn, Tony Roberts, and, in his more carefree days, Adnan Khashoggi. Some 90% of the Americans who come to Ibiza opt for this hideaway, the island's only five-star property and a member of the Relais et Châteaux network. At once luxurious and laid back, it is also favored by honeymooners seeking a paradise of privacy.

Its numerous nooks and crannies are tailor-made for sitting and doing absolutely nothing. The focal point of the hotel's call to leisure is the large, gracious pool where, weather permitting, breakfast, lunch, and dinner are served. Any guest who has spent more than 365 days in the hotel is awarded a silver medal—42 have been granted so far. I guess it's true what they say about a satisfied customer!

The Hacienda's light, airy rooms are varied of decor and range from the simple to the sublime. Top of the line is the two-bedroom Presidential Suite (no. 607), a real stunner with a sea view from the separate shower and tub in the master bath as well as from the Jacuzzi out on the terrace. All rooms have one of the finest sunset views in the annals of travel.

Dining/Entertainment: The hotel's fine restaurant was the recipient of the 1988 "Golden Fork Award" bestowed by the International Food, Wine, & Travel Writers Association. The menu is varied and, in the words of hotel owner Ernesto Ramón Fajarnés, "only an indication" of what's available. For example, a fine pepper steak flambéed with cognac is not on the menu but almost always available on request. Similarly, available for up to 12 people is an authentic Carthaginian meal served in the restaurant's special alcove. In keeping with the family tradition of chronicling the island's history, Don Ernesto has personally documented the authenticity of a dozen or so recipes of that remote period. Evenings in the hotel bar feature a variety of musical entertainment, including South American and Spanish music and Asian dance.

Facilities: Indoor and outdoor pool.

RATES (INCLUDING BREAKFAST): 12,200–17,700 ptas. ($102–$148) single; 15,500–23,800 ptas. ($129–$198) double; 18,800–29,300 ptas. ($157–$244) junior suite; 25,000–85,000 ptas. ($208–$708) suite. Closed Nov–Mar.

• **Hotel Galeón,** 07815 Port Sant Miquel (Puerto de San Miguel), Ibiza (tel. 971/33-30-19). 182 rms.

This is one of two cliff-hanging hotels overlooking this lovely bay. All the rooms have terraces and sea views, but beyond that, this is your basic dormitory-style tourist accommodation—simple, clean, comfortable, and rather nondescript. Ditto the restaurant.

Facilities: Tennis courts, water sports.

RATES (INCLUDING IVA): 2,445–3,100 ptas. ($20.50–$25.75) single; 4,180–5,845 ptas. ($34.75–$48.75) double. Closed Nov–Apr.

• **Hotel Cartago,** 07815 Port Sant Miquel (Puerto de San Miguel), Ibiza (tel. 971/33-30-24). 196 rms.

The Cartago is very similar to its counterpart next door, the Hotel Galeón (see above). Together these two massive hotels have procured a good view for themselves but in turn have destroyed the view for others from below as they are quite out of proportion to this lazy little bay. The rooms here are slightly inferior to those at the Galeón.

Facilities: Tennis courts, water sports.

RATES (INCLUDING IVA): 2,445–3,100 ptas. ($20.50–$25.75) single; 4,180–5,845 ptas. ($34.75–$48.75) double.

• **Hotel Imperio Playa,** 07469 Cala San Vicente, Ibiza (tel. 971/33-30-55). 210 rms. TEL

Cala San Vicente is a pretty bay on the northeastern tip of the island and the winding drive out there through the lovely pine forests is beautiful. The wide, 350-meter-long (1,150-ft.) beach curves at the foot of some steep hills dotted with traditional houses. The sand and water are lovely and the beach is among the best cared for on the island. (Windsurfing, waterskiing, and pedalboats are available at the beach.)

Of the several package-tour hotels on the beach, the Imperio Playa and the Hotel Cala San Vicente (see below) belong to the Insotel Group. The public lounges here at the Imperio Playa are spacious; the rooms are functional and friendly.

Facilities: Restaurant, bar, snackbar, disco, beauty parlor, boutiques, pool, tennis court, children's playground.

RATES (INCLUDING BREAKFAST, DINNER, AND IVA): 2,095–2,885 ptas. ($17.50–$24.25) single; 1,695–2,483 ptas. ($14.25–$20.75) per person double occupancy. Closed Nov–Apr.

• **Hotel Cala San Vicente,** 07469 Cala San Vicente, Ibiza (tel. 971/33-30-21). 116 rms. TEL

The second Insotel hostelry at Cala San Vicente, this one has similarly functional rooms and virtually the same facilities.

RATES (INCLUDING BREAKFAST, DINNER, AND IVA): 2,055–2,845 ptas. ($17.25–$23.75) single; 1,655–2,425 ptas. ($13.75–$20.25) per person double occupancy. Closed Nov–Apr.

DINING

As in the matter of hotels, there are fewer restaurants in the northern part of the island than to the south and west, but those that are here are rather exceptional.

• **Restaurante Ama Lur,** Carretera San Miguel, km. 2.3 (tel. 31-45-54). *Prices:* Entrées 1,850–3,500 ptas. ($15.50–$29.25).

Installed in a 200-year-old farmhouse, Ama Lur has several small interior dining areas and a stylish al fresco terrace. The cuisine is primarily Basque and includes such unusual dishes as filet of sole with oysters in champagne and duck escalopines with red-currant sauce.

Open: Mar–Nov, daily 8pm–midnight. *Closed:* Dec–Feb. *Reservations:* Imperative in July and Aug. BASQUE

• **Can Pau,** Carretera San Miguel, km. 3 (no phone). *Prices:* Meals average 2,300 ptas. ($19.25).

This pleasant, lively place with a large outdoor patio is a favorite among the yachting crowd who, according to owner Narcís Pau, consider the house specialty, conejo al cau (rabbit stew with onions, tomatoes, and more), well worth the trip—especially at only 825 ptas. ($7). Don Narcís uses only fresh (never frozen) meats and wild, not farm-bred, rabbits. Another house specialty is roast lamb.

Open: June–Sept, daily 8pm–1am; Sept–June Tues–Sun 1–3:30pm and 8pm–midnight. *Closed:* Jan. SPANISH/IBICENCO

• **Restaurante Can Gall,** Carretera Ibiza–San Juan, km. 11.6 (tel. 33-29-16). *Prices:* Meals average 2,500 ptas. ($20.75).

Located in the countryside in a 125-year-old farmhouse, Can Gall is a rustic restaurant offering largely Spanish dishes sprinkled with some local fare. Among the house specialties are cochinillo de San Lorenzo (suckling pig), a delicious grilled quarter chicken, and suckling rabbit. In winter, the menu features game and sofrito pagés (chicken, lamb, and pork sautéed with sausage).

Open: Wed–Mon 1–3:30pm and 8–11:30 pm. *Closed:* Nov 20–end of Dec. *Reservations:* Strongly urged for dinner in July and Aug. SPANISH/IBICENCO

THINGS TO SEE AND DO

Near the Hotel Hacienda is the **Taller de Arte** (no phone), where J. Mateo creates and sells paintings, ceramics, and bronze sculptures of great grace and striking visual appeal. Open April to October, Thursday through Tuesday from 10am to 1pm and 4:30 to 8pm.

Off the road leading into Puerto de San Miguel is the **Cova de "Can Marça,"** about 100 meters (300 ft.) from the Hotel Galeón. There is a fine view of the bay from the snackbar. After a stunning descent down stairs that cling to the face of the cliff, you enter a cave that's over 100,000 years old and forms its stalactites and stalagmites at the rate of about one centimeter (0.4 in.) per 100 years. A favored hiding place for smugglers and their goods in former days, today it's a beautifully orchestrated surrealistic experience—including a sound-and-light display—not unlike walking through a Dalí painting. Many of the limestone formations are delicate miniatures. The half-hour tour is conducted in several languages for groups up to 70. In the summer, tours are offered every half hour from 10:30am to 7pm (except at 2pm and 2:30pm); out-of-peak season, tours are conducted hourly. The cave opens just before Holy Week and closes the end of October. Admission is 475 ptas. ($4) for adults, 250 ptas. ($2) for children.

At the island's northern tip is **Portinatx,** a pretty series of beaches and bays now marred by a string of souvenir shops and haphazardly built hotels. For a taste of its original, rugged beauty, go past all the construction to the jagged coast along the open sea.

Every Saturday throughout the year there is a **flea market** just beyond San Carlos on the road to Santa Eulalia (you'll know where it is by all the cars parked along the road). Open from about 10am until 8 or 9pm, it offers all kinds of clothing, (both antique and new), accessories, crafts, and the usual odds and ends of a combination craft fair and flea market.

If you want to escape to a lovely beach that remains a stranger to hotel construction, head for **Playa Benirras** just north of Puerto de San Miguel. An unpaved but passable road leads out to this small, calm, pretty cove where lounge chairs are available and pedalboats are for rent. There is also a snackbar here, as well as two good restaurants, Roca y Mar and Restaurante 2000, which feature traditional Spanish cuisine. The latter one specializes in paella.

Santa Gertrudis

Santa Gertrudis, just off the main road between Ibiza Town and San Miguel, is a small village primarily of shops offering high-quality handcrafts, antiques, jewelry, artwork, and more. **Te Cuero,** Plaza del Banco s/n (no street number) (no phone), specializes in fine leather goods from the island and carries unusual belts, wallets, skirts, and pants. It also offers belt buckles, scarves, and at times, a glimpse of the world's oldest bonsai specimen, the pride and joy of shop owner Klaus, a transplanted German. His petite marvel is over 1,000 years old and documented in the *Guinness Book of World Records.* The store is open in summer Monday through Saturday from 6 to 11pm and in winter Monday through Saturday from 11am to 2pm and 5 to 9pm; closed two weeks in January.

El Almacen, in the main plaza (tel. 31-03-09), is a home-decor shop with ceramics, furniture, glassware, candles, and assorted other decorative items. Open Monday through Friday from 4 to 8pm; closed January 15 to February 28.

Punto A, Plaza de la Iglesia (no phone), is an eclectic, upscale shop offering artwork, leather goods, textiles, belts, and jewelry. Open April to November daily from 6 to 11pm and also from noon to 2pm in July and August.

Casi Todo (literally, "almost everything"), also in the main square (tel. 31-09-08), is an aptly named shop that is a browser's paradise. Antiques and all manner of interesting odds and ends find their way here. Open in summer daily from 11am to 2pm and 6 to 10pm; the rest of the year, daily from 11am to 6pm; closed several days at Christmas.

Galeria Can Daifa (tel. 31-21-33) offers unique antique and modern jewelry, antique lamps, paintings, sculptures, and fans old and new. Open May to October; in summer, 6 to 11pm; the rest of the time, 5 to 10pm.

Portobello, on the second floor above the bar next to Punto A (tel. 31-64-25), is a secondhand clothing store run by Lise, a Norwegian woman who succumbed to the island's call after coming here for 15 years on vacation. Here you'll be able to dress yourself in madcap Ibiza fashions at more affordable prices. Open all year, except February: in summer, Tuesday through Sunday from 10:30am to 2:30pm and 6pm to whenever; the rest of the year, Tuesday through Sunday from 11am to 8pm.

4. Santa Eulalia and the Eastern Coast

Fourteen kilometers (nine miles) from Ibiza Town on the estuary of the island's only river is Santa Eulalia del Río. Crowning the Puig de Missa at the town's entrance is a typical, gleaming white ibicenco fortress church of the 16th century. Its *porche,* which provides shelter from the sun, reflects the Arab architectural influence on the island. Prettier, more tranquil, and less plastic than San Antonio Abad, Santa Eulalia predominantly attracts middle-class northern Europeans.

One of the best hotel bets in the area is the **Hotel S'Argamassa Sol,** Urbanización S'Argamassa, 07849 Santa Eulalia del Río (tel. 971/33-00-51); to make reservations Stateside, contact Marketing Ahead, 433 Fifth Ave., New York, NY 10016 (tel. 212/686-9213). A brief walk from a sandy beach, this hotel, with its own small dock, is three kilometers (two miles) outside the town of Santa Eulalia del Río. Its 230 rooms all have a bath, telephone, terrace, and sea view; some triples are available as well. Though a bit stark, these rooms are clean and comfortable. A lobby lounge and bar, swimming pool, games room, TV room, playground, restaurant, lit tennis court, and waterskiing from the hotel dock complete the offering. Rates (including breakfast) are 2,635 to 4,890 ptas. ($22 to $40.75) per person per day; closed November to April.

One of the best restaurants in town is **Doña Margarita,** Paseo Marítimo s/n (no street number) (tel. 33-06-55), located on the curved seaside promenade in Santa Eulalia. The cuisine is traditional Spanish with some Catalan accents, such as the esqueixada de bacallà. Other specialties include the arròs de peix (rice with fish), chicken liver pâté, and Mexican-style avocados. There is also a special market menu daily plus an ample selection of standard fish and meat dishes. The outdoor terrace offers a splendid view of the bay. In summer it is open Tuesday through Sunday from 1 to 3:30pm and 8 to 11:30pm; in winter, daily from 1 to 3:30pm, with Friday and Saturday evening hours from 8 to 11:30pm; closed four weeks around November and December.

---

5. Excursion to Formentera

You can see the ocean from any point on Formentera. Some say the island has the best beaches in the Mediterranean—the opinion has much merit. Recently, Formentera was declared a "World Treasure" by UNESCO, one of four places thus honored due to its special character as an ecological and wildlife preserve. This designation implies an indirect control by UNESCO of activities that could jeopardize the island's ecological well-being.

Meanwhile, day trippers from Ibiza have fun sampling its long, sedate beaches and solitary coves before returning to Ibiza's ebullience in the evening.

Historically, Formentera's political fate has been much the same as Ibiza's—the same succession of conquering cultures. The southernmost of the Balearic Islands, Formentera has a total area of 82 square kilometers (30 square miles), excluding the two interior lakes (Estany Pudent and d'es Peix). The island is flat except for the two plateaus, Es Cap de Barbaria and La Mola. Its population is approximately 5,000 but triples in the summer. The island's scrub pines and dune beaches are reminiscent of parts of Long Island's Hamptons and sections of the New England coast, albeit with the important added attractions of milder temperatures and dazzling Mediterranean waters in varying shades of aquamarine.

GETTING THERE

Trasmediterránea, Avenida Bartolomé Vicente Ramón s/n (no street number) (tel. 971/31-50-11), runs a half-hour **hydrofoil service** from Ibiza Town to the port of La Sabina on Formentera in March and April daily at noon and from La Sabina to Ibiza Town daily at 1pm. From May 1 to early September there are two boats daily from Ibiza (at 10:30am and 4:50pm) and two boats daily from Formentera (at 11:15am and 5:35pm). The one-way fare is 800 ptas. ($6.75). For the latest schedule information and reservations in Ibiza, call Trasmediterránea.

In summer, regular **ferry service** to Formentera is frequent (check daily listings in *La Prensa de Ibiza, Diario de Ibiza* and *Ibiza Now*); one-way fares run 700 ptas. ($5.75) for adults and 353 ptas. ($3) for children ages 2 to 12.

GETTING AROUND

On Formentera you can rent a car, various forms of two-wheeled motorized transport, or a bicycle. Two-wheeled traffic is common on the island, and the trunk roads have separate bike lanes to accommodate it. You can also take a **taxi** to the beach of your choice; rates run from 750 ptas. ($6.25) to Es Pujols to 1,500 ptas. ($12.50) to the far end of Playa Mitjorn. If you do this, be sure to arrange a return pickup or call well in advance for a return taxi (tel.

32-00-52 in La Sabina or 32-00-16 in Es Pujols) as it may take 20 minutes until it gets to you.

However, it's better to get your own wheels and sample several beaches before settling in at the one that most appeals. When you arrive at La Sabina, taxis will be waiting and all the vehicle-rental offices will be open. Open, too, will be the **tourist office kiosk** at the dock with maps and general information about the island. **Bicycles** rent for about 350 ptas. ($3) a day, **mobilettes** for about 1,000 ptas. ($8.25), and **motorbikes** for about 2,900 ptas. ($24.25).

THE BEACHES

Along Platja de Mitjorn, which is several kilometers long, the current is stronger and things get dangerous faster than on the Es Caló side of the island, which is, however, more rocky. To help you find the beach that will suit you best, here is a quick survey of what's most accessible to the day tripper, beginning at the easternmost end of the island farthest from La Sabina.

If you follow the main trunk road down the island to the eastern end of **Platja de Mitjorn,** you will see signs for Club La Mola Hotel and Club Maryland that will eventually lead you to **Es Copinyar beach,** which is very pleasant and long, and offers the services of several snackbars and restaurants. On the other side of this end of the island, which is very narrow at this point, is the beach near the town (just a few buildings, really) of **Es Caló.** As you head back toward La Sabina, it is on your right just beyond the "town" and indicated by a simple, faded wooden sign and a cement-block walkway leading down to the sea (watch for bikes and Vespas parked along the road). Although the beach is rocky, the cliffs in the background add drama and there are numerous sandy areas where you can settle in with a good book. When you get hungry or thirsty, there's a small snackbar.

Heading again along the main trunk road toward La Sabina, you will see a sign for "Las Dunas Playa," which will lead you to the adjoining beaches of **Las Dunas** and **Els Arenals.** The road out is bumpy at best, but the mile-long beach with thatched umbrellas is worth the jostle. The water here remains shallow quite far out and there are few rocks. There is also the commendable Flipper restaurant for food and drink. The remaining, more westerly portions of Platja de Mitjorn are less appealing.

At **Cala d'es Pujols** you'll find one rock-rimmed cove next to a sandy cove lined with shops, bars, and other tourist amenities abutting the beach. This is much the same as what you'll find on some of Ibiza's more crowded beaches—there is really no need to come to Formentera for it.

By far Formentera's pièce de résistance beach-wise is the **Platja de Ses Illetas,** stretching along the slender northern tip of the island. As you leave La Sabina, take the "Pujols" turnoff to the left and continue straight, entering the dirt road when the paved road curves right toward **Es Pujols.** This road, which passes the salt flats, gets very bumpy but remains navigable at slow speeds until it terminates in a restaurant/bar (there are also several others along the way). The sea and sand are idyllic here with beaches on either side of the slender finger of land trailing soft and white out into the Mediterranean. When the waters on one side are rough, they are calm on the other. All along you will see yachts moored out in the blue-green waters of the curving coves. In the annals of sea and sand one couldn't ask for more.

If you wish to spend a night or two on Formentera, the Insotel Group has several **hotels along Platja de Mitjorn** in varying price ranges. For information and reservations, contact their central office at Avenida España 20, 07800 Ibiza Town (tel. 971/30-01-00), or Viajes Ebusus, Calle Conde Rosellón 10, 07800 Ibiza Town (tel. 971/31-01-11). Club La Mola, Platja de Mitjorn (tel. 971/32-80-69), is also a good choice, with per-person rates in a single or double ranging from 3,320 to 9,560 ptas. ($27.75 to $79.75); closed November to April.

MAÓ (MAHÓN)

A polite, provincial city, Maó (Mahón) is a curious hybrid of Georgian, bay-windowed town houses and unpretentious Spanish structures sharing a warren of narrow streets. Unlike most other port cities in the world, Maó has no district of vice, no seamy side to balance its propriety.

It has been the capital of Minorca since the British saw the potential of its deep-water channel as a naval base during the War of the Spanish Succession (1702–14) and managed to have the island ceded to them under the Treaty of Utrecht in 1713. Although Spain regained possession in 1782, the Napoleonic threat in the Mediterranean gave rise to a new British base under the command of Admirals Nelson and Collingwood. While the British legacy has blended with the Spanish, it is still distinguishable, especially in such architectural features as the Georgian sash windows sometimes still referred to locally as *winderes*.

Situated atop the cliffs of a natural harbor on Minorca's southeastern shore, Maó is prettiest when viewed from the port. Its population is nearly 22,000, and it is the focal point of island commerce.

As the capital and the city closest to the airport, Maó is the center for most tourist services. But Ciutadella (Ciudadela), the long-ago capital, runs a close second in terms of tourist activity, and many of the "Fast Facts" below mention both these cities that flank the island like urban bookends.

1. Orientation

GETTING THERE

Aviaco (36-56-73) offers direct flights from Palma and Barcelona.

There are also **ferries** from Palma, Barcelona, and Ibiza that sail into Maó Port. The trip from Barcelona is about seven to eight hours aboard a moderately luxurious liner. For about the same cost as a chair in the lounge, you can purchase a bunk in a quad cabin.

In 1989 the new **hydrofoil** *El Leopardo* began operating between Barcelona and Majorca and Minorca. Travel time is only three hours, and the luxury craft has a capacity of 280 passengers, including 80 in the extra-luxurious first-class section.

Trasmediterránea, Estación Marítima, Port of Maó (tel. 36-29-50), is open Monday through Friday from 8am to 1pm and 5 to 9pm, but all ferry arrangements are just as easily made at any travel agency.

UPON ARRIVAL

The **airport,** five kilometers (three miles) from Maó, has no tourist office, no money exchange facilities, and no bus service. To get anywhere by bus, you have to take a taxi into Maó and catch the buses that radiate from there throughout the island.

CITY LAYOUT

The **Plaza de la Constitución,** with its neoclassical Casa Consistorial, is the nucleus of Maó. Nearby in **Plaza Alfonso III** is a sculpture commemorating the king who took Minorca from the Moors in 1287. Also in this plaza is the notable Ca'n Mercadal, a Minorcan mansion of 1761 now housing the Biblioteca Pública.

The **port** is the city's northern boundary and is lined with restaurants and shops. From there, the **Costa de Ses Voltes** winds its way to **Plaça d'Espanya** at the edge of the town nucleus, composed of narrow, crisscrossing streets. Marking the other extreme of "center city" is the **Plaça de S'Esplanada (Plaza Explanada),** where the tourist office is located.

Like Ibiza Town, Maó has no beach and is not a resort city but rather a center for shopping and nightlife. Nearby **Villacarlos,** a virtual continuation of the capital stretching east along the port, comes closer to being a resort, but also has no beach. You'll find some of the island's more popular hotels there, however, and at Calas Fons, a very popular nightlife niche. **Cala Mesquida** and **Punta Prima** offer two fine beaches nearby.

2. Fast Facts

BUSINESS HOURS: Banks are open June to September Monday through Friday from 9am to 2pm; hours are extended to Saturday

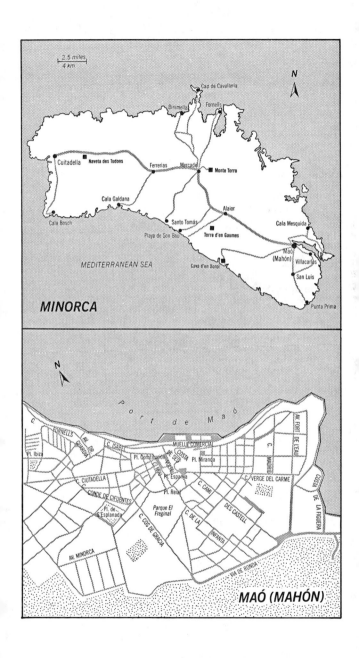

the rest of the year. You can exchange money at most banks during normal banking hours, but many stores and most hotels will also change money for you after hours or on the weekend. **Shops** are generally open Monday through Saturday from 10am to 1:30pm and 5 to 8pm.

CONSULATES: The **British Vice Consular office** is at Torret 28, San Luis (tel. 36-64-39). The nearest **U.S. Consulate** is in Barcelona (tel. 93/319-95-50) (see Section 4, "Fast Facts," in Chapter II).

ELECTRICITY: Primarily 220V, but some 125V outlets are still to be found.

EMERGENCIES: For **hospital attention** or an **ambulance,** call 36-35-00 or 36-11-80 in Maó; 36-06-87 or 38-19-93 in Ciutadella. The **Red Cross** numbers in the two cities are 36-11-80 and 38-19-93, respectively. The **police** in Maó can be reached at 091; in Ciutadella at 38-10-95. In the event of **fire,** call 36-39-61 in Maó or 38-07-87 in Ciutadella.

HOLIDAYS: Besides the nationwide holidays (see Section 4, "Fast Facts," in Chapter II), the following fiestas honoring local patron saints are observed throughout the island: September 7, 8, and 9 Maó stages horse processions in the streets; June 23, 24, and 25 much the same occurs in Ciutadella; August 12 and 13 in Alayor; July 24, 25, and 26 in Villacarlos; August 23, 24, and 25 in Ferreries; July 15 and 16 in Mercadal; August 26 and 27 in San Luis; and July 8, 9, and 10 in Es Migjorn.

LANGUAGE: See Section 2, "Fast Facts," in Chapter VIII. "Menorca" is the prevailing, Spanish spelling of the island's name. The local subdialect of Catalan is *menorquín.*

MAIL: The post office in Maó is at Buen Aire 15 (tel. 36-38-92) and in Ciutadella at Plaça Constitutción (tel. 38-00-81). Hours are Monday through Friday from 9am to 2pm and on Saturday from 9am to 1pm; closed holidays.

NEWSPAPERS: The local Spanish- and Catalan-language daily is *Minorca Diario Insular.* A monthly English-language magazine called *Roqueta* provides information on what's happening on the island. Also available locally is the English-language *Majorca Daily Bulletin.* As in Ibiza and Majorca, foreign papers are readily available.

PHARMACIES: For the daily listing of pharmacies open around the clock, consult the *Minorca Diario Insular.*

SAFETY: Whenever you're traveling in an unfamiliar city or area, stay alert. Be aware of your immediate surroundings. Wear a moneybelt and don't sling your camera or purse over your shoulder; wear the strap diagonally across your body. This will minimize the possibility of your becoming a victim of crime. Every society has its criminals. It's your responsibility to be aware and alert even in the most heavily touristed areas.

TAXIS: Taxis do not have meters here. An official list indicates fares from the airport and Maó; prices vary from other departure points. Supplementary charges are levied on Sunday, holidays, at night, and for luggage. For a radio taxi, call 36-71-11 in Maó, 38-28-96 in Ciutadella. Elsewhere on the island, ask at the hotel for local taxi service.

TELEPHONE: There are telephone booths all over the island. Many bars also have telephones available for public use with meters indicating the number of units for which you must pay. Local calls require a minimum of two 5-pta. coins.

In Maó you can make international calls at Hallo, Calle Cos de Gracia 5, in the central shopping area (tel. 36-56-84). Summer hours are Monday through Friday from 9am to 1:30pm and 5 to 10pm, and on Saturday from 9am to 1:30pm and 5 to 9pm; winter hours are Monday through Friday from 9:30am to 1:30pm and 5 to 9pm, and on Saturday from 9:30am to 1:30pm and 5 to 8:30pm; closed holidays.

TELEVISION/RADIO: TVE 1 and TVE 2, the national Spanish-language TV stations, and TV-3, TVE-2 Cataluña, and Canal 33, the regional Catalan-language stations, broadcast to the island.

TIPPING: See Section 4, "Fast Facts," in Chapter II.

TOURIST INFORMATION: The **tourist office** in Maó at Plaça de S'Esplanada 40 (tel. 971/36-37-90) is open all year Monday through Friday from 9am to 2pm and 5 to 7pm, and on Saturday from 9:30am to 1pm; closed holidays. For **airport information,** call 36-01-50.

For information on **flight and ferry schedules,** consult the *Minorca Diario Insular.*

Two publications worth picking up are *12 Walks in Minorca* by Dodo Mackenzie (400 ptas., $3.25) and the *Archaeological Guide to Minorca* by a trio of Spanish authors sponsored by the Consell Insular de Minorca (650 ptas., $5.50), available at most bookstores.

3. Accommodations

In July and August hotel space is at a premium, so book well in advance. The hotel offering in town ranges from pensions to the four-star Port Mahón. There are no luxury hotels to compare with the upper-echelon accommodations of Ibiza and Majorca, however, as Minorca is the sleeper of the Balearic Islands in tourist terms and caters primarily to package-tour travelers from Britain and Germany.

The posted rates at most lodgings are the official maximums the place can charge. Often you can negotiate at least a 10% discount—sometimes more in the off-season. For the purposes of this guide, "expensive" hotels charge 8,500 ptas. ($71) and up for a double room; "moderate" hotels, 5,000 to 8,500 ptas. ($42 to $71); and "budget lodgings" less than 5,000 ptas. ($42). *Note:* Unless otherwise indicated, all accommodations have private bath or shower, all hotels are open year round, and all rates given include service charge but *not* IVA.

EXPENSIVE

■ **Hotel Residencia Capri,** San Esteban 8, 07703 Maó, Minorca (tel. 971/36-14-00). 75 rms. A/C MINIBAR TV TEL

Located in the center of Maó, the Capri is a Best Western affiliate that has recently renovated its rooms and by now may have renovated its lounge, bar, cafeteria, and reception areas as well. As it is geared more to businesspeople than tourists, it offers no pool. Otherwise, its facilities are the best in town.

Facilities: Garage.

RATES: 4,800–6,800 ptas. ($40–$56.75) single; 8,500–10,000 ptas. ($70.75–$83.25) double.

MODERATE

■ **Hotel Port-Mahón,** Avenida Fort de L'Eau s/n (no street number), 07701 Maó, Minorca (tel. 971/36-26-00). 74 rms. TEL

Perched on a cliff above the port, the Port-Mahón represents a bit of old-world elegance surrounded by well-maintained gardens and charmingly captivating public spaces. Built in the 1950s, this grand dame of Minorca hotels has a colonial English mien steeped in Spanish graciousness. A young British couple staying here said that they felt a bit out of place, however, among the "old colonial types" who seemed to compose the bulk of the clientele.

Though some of the rooms live up to the grand-dame image, others are slightly worn around the edges; some have terraces and sea views.

Dining/Entertainment: The restaurant has a lovely view of the port, and there is a very inviting piano bar.

Facilities: Pool.

RATES: 3,800–5,300 ptas. ($31.75–$44.25) single; 4,500–7,900 ptas. ($37.50–$65.75) double with shower, 5,000–14,100 ptas. ($41.75–$118) with full bath; 12,800–17,300 ptas. ($107–$144) suite.

■ **Hotel del Almirante** (also known as the Collingwood House), Carretera de Villacarlos (along the road from Maó to Villacarlos), 07700 Maó, Minorca (tel. 971/36-27-00). 40 rms. (with toilet).

A decidedly English ambience prevails as well at this small, cozy inn whose main building is the former residence of Lord Collingwood, chief admiral of the British Mediterranean Squadron and close friend of Admiral Nelson. It dates from the early 18th century and combines an English Georgian style with Minorcan accents of the period. At various times it has served as a convent, the home of a German sculptor, and the German embassy.

Since 1964 it has been a hotel with 30 "bungalow" rooms of recent vintage complementing the more uniquely furnished rooms in the house proper, which contains an assortment of antiques, memorabilia from the British Empire, and the occasional tasteless modern furnishing. Upstairs is an eccentric parlor with an old upright piano. Some rooms have a shower only (no tub), but all at the Almirante is immaculate and well kept.

Facilities: Pool, bar.

RATES (INCLUDING HALF BOARD): 2,850–5,600 ptas. ($23.75–$46.75) single; 5,700–11,200 ptas. ($47.50–$93.25) double. Closed Nov–Apr.

- **Hotel Agamenon,** Paraje Fontanillas 16, 07720 Villacarlos, Minorca (tel. 971/36-21-50). 75 rms. TEL

Go beyond the Almirante (see above) along the Maó–Villacarlos road and take the first turn off to Villacarlos to reach this gleaming-white, five-story structure in a quiet setting. The Agamenon's sizable rooms are pleasant and all have a terrace overlooking the sea.

Facilities: Pool, restaurant, two bars.

RATES: 4,000–5,500 ptas. ($33.25–$45.75) single; 5,000–7,600 ptas. ($41.75–$63.25) double; 7,350–10,000 ptas. ($61.25–$83.25) suite. Closed Nov–Apr 30.

- **Hotel Rey Carlos III,** Cala Corp, 07720 Villacarlos, Minorca (tel. 971/36-31-00). 87 rms. TEL

Just a few blocks from the Agamenon (see above), the Rey Carlos greets you with old-fashioned charm. The spacious rooms, spread across three floors, are all doubles with sea views from their terraces. The decor varies from room to room, but each is clean and pleasant. Overall, a very good choice in a great setting.

Facilities: Pool, restaurant.

RATES (INCLUDING BREAKFAST AND IVA): 4,500–5,550 ptas. ($37.50–$46.25) single use of double; 6,100–7,800 ptas. ($50.75–$65) double. Closed Nov–Holy Week.

BUDGET

- **Residencia Jume,** Concepción 6, 07701 Maó, Minorca (tel. 971/36-32-66). 35 rms.

This very clean, comfortable, and commendable in-town option has spacious, cheerful rooms and a TV sitting room by the reception area. Triples and quads are also available. When I was last there they were installing a cafeteria.

RATES: 1,400–1,550 ptas. ($11.75–$13) single; 2,750–3,000 ptas. ($23–$25) double. Closed Dec 15–Jan 7.

4. Dining

The majority of the capital's restaurants are, of course, gathered around the port and serve lovely maritime vistas with their meals.

The most popular Minorcan dishes are the *calderetas,* rich soup/casseroles of fish, shellfish, or the local spiny lobster. Though common to all the Balearic Islands, the calderetas of Minorca enjoy a special cachet. King Juan Carlos of Spain is reported to have a special fondness for them and often sojourns to Fornells to indulge it.

Minorca's *escopinyes* ("venus" clams) are also touted, along with the whole range of its Mediterranean fish and shellfish. Also typical local fare are the *oliagua* (a tomato-based vegetable soup), baked eggplant, partridge-and-cabbage casserole, and *formatjades* (pastry turnovers) with various fillings.

Traditional Minorcan cured sausages include the spreadable *sobrasada, camot* (large black sausage), and *carnixua* (coarsely cut salami-type sausage). Another local specialty is Maó cheese.

As with all the Balearic Islands, meals are generally not cheap in Minorca because almost everything must be flown in. Fish is one exception, of course, but demand keeps prices high in summer (they drop off considerably in winter, however). All the better restaurants are more or less on a par when it comes to price, with the average meal costing about 2,500 ptas. ($20.75). Eating cheaply means grabbing a sandwich or snack at a pub or fast-food stand. Where prices below are indicated for "meals," they refer to an average three-course meal without wine. As with the hotels, service is usually included in the prices, but IVA is *not.* Many restaurants offer economical three-course luncheon menus, including bread and house wine. At cafeterias, tapas bars, and other informal eating establishments, it often costs less to eat at the bar than at a table.

Most of the island's classiest and priciest restaurants are in Maó and Fornells, along with one or two first-class offerings in Ciutadella.

For trivia buffs, here's an interesting culinary footnote—mayonnaise (*mahonesa* in Spanish) was allegedly invented in Maó.

EXPENSIVE

• **Restaurante Rocamar,** Cala Fonduco 32 (tel. 36-56-01). *Prices:* Entrées: 1,200–5,500 ptas. ($10–$45.75); three-course menu of the day featuring the caldereta 5,000 pesetas ($41.75); six-course degustation menu 4,000 ptas. ($33.25); children's menu under 1,000 ptas. ($8.25).

Located at the western end of the port, Rocamar is deemed the island's best restaurant by most locals. A Michelin recommendation seconds that notion. Situated on the first (to Americans, second) floor of the Hostal Rocamar, the restaurant boasts a classically elegant decor with lots of wood.

The menu stresses seafood. Top choices are the caldereta de langosta (lobster), caldereta de pescado (fish), fish stew with thyme sauce, salmon tartare with vodka, and the fish carpaccio marinated with hazelnut vinaigrette. Meat entrées include lamb, rabbit, and magret. Live music accompanies evening meals daily except Thursday and Sunday.

Open: Summer, daily 1–3:30pm and 8:30–11pm. *Closed:* Nov and Mon in winter. *Reservations:* Recommended. SPANISH/MINORCAN

• **Jagaro Restaurant,** Port de Maó (tel. 36-46-60). *Prices:* Meals begin at 3,000 ptas. ($25).

Jagaro's outdoor terrace topped by a tent canopy is reminiscent of a luxurious jungle setting. Its smaller indoor dining area is an elegant array of wood and greenery.

The menu, written on pages of leather, is Minorca's most varied and interesting, and includes many unusual house specialties. Among them are carparcho de mero (grouper) with a green-mustard sauce, ensalada templada con cigalitos y setas (a bed of lettuce topped with warm prawns and wild mushrooms), red pepper stuffed with cuttlefish, a unique variation of gazpacho containing melon and shrimp, fish-and-vegetable mousse, Iranian caviar, and a long list of seafood dishes headlined by the caldereta de langosta and caldereta de marisco y pescado. Fish here is primarily prepared one of two ways—al horno (baked) or al espalda (baked first with wine, then topped with a wine-and-garlic sauce).

The meat offering includes duck magret in an orange sauce and small magret hamburgers with a sweet-and-sour sauce. All the desserts are homemade, including the honey and almond ice creams and sorbets. The wine list is mostly Spanish and offers reds dating from 1935. And as if all this weren't enough, the service is impeccable, with one waiter for every three tables. All in all, a very sybaritic dining experience for those with a gourmet palate and budget.

Open: Daily 1–4pm and 8pm–midnight. *Reservations:* Imperative; reserve the day before in July and Aug. ECLECTIC

• **Gregal Restaurant Bar,** Mártires del Atlante (also called Anden de Levante) 43 (tel. 36-66-06). *Prices:* Entrées 935–5,500 ptas. ($7.75–$45.75).

This small, pleasant restaurant with a beamed ceiling and checkered tablecloths specializes in seafood. Some of the day's wares are on display for the choosing. Gregal also serves meat and fowl dishes in a Spanish, Catalan, French, and international vein, along with a sprinkling of Greek dishes including dolmades, taramosalata, and moussaka.

Open: Daily 1–3:30pm and 8–11:30pm. SEAFOOD/INTERNATIONAL

MODERATE

‣ **Pilar Restaurant,** Forn 61, Mao (tel. 36-68-17). *Prices:* Appetizers 700–1,200 ptas. ($5.75–$10); main dishes 1,400–1,800 ptas. ($11.75–$15).

At this small, stylish restaurant in the center of Maó, you'll feel you're dining in somebody's home. Even the small kitchen where owner-chef Pilar Pons works her culinary wonders looks more like a domestic kitchen than a restaurant kitchen. There are about half a dozen tables indoors and another half a dozen spread around the rear patio in the summer. Some antique furnishings and impressionistic artwork contribute to the coziness.

The menu is understandably limited, but not the quality and care taken in preparation. The cuisine is largely menorquín with innovative variations. Try the berenjenas rellenas (stuffed eggplant) and conejo a la menorquina (rabbit in an onion-and-thyme sauce).

Open: Summer, Mon–Sat 8–11pm; Oct–Dec, Wed–Sat 8–11pm. *Closed:* Jan and Feb. MINORCAN

BUDGET

▪ **La Tropical,** Calle Luna 36 (tel. 36-05-56). *Prices:* 1,000–1,600 ptas. ($8.25–$13.25); daily three-course menu 950 ptas. ($8).

La Tropical is a three-in-one eatery. You can have snacks at the bar, platos combinados in the informal dining room, or full-fledged restaurant fare in the more formal dining area. The restaurant offers a good selection of Minorcan specialties, including a reasonably priced fish-and-shellfish caldereta. There is also a daily market menu and an assorted selection of Spanish and international dishes.

Open: Daily 8am–4pm and 8–11pm for meal service in the restaurant (8am–midnight for bar and snack service). *Closed:* Feb. SPANISH/MINORCAN

▪ **The American Bar,** Plaça Reial 8 (tel. 36-18-22). *Prices:* Meals 1,000–1,500 ptas. ($8.25–$12.50).

This is as close as Maó comes to a diner. Located in the heart of the central shopping district, it offers a square meal in a no-nonsense indoor or outdoor setting. The down-home Spanish menu is sprinkled with international footnotes like lasagne, spaghetti, and hot dogs. It also serves snacks and ice cream.

Open: Mon–Sat 6:30am–10pm (to 11pm in summer). SPANISH/INTERNATIONAL

---

5. Things to See and Do

There is really little need to spend much time in Maó, except perhaps to shop in the center of town or spend your evenings in the restaurants and bars along the port. The **Cathedral of Santa María,** however, does have an unusual organ whose inner workings, built in Barcelona, are the work of Swiss artisan Johan Kyburz; its outer cabinetry and sculpture are the work of Maó artists. Inaugurated in 1810, it consists of four keyboards and 3,210 pipes, 215 of them wooden and the rest metal. In the summer, special daily half-hour concerts are held at 11am to show off its special musical charms. Admission is 200 ptas. ($1.75). At other times there is no charge for visiting the church and organ.

Just off the Plaça de S'Esplanada on Calle Conde de Cifuentes is the **Ateneo Científico, Literario y Artístico,** essentially a retired men's club but with a small, offbeat museum boasting "the most comprehensive collection of dried seaweeds in southern Europe."

Off the Maó–Villacarlos road is a marked turnoff for the *taula* and *talayot* of Trepucó. The taula (see the box on archeological sights in Section 2, Chapter XIII), one of the island's largest, probably dates from the middle of the millennium before Christ.

From Cales Font in Villacarlos there are **boat excursions** around Maó Harbor and to surrounding bays leaving daily in summer at 3pm (boarding at 2:30pm); the cost is 700 ptas. ($5.75) for adults, half that for children.

Maó itself and the adjacent Villacarlos have no beaches. Some fine sandy property is not far away, however, both to the north and south.

North of Maó is **Cala Mesquida,** one of the best beaches on the island. After turning off the road toward Cala Llonga, follow the "Playa" signs through the sleepy fishing village and continue along the dirt track to this beautiful, long beach flanked by rocky bluffs, one of which is topped with the ruins of a tower. There are no snack stands or restaurants here, but there are some in the village. Also north of the capital en route to Sant Antoni is Golden Farm, the Georgian mansion where Admiral Lord Nelson and Lady Hamilton allegedly cohabited.

South of Maó is San Luis, a small town of two-story, whitewashed buildings. **Punta Prima,** a large, sandy beach known to have some rigorous surf, is below San Luis to the east. A full complement of bars and eateries caters to bathers nearby. Another attractive beach in this area is at **Cala de Binibeca.** The sand is lovely, white, and fine here, and there is a very inviting thatch-roofed bar/restaurant terraced across the rocks.

At kilometer-stone 4 of the Maó–Ciutadella road, a marked turnoff to the left leads to the **Talatí de Dalt.** From the small parking indentation, some rudimentary steps in the stone wall facilitate your climbing over it so you can follow a rudimentary path to the taula, hypostylic chambers, and subterranean caves of this prehistoric village. Most noteworthy is the taula with a pilaster leaning on the capital stone. As it's not there for support, one can surmise that it was a vertical stone that broke loose and toppled into its present position.

---

6. Shopping

Maó offers the most extensive and most sophisticated shopping on the island. The primary shopping streets that wind their way through the heart of town are Sa Ravaleta (with a series of open-air terraces in the middle), Carrer Nou, Carrer Hanover (also called Costa de Sa Plaça), and Carrer del Dr. Orfila (also Carrer de Ses Moreres). In nearby Villacarlos, **Ecco Bisuteria,** Cales Fonts 24 (no phone), stands out for its fine offering of costume jewelry designed by Barcelona-based Carlos Martini.

Es Portal, Sa Ravaleta 23 (tel. 36-30-36).

Features fashions for both men and women by Spain's leading designers—Manuel Piña, Jesús del Pozo, Adolfo Dominguez, and Sybilla; and if you've been to Ibiza, you'll recognize the fashions of designer Armin Heinemann of Paula's in Ibiza Town. It also carries unique accessories and shoes.

Open: Summer, Mon–Fri 10am–1:30pm and 5:30–9pm, Sat 10am–1:30pm; winter, Mon–Fri 10am–1:30pm and 5–8:30pm, Sat 10am–1:30pm.

Looky Boutique, Dr. Orfila 43 (tel. 36-06-48).

Purveyor of some of the island's most stylish and sophisticated leather goods manufactured in its factory in Ciutadella. The offering includes shoes, handbags, leather clothing for men and women, and luggage. They also have a shop in Ciutadella at José María Quadradro 14 (tel. 38-19-32).

Open: Mon–Fri 10am–1:30pm and 5–8pm, Sat 10am–1:30pm.

Patricia, Calle de Ses Moreres 31 (tel. 36-91-78).

Also offers leather goods of its own local fabrication, featuring stylish coats, jackets, and suede skirts and suits. Shops can also be found in Ciutadella at Camino Santandria/Ronda Baleares (tel. 38-50-56) and Fornells, Calle Poeta Gumersindo Riera 1 (tel. 37-65-73).

Open: Mon–Fri 9:30am–1:30pm and 5–8pm, Sat 9:30am–1:30pm.

Toledo, Calle Nou 17 (tel. 36-57-84).

Sells primarily Lladró and Majórica pearls along with some crystal and silver.

Open: Mon–Fri 9:30am–1:30pm and 5–8pm, Sat 9am–2pm.

7. Nightlife

The nightlife offering in the port of Maó stretches piecemeal along the waterfront in sections intermittently developed for diversion; the majority of nightspots are grouped at the western end of the port. The tone is more upscale and subdued than in Ciutadella (see Chapter XIII). The principal diversion of an evening is conversation with friends over a few drinks, accompanied by a little music, on the terrace of a bar.

For dancing, there are several discos in town and in the neighboring developments. One curious spot at the eastern extremity of the port is the **Disco Pub Acuarium Minorca,** Andén de Poniente 73 (no phone), with aquariums lining the walls, a billiard room, and loud music. It's open in summer daily from 10am to 4:30am and in winter daily from 6pm to 3:30am.

One of the most pleasant places to spend an evening is at **Cales Fonts** (Calas Fons) in nearby Villacarlos. This snug little cove is rimmed with diminutive, whitewashed houses that from May to October blossom with boutiques, assorted eateries, and informal entertainment. At least a dozen open-air restaurants and several snackbars are strung along the Cales Fonts waterfront, so just stroll along, look at the menus and plates of food on the tables, and choose what looks best. Most of these establishments offer a mixture of Spanish and international cuisine and, of course, stress the seafood.

Two places that deliciously deviate from the mainstream here are the **Restaurante Pizzería,** Muelle Cala Fonts 44 (tel. 36-61-58), at the far end of the cove, and **Groucho Creperie,** Calas Fons (no phone), at the near end. The former has grilled fish and meat dishes ranging from 550 to 1,300 ptas. ($4.50 to $10.75), basic pasta dishes for under 700 ptas. ($5.75), and outstanding pizzas. It's open May to October daily from 1 to 3:15pm and 7pm to past midnight; closed Sunday at lunch. At Groucho Creperie, the crêpes come savory, sweet, flambéed, or with ice cream, each for under 500 ptas. ($4.25). Open May to October daily from 7pm until the night owls retire to their beds.

After dinner, head for **Chéspir Bar,** Cales Fonts 47 (no phone), to listen to recorded jazz music. This small place embedded in the cliff has made the most of its cave environment, lining the rock walls with billowy cushions and providing a cozy little bar at the entrance. All conducive to a very mellow evening. Open May to October daily from 7pm to about 3am.

AROUND MINORCA

1. GETTING AROUND
2. CIUTADELLA AND THE WEST
3. CENTRAL AND SOUTHERN AREAS
4. FORNELLS AND THE NORTHERN COAST

Maó and Ciutadella are the urban cornerstones of Minorca. The former, the current capital, is more British of aspect and subdued of demeanor. The latter, the former capital, more earthy and flamboyantly Spanish. In tandem they represent the two cultural faces of the island.

Physically speaking, Minorca is 55 kilometers (34 miles) long and an average 16 kilometers (10 miles) wide. Of the Balearic Islands, Minorca has best preserved its natural habitat. Much of its 175-mile coastline remains undeveloped and, in some cases, accessible only by all-terrain vehicle or on foot. Those who make the effort are amply rewarded with virgin vistas of crystal-clear water and shimmering white sand.

Beyond that, much of Minorca's enchantment lies in a landscape that variously echoes the English countryside, the highlands of Scotland, and the rocky, arid terrain of certain parts of Spain's Andalucía region. From the pinnacle of its most dazzling and dramatic scenic beauty at Cap de Cavalleria in the north, the island's terrain tapers off to the softer, gentler landscapes of the south that, in certain lights, take on overtones of Thomas Hardy's ominous moors.

All across the island there are dry-stone walls that reinforce the innate "Englishness" of the countryside and recall the agricultural strength of the island in the days before tourism. Once they sheltered field after field of staple crops from the *tramontana* (a vicious north wind); now only a handful of them keep watch over a few meager acres of rape and corn.

Tourism is the economic beacon of tomorrow, and in one or two places around the island it's already beginning to shine rather too brightly. Fortunately, the island seems to have taken note of the sins of rampant exploitation committed against parts of Majorca and Ibiza and is attempting to steer a more rational and far-sighted course into its touristic future.

1. Getting Around

Several bus and boat tours (primarily conducted in German) are offered from May to October. For full information, contact **Ultramar Express,** Vassalo 31, Maó (tel. 36-16-16), Monday through Friday from 9am to 1pm and 4 to 7:30pm, and on Saturday from 9am to 1pm.

Transportes Minorca, S.A., José María Quadradro 7, Maó (tel. 36-03-61), and Calle Barcelona 8, Ciutadella (tel. 38-03-93), operates the red-line buses servicing the island and departing Maó from either the Plaça de S'Esplanada or in front of the station itself near this plaza. The station opens half an hour before departure times, as those buses leaving from the station require advance purchase of tickets. Tickets are sold on board the buses leaving from the plaza. Schedules are highly volatile, so pick up the latest one at the tourist office, the station itself, or check the listings in *Roqueta.*

Since most of Minorca's better beaches are off the major public transportation routes and the island's major arteries, renting a car will greatly enrich your stay. You can also rent a motor bike or bicycle, but some of the remote roads can get rather bumpy. Real explorers will want to rent an all-terrain vehicle. There are several **rental-car agencies** at the airport that also have offices in Maó and at various points around the island, as follows:

Atesa: At the airport only (tel. 36-62-13), open daily from 8am until the last flight of the night.

Avis: At the airport (tel. 36-15-76), open in summer daily from 7:30am to 10:30pm, and in winter daily from 8am to 10pm; Plaça de S'Esplanada 53, Maó (tel. 36-47-72), open in summer only, daily from 9am to 1pm and 4:30 to 7pm.

BC Betacar: At the airport (tel. 36-64-00), open in summer daily from 8am to 11pm, and in winter daily from 8am to 10pm; Plaça de S'Esplanada 9, Maó (tel. 36-06-20), open Monday through Saturday from 8am to 1pm and 4 to 8pm, and on Sunday from 9am to 1pm and 5 to 7pm.

At presstime, base rates began at about 2,700 ptas. ($22.50) a day, but special rates apply for rentals of more than one week.

There are only about half a dozen gas stations scattered around the island, so try to keep the tank topped off. Only one station in Maó and (sometimes) one in Ciutadella are open after 9pm, and only selected ones are open on a rotating basis on weekends and holidays.

2. Ciutadella and the West

Located at the western end of the island, Ciutadella has a typically Mediterranean air about it. Lining the narrow streets of the old city are noble mansions of the 17th and 18th centuries and numerous churches. It was the capital until 1722, when the British chose Maó instead, largely because its harbor channel is eminently more navigable than the one at Ciutadella. Subsequently, the British built the main island road to link the two cities.

Like Maó, Ciutadella perches high above its harbor, which is smaller than Maó's. The seat of Minorca's bishopric, Ciutadella pontificates while Maó administrates. Its population is 19,000—again, just a few thousand less than Maó's head count.

Known as "Medina Minurka" under the Muslims, Ciutadella retains some Moorish traces despite the 1558 Turkish invasion and destruction of the city. An obelisk in memory of the city's futile defense against that invasion stands in the pigeon-filled Plaça d'es Born (Plaza del Born), the city's main square overlooking the port.

The **tourist office** (tel. 38-10-50) is housed in a mobile home parked in the Plaça d'es Born, May to October every morning from 9am to 1:30pm. In the afternoon from 5 to 9pm it stations itself in the various tourist developments around Ciutadella on a rotating basis.

You can **change money** at Friend's Cars, Plaça d'es Born 27 (tel. 38-60-67), Monday through Friday from 9am to 2pm and 5 to 9pm, on Saturday from 9am to 2pm, and on Sunday from 11am to 1pm.

All along Plaça Colón at the edge of Plaça d'es Born are **bus stops** serving various parts of the island. Destinations and departures are clearly marked and there is a ticket kiosk in the square. **Ferry service** runs between Majorca and Ciutadella. See any travel agency for information.

ACCOMMODATIONS

In general, the hotel offerings in and around Ciutadella are a cut above those in and around Maó. Along the coast from Los Delfines to Cala Blanca are a number of tourist resorts with fine beaches, and in Ciutadella itself there are several commendable hostelries, some bordering on the luxurious. At night, many of the travelers staying at the nearby beaches head into Ciutadella to enjoy the fine restaurants and nightlife, which is a bit more boisterous than in Maó.

• **Patricia Hotel,** Paseo San Nicolás 90–92, 07760 Ciutadella, Minorca (tel. 971/38-55-11). 44 rms. A/C MINIBAR TV TEL

This is probably the island's most luxurious accommodation. Located near the Plaça d'es Born, it is primarily a businessperson's enclave, but is just one kilometer from the beach at Playa de La Caleta and, if all went well, should by now have a pool to offer guests. The carpeted rooms are done in pleasant pastels and feature large baths.

Dining/Entertainment: The La Cúpula restaurant offers both Minorcan and international cuisine.

Facilities: Hopefully by now, a pool.

RATES: 5,800–7,000 ptas. ($48.25–$58.25) single; 6,800–10,600 ptas. ($56.75–$88.25) double; 10,500–12,600 ptas. ($87.50–$105) triple.

• **Mediterrani,** Cala Blanca (Apartado de Correos 1.E), 07760 Ciutadella, Minorca (tel. 971/38-42-03). 180 rms. TEL

The best of the package-group hotels on the island, the Mediterrani is a brief walk from the small, sandy beach at Cala Blanca. Its public areas are well laid out, its very pleasant rooms are simply but invitingly outfitted with tiled floors and terraces, and the property is so well cared for that I thought it was brand new when, in fact, it was in its fourth season.

Facilities: Pool, bar, dining room, TV lounge, games room, tennis courts.

RATES (INCLUDING BREAKFAST AND IVA): 3,900–6,400 ptas. ($32.50–$53.25) single; 6,300–11,100 ptas. ($52.50–$92.50) double. Half and full board also available. There's a 25% discount for children ages 2 to 11 staying in a double with their parents. Closed Nov–Apr.

- **Hotel Esmeralda,** Paseo San Nicolas 175, 07760 Ciutadella, Minorca (tel. 971/38-02-50). 161 rms. TEL

The Esmeralda is Ciutadella's answer to Maó's Hotel Port-Mahón. Similarly located at the mouth of the harbor, it's about 15 minutes away from the nearest beach. Unlike the Port-Mahón, the clientele here is a heterogeneous mix of young and old.

The rooms, though large, are sparsely furnished, but the baths are big and bright. Some rooms have a shower only, some have a terrace, and some have a sea view.

Facilities: Pool.

RATES: 3,700–5,550 ptas. ($30.75–$46.25) single; 5,550–8,900 ptas. ($46.25–$74.25) double. Closed Nov–Apr.

- **Hotel Almirante Farragut,** Cala'n Forcat, 07760 Ciutadella, Minorca (tel. 971/38-28-00). 472 rms.

Located five kilometers (three miles) outside Ciutadella on a small, rocky inlet in the development of Los Delfines, the Almirante Farragut has large, amorphous public areas. The rooms, however, are pleasant enough, with patio flooring, baths (some singles with shower only), and terraces with a view of the inlet or the open sea.

Facilities: Two saltwater pools for adults, one pool for children, bars, restaurant, cafeteria, disco, TV and video room, tennis courts, mini-golf, shops, beauty parlor, supermarket, diving school, access to the bay.

RATES: 2,800–4,600 ptas. ($23.25–$38.25) single; 3,450–8,250 ptas. ($28.75–$68.75) double. Closed Nov–Apr.

- **Hotel Alfonso III,** Camí de Mao 53, 07701 Ciutadella, Minorca (tel. 971/38-01-50). 52 rms. TEL

The Alfonso III sits at the far end of the main shopping street leading off Plaça d'es Born and offers simple, dormitory-style accommodations at economical rates. Some rooms have a shower only (no tub). There is a dining room and cafeteria/snackbar.

RATES: 1,400–1,600 ptas. ($11.75–$13.25) single with shower; 2,500–3,000 ptas. ($20.75–$25) ptas. double with shower, 3,300–3,900 ptas. ($27.75–$32.50) with complete bath and terrace.

- **Hostal Residencia Ciutadella,** Calle Sn. Eloy 10, 07701 Ciutadella, Minorca (tel. 971/38-34-62). 17 rms. TEL

This solid, in-town choice near Plaça Alfonso III just off the main shopping street has sizable rooms and floor-length windows fronting a rather quiet street. The floors are tiled and the upholstered furnishings covered in cheery, floral prints. The rooms are spread across three floors, but there is no elevator.

RATES: 1,650–2,500 ptas. ($13.75–$20.75) single; 3,400–3,950 ptas. ($28.25–$33) double; 3,950–4,850 ptas. ($33–$40.50) triple.

- **Hostal Madrid,** Calle Madrid 60, 07760 Ciutadella, Minorca (tel. 971/38-03-28). 20 rms.

Tucked away on a residential street near the Hotel Esmeralda, the Hostal Madrid offers comfortable rooms on three floors (no elevator), all with terraces. Playa des Degollador, a 10-minute walk away, is the nearest beach. It's also a short walk into town and to the port. At this writing there were plans to renovate the rooms for the upcoming season.

Facilities: Pool, bar/cafeteria.

RATES: 2,300–3,080 ptas. ($19.25–$25.75), single or double. Closed Nov–Apr.

- **Hotels Cala Bona and Mar Blava,** Urbanización Son Oleo, 07760 Ciutadella, Minorca (tel. 971/38-00-16). 44 rms.

These two neighboring hotels under the same management are at a cozy, half-kilometer remove from the center of Ciutadella. Stairs lead down to the pretty, rock-rimmed bay below for sunbathing by the sea. The decor throughout both hotels is ad hoc but homey.

The rooms in both are clean and comfortable and all have a sea view. The rooms at the Mar Blava are more cramped; the 18 rooms at the Cala Bona are nice and bright. Triples and quads available.

Facilities: The bar, pool, reception area, and outdoor terrace are all at the Mar Blava.

RATES: 1,700–2,000 ptas. ($14.25–$16.75) single; 2,500–3,500 ptas. ($20.75–$29.25) double. Cala Bona closed Nov 1–Mar 31.

DINING

The port of Ciutadella offers a great selection of restaurants for all palates and prices.

- **Casa Manolo,** Marina 117–121, Port de Ciutadella (tel. 38-00-03). *Prices:* Entrées 1,500–6,000 ptas. ($12.50–$50).

Situated at the far end of the port where all the bigger yachts are docked, Casa Manolo tops the list of Ciutadella restaurants in quality and cost. King Juan Carlos has been known to drop in here from time to time for the fresh seafood and lobster specialties. Spanish and local cuisine are featured, along with a unique trademark dish —arroz de pescado caldoso, a kind of fish paella but with more broth. The outdoor dining area is small and sophisticated; the indoor area is carved out of rock. But owner Manuel Plens-Guiu says that even indoor diners will soon enjoy a sea view.

Open: Mar–Sept, daily 1–4pm and 8–11pm; Oct–Feb, Mon–Sat 1–4pm and 8–11pm. *Closed:* Dec 10–Jan 10. *Reservations:* Imperative. SPANISH/MINORCAN

- **Restaurant El Comilon,** Plaza Colón 47, Ciutadella (tel. 38-09-22). *Prices:* Meals average 3,000 ptas. ($25).

This is another upscale eatery featuring fresh seafood—mostly grilled—and beef dishes with a French accent, including entrecôte with a roquefort, pepper, or Normandie sauce (a sweet-and-sour sauce made with apples, whiskey, honey, and vinegar). The tournedos belle époque are served with fresh vegetables. The dozen or so indoor tables are topped with pink linen, and there is covered patio dining in the back.

Open: Summer, Mon–Sat 1–3:30pm and 7–11pm, Sun 7–11pm; winter, Tues–Sat 1–3:30pm and 7–11pm, Sun 1–3:30pm. *Closed:* Christmas through Jan. SEAFOOD/FRENCH

- **Cas Quintu,** Plaza Alfonso III no. 4, Ciutadella (tel. 38-10-02). *Prices:* Meals average 2,500 ptas. ($20.75).

Cas Quintu offers informal tables by the bar or a more handsome and formal setting in the back. Seafood is the specialty, and the day's fare is on display near the bar. The calderetas share top billing with other traditional Spanish fish dishes. There is also a seasonal menu with an assortment of Spanish and Minorcan dishes, among them several meat offerings.

Open: Daily 1–4pm and 7:30–11pm; bar open 9am–1am. SPANISH/MINORCAN

- **Es Caliu Grill,** Carretera Cala Blanca, Ciutadella (tel. 38-01-65). *Prices:* Entrées up to 1,800 ptas. ($15).

Along the main road between Cala Santandria and Cala Blanca, Es Caliu is the place to come when you've had your fill of seafood. Specializing in grilled meats of the first and freshest quality, it offers veal, pork, rabbit, quail, and spit-roasted suckling pig and lamb. But beyond fine food, you get a very special ambience here. Above the bar hang hams and garlic braids, and off to the side are stacked wine barrels. The family-style tables and benches are made of cut and polished logs. The outdoor terrace is roofed and smothered with cascading flowers. Indoors there are two rustic dining areas, one with a fireplace.

Open: May–Oct, daily 1–4pm and 7:30pm–12:30am; Oct–May, Fri–Sun 1–4pm and 7:30pm–12:30am.

- **Funky Junkie,** Passeig Sant Joan 15, in the port (tel. 38-55-97). *Prices:* Meals average under 1,200 ptas. ($10).

Billing itself as "Junk-Food Heaven" and "Home of the Junker —The Best Junk Food from Around the World," Funky Junkie is owned and operated by Ed Wall, a transplanted Philadelphian who makes fast friends with his customers and is always glad to see a fellow American. He also knows a lot about the island and can fill you in on the latest nightspots. Meanwhile, his fast-food eatery serves up 17 versions of a hamburger with Ed's special sauce, club sandwiches, Philadelphia steak sandwiches, Sloppy Joes, spareribs, and some Italian and Mexican dishes. Naturally, the food doesn't taste the same as back home, but Ed's hospitality is 100% American.

Open: Apr–Oct, daily 11am–4pm and 7pm–4am; Nov–Mar, Thurs–Sun 7pm–3am. AMERICAN

- **La Granja,** Plaça Colón 48, Ciutadella (tel. 38-40-81). *Prices:* Tapas under 800 ptas. ($6.75) a plate.

Popular with both locals and tourists, La Granja is a stylish, modern tapas bar offering both indoor and outdoor "grazing." You'll find no menu here, only a verbal explanation in diverse languages of the selection of fresh, high-quality tapas and sandwiches available that day, some of which are on appetizing display.

Open: Mon–Sat 10am–3am.

- **Bar Triton,** Muelle Ciutadella (tel. 38-00-02). *Prices:* Tapas 250–1,500 ptas. ($2–$12.50) per plate.

Another fine tapas spot, Triton, in the port, offers a wide range of snacks including sausages, tortillas (Spanish omelets), meatballs, and a dozen or so seafood tapas, among them baby octopus, stuffed squid, and escupiñas (Minorcan clams). On the wall inside are photos and illustrations of the port before it was a haven for holidaymakers. As in those days, fishermen still make up an important part of the clientele, and you'll often find the local men engaged in a friendly game of cards of an afternoon.

Open: Daily 4:30am–midnight.

THINGS TO SEE AND DO

Ciutadella's municipal center of gravity is the **Plaça d'es Born,** which contains two magnificent palaces (the Conde de Torresaura and Casa Salort, now a theater), the Real Alcázar (now the Town Hall), and the San Francisco Church. In the center of the square stands an obelisk commemorating the heroic but ineffectual defense of this former capital against the Turkish invasion in 1558.

Leading off this square is Calle Mayor, where on the right you will find the **Palacio Salort,** privately owned but uninhabited and open to the public July to October Monday through Saturday from 10am to 2pm; admission is 150 ptas. ($1.25). Part of this palace dates from the 16th century and the rest from the 19th. The facade is neoclassical, but the arcades facing the Plaça d'es Born are in a Renaissance style. On the ceiling of the main entrance you can see the coats of arms of the Salort and Martorell families, the latter having enlarged the house to its current size in 1813. Of particular note in this two-story structure are the French tapestries, English chairs, and Louis XV– and XVI–style console tables. Downstairs is a patio garden and garage with a vintage 1920s Buick on display, the second car to come to Ciutadella.

Farther along this same street is the **cathedral,** which was built in a Gothic style atop a former mosque upon the orders of King Alfonso III of Aragón some 700 years ago; its neoclassical facade dates from 1813, however. Completely sacked in 1936 at the onset of the Civil War, its current aspect is the result of subsequent restoration. Notable are its fine vaulting and the width of the nave flanked on either side by six chapels. The choir, formerly in the center of the nave, was moved to either side of the episcopal chair during the post–Civil War restoration

From the aristocratic Plaça d'es Born to the quaint Plaça d' Alfonso III stretches a pedestrian zone lined with shops. While some Maó shops have branches here, the shopping is generally better in the capital.

The surrounding streets make up the heart of the old town and are lined with whitewashed houses dabbed with accents of color. To sweeten your stroll through this area, stop at **Baixamar** in the Plaça de la Catedral for some homemade ice cream; open March to October daily from 10am to 11pm.

As with Maó, the pulse of life in Ciutadella emanates from the port, where the fishermen's quays are animated with sailboats and yachts and a wide range of restaurants, terrace bars, handcraft stalls, pubs, and the occasional discotheque. Ciutadella doesn't have a beach either, but there are some good ones in the vicinity, along with a number of other worthwhile sights.

Archeological Remnants

Archeologists posit that Minorca was first inhabited as long as 7,000 years ago by a strong, athletic race that relinquished its caves to construct underground villages. Scattered across the island's countryside are significant archeological remnants dating back over 3,000 years that have, unfortunately, been largely neglected. Collectively, however, these numerous *talayots, taulas, navetas,* and prehistoric cave villages make up a valuable open-air museum. Thought to have some link with similar remains in Sardinia, they are believed to date primarily from the Talayot Culture of the second millennium B.C.

Talayots are the round rock mounds found all over Minorca. Were they watchtowers as some suggest? Probably not—they have no interior stairway and only a few are found along the coast. The best-preserved one is at Torello, near Maó airport, which you can drive up to (but it's closed to the public). The megalithic **taulas** are huge Stonehenge-esque, T-shaped stone structures about four meters (12 ft.) high and apparently peculiar to Minorca. Dating from pre-Roman times, their purpose is unknown and they are almost always found alongside a talayot.

The **navetas,** dating from 1400 to 800 B.C., are stone constructions in the shape of inverted boats (hence the name derived from *nave,* Spanish for "boat"). Many have false ceilings, and often you can walk inside. Perhaps the island's best known is the **Naveta d'es Tudons** near Ciutadella, a funerary building belonging to the Talayotic Age (1500–1400 B.C.).

Another archeological must on Minorca is the prehistoric village of **Torre d'en Gaumes** (see Section 3, "Central and Southern Areas," below) with its notable variety of monuments. Also of interest are **Trepuca** and **Talati de Dalt** near Maó, and the Paleo-Christian basilica at Son Bou (again, see Section 3, "Central and Southern Areas," below).

Some four kilometers (2.5 miles) before reaching Ciutadella on the main Maó–Ciutadella road, there is a well-marked track leading south to the **Naveta des Tudons,** a two-story tomb from the Bronze Age containing the remains of about 50 bodies. In 1968 the naveta (so called because it's shaped like an upturned boat) was restored and excavations carried out that turned up invaluable prehistoric artifacts including arms, jewelry, and crockery. Another track nearby leads to a prehistoric cave with pillars and niches in the wall similar to those described below at Cala Morell.

Some eight kilometers (five miles) northeast of Ciutadella at **Cala Morell,** along a well-marked road, is one of the most important groups of prehistoric caves on Minorca. One of them has an isolated pilaster cut separate from the rock face with a horn-shaped capital, and another has high-relief ornaments decorating its facade and framing the trapezoidal portal. Also found here are numerous hollows, usually oval in shape, about half a meter up the cliff sides. Speculation is that they were receptacles for offerings to the dead entombed here. Not all these caves were exclusively burial chambers, however; some served as dwellings as well, but it is unclear whether they ever served both purposes simultaneously.

If you continue along the road past the caves down to the playa, you'll come to one of the island's prettier, more peaceful bays, framed with cliffs and unusual rock formations. There is a small sand beach here, as well as cement platforms for sunbathing and a snackbar and restaurant. Housing developments are rapidly cropping up on the hillside—so far they blend in nicely.

South of Ciutadella at **Cala de Santandria and Cala Blanca** are two small bays with vest-pocket beaches and a smattering of hotels, hostels (see "Accommodations," above), snackbars, restaurants, and shops.

On the island's southwestern coast between Son Xoriguer and Cala Galdana, a series of aboriginal beaches sheltered by pinewoods includes the sandy double bay of **Son Saura** and the lovely inlets of **Cala Turqueta** and **Macarella.**

NIGHTLIFE

Ciutadella is more popular with the younger crowd than Maó. At night its port blossoms with handcraft stands and diverse musical establishments in addition to the bars and restaurants open all day. Also in the vicinity are a number of popular discos.

Bar La Escalera, Calle de Pere Capllonch s/n (no street number) (tel. 38-52-42).

This is the first place you'll come to as you descend the steps down to the port. Like many other nightspots around the island, it's installed in a cave and it has a billiard table and loud music. The crowd is largely offbeat.

Open: Daily 9pm–4am.

Aladino, Port de Ciutadella (no phone).

Another cave bar with darts, billiards, loud music, and a largely young crowd.

Open: June–Sept, daily 8:30pm–4am; Sept–June, Fri and Sat, 8:30pm–3am.

Burinot, next to the Bar Triton, Port de Ciutadella (tel. 38-49-68).

Here you'll find outdoor tables, a small indoor bar, and a billiard table downstairs. The loud music is a mixed bag of popular Spanish and international tunes. The crowd is similarly mixed.

Open: Daily 8pm–4am.

Zona B, Plaça Sant Joan s/n (no street number), Port de Ciutadella (tel. 38-43-20).

This bar can arguably be said to have the loudest music of all, though the competition is fierce. Again, billiards upstairs.

Open: Summer, daily 9pm–4am; winter, Fri and Sat 9pm–4am.

El Rincón de Martin, along Plaça Sant Joan, Port de Ciutadella (tel. 38-62-88).

A small, smoky, cave bar one flight up, El Rincón de Martin offers live South American music most often performed by the bar's Argentinian owner. After a few soothing, haunting songs, things get pleasantly mellow.

Open: Summer, daily 9pm–4am; winter, Fri and Sat 9pm–4am. The music starts anytime between 11:30pm and 1am.

Lateral, across the way from El Rincón de Martin (no phone).

This is the port's disco. A subterranean, cellar atmosphere prevails downstairs. Upstairs is a terrace bar and, yes, a billiard table. Attracts a mixed crowd.

Open: Summer, daily 10pm–5am; winter, Fri and Sat 10pm–5am.

Café de Paris, San Sebastian 8 (in the vicinity of the cathedral), Ciutadella (no phone).

For those who like their music sedate and their ambience upscale and sophisticated, the art-deco echoes here make a pleasant setting for a drink and conversation. You can take your pick among many small, intimate conversational areas or perch yourself at the gracefully curving bar at the entrance. No billiard table, no loud music—just a pleasant place to sit and chat. The crowd is mostly local.

Open: Daily 6:30pm–whenever.

Adagio's, along Cala Degollador just outside Ciutadella (tel. 38-47-27).

This is a somewhat sophisticated disco with large cushions along the wall and a spacious dance floor.

Open: July–Sept, daily midnight–5am; Sept–July Fri–Sun midnight–5am. *Prices:* Cover charge 700 ptas. ($5.75), including one drink. All year Sat and Sun "matinee" session 7–10pm for teens 16 and up, admission 400 ptas. ($3.25).

Macho, Santandria (tel. 38-63-59).

A little farther out of Ciutadella than Adagio's, Macho is a disco experience endowed with four bars, a billiard table, and a lively mixed crowd that corresponds to the mixture of old and new music offered. A special feature here are the occasional "foam" parties reported to be quite a sensual experience.

Open: May 1–Oct 30, daily 11pm–6am; the rest of the year, Sat 11pm–6am. *Prices:* Cover is 500 ptas. ($4.25).

---

3. Central and Southern Areas

Topographically and climatically, this is the more tranquil part of the island. The beaches are more accessible, the winds blow less strongly, and as a result, tourism has taken a firmer foothold here than in the north. Santo Tomás, Cala Galdana, Playa de Son Bou, Cala Bosch, and Punta Prima are some of the focal points for travelers.

ACCOMMODATIONS

Most of the hotels in this area cater to tour groups. Some are better than others.

• **Hotel Santo Tomás,** Playa Santo Tomás, 07749 San Cristóbal, Minorca (tel. 971/37-00-25). 85 rms. TEL

On this beach, the Santo Tomás has seniority, and in this case older is better and more charming. Its dining room, poolside bar, and other communal spaces have the bright, breezy feel of a lazy, summer retreat.

The pleasant, though more prosaic, rooms are carpeted, comfortable, and very well kept. The majority have terraces with sea views. The clientele is mostly British and German.

Facilities: Pool (an especially nice area featuring thatched umbrellas scattered throughout a terrace garden), rudimentary mini-golf course, and a smattering of water sports offered on Santo Tomás Beach.

RATES (INCLUDING IVA): 5,443–6,653 ptas. ($45.25–$55.50) single; 9,072–11,974 ptas. ($75.50–$99.75) double; 12,096–14,516 ptas. ($101–$121) suite. Closed Nov–Apr.

• **Hotel Los Cóndores Sol,** Plaza de Santo Tomás s/n (no street number) 07749 San Cristóbal, Minorca (tel. 971/37-00-50) 188 rms. TEL

Right next door to the Santo Tomás, this is another Sol group property with lots of stone, wood, and tiles creating a friendly, hacienda atmosphere. The attractive rooms have pretty balconies with wooden doors, louvered shutters, and sea views.

Facilities: Pool, shops, beauty parlor, mini-golf, dining room.

RATES (INCLUDING BREAKFAST): 5,300–6,800 ptas. ($44.25–$56.75) single; 7,800–10,800 ptas. ($65–$90) double. Closed Nov–Apr 30.

• **Hotel Victoria Playa,** Playa Santo Tomás, 07740 Mercadal, Minorca (tel. 971/37-02-00). 266 rms.

The Victoria Playa belongs to the Med Playa group of hotels that owns the Cartago and Galeón in Puerto de San Miguel, Ibiza. Its rooms all have terraces, sizable baths, patio flooring, and a light, cheery decor. The public areas and bar are geared to tour groups, and overall the hotel has an institutional feel about it, with hallways that recall college dorms.

Facilities: Pool.

RATES (INCLUDING BREAKFAST AND IVA): 2,600–4,700 ptas. ($21.50–$39.25), single or double. Closed Nov 1–Apr 30.

■ **Hotel Lord Nelson,** 07749 Playa Santo Tomás, Minorca (tel. 971/37-01-25). 145 rms. TEL

This more intimate property has an attractive swimming pool bordering the dunes of the beach. All the compact but comfortable rooms have terraces with a sea view.

RATES (INCLUDING IVA): 5,000–6,600 ptas. ($41.75–$55) single; 6,600–9,450 ptas. ($55–$78.75). In peak season there are also 32 bungalow accommodations where three can stay for the price of two. Closed Nov–Apr.

■ **Hotel Los Gavilanes Sol,** Urbanización Cala Galdana s/n (no street number), 07750 Ferrerias, Minorca (tel. 971/37-31-75). 357 rms. TEL

The original beauty of Cala Galdana has been substantially marred by tourist construction, but you can enjoy the best end of its sandy, crescent beach and beautiful turquoise waters by staying at the Gavilanes. A member of the Sol hotel group, this one offers sizable, functional rooms and the standard amenities of a large tour-group hotel.

Facilities: Pool, children's playground, TV and games rooms, gift shop, supermarket, water sports.

RATES (INCLUDING BREAKFAST): 5,450–6,850 ptas. ($45.50–$57) single; 4,100–11,000 ptas. ($34.25–$91.75) double. Children ages 2–6 get a 25% discount. Half and full board available.

DINING

Some of the best dining in this area is offered in the inland villages rather than along the coast. Mercadal, in particular, has a few choice restaurants.

■ **Costa Sur,** Playa de Santo Tomás (tel. 37-03-26). *Prices:* Meals begin at 2,500 ptas. ($21).

The sophisticated aspirations of Costa Sur are hampered by a rather starkly modern decor. The Spanish/Catalan menu is equally divided between seafood and meat dishes, and the house prides itself on unusual sauces like the peach sauce served with the loin of pork and the steak Café de Paris whose sauce is a blend of some two dozen ingredients.

Open: May–Oct, daily 7–11pm. *Closed:* Nov–Apr. CONTINEN-TAL

■ **Ca N'Olga,** Pont. Na Macarrana, Calle d'es Sol, Es Mercadal (tel. 37-54-59). *Prices:* Entrées 875–2,500 ptas. ($7.25–$21).

A stylish, sophisticated spot that attracts a similar clientele, Ca N'Olga is warm, winsome, and intimate. Occupying a typical white-stucco Minorcan house some 150 years old, this restaurant offers outdoor dining in a pretty patio garden and a handful of tables indoors.

The eclectic menu draws from Spanish, Catalan, and a more universal Mediterranean cuisine, changing frequently with the market offering. The day I was there the menu included quail with onion and sherry vinegar, osso buco, veal-and-peach casserole, and squid stuffed with onion-and-saffron sauce. For dessert I had a fine local melon served in cream topped with sprigs of mint.

Open: May–Sept, Wed–Mon 8–11pm; the rest of the year, Thurs–Sun 1–3:30pm and 8–11pm. *Closed:* Jan and Feb. MEDITERRANEAN

- **Restaurant Molí d'es Reco,** Es Mercadal (tel. 37-53-92). *Prices:* Meals begin at 1,500 ptas. ($12.50).

Easily spotted by the windmill that inspired its name, Molí d'es Reco has a pleasant outdoor patio but a rather plain indoor dining area. Overall, the place is a bit touristy, but it offers hearty Minorcan fare including stuffed eggplant, oliaigua amb tomatecs (a soup with tomato, onion, parsley, green peppers, and garlic), snails with spider crab, partridge with cabbage, and stuffed squid.

Open: Daily 1–4pm and 7–11pm. MINORCAN

- **Restaurante Bar Sa Plaça,** Calle Denmig 2 (tel. 37-50-48). *Prices:* Meals average under 2,000 ptas. ($16.75).

This budget alternative under the same ownership as Molí d'es Reco serves traditional Spanish fare in a lively, family setting with an odd-lot assortment of tables indoors and out. Clearly a local favorite not only for dining but for snacks.

Open: Summer, daily 6am–1am; winter, daily 6am–midnight. *Closed:* Feb.

- **58,s'engolidor,** Calle Major 3, Es Migjorn (San Cristóbal) (tel. 37-01-93). *Prices:* Meals average 2,000 ptas. ($16.75).

Between Mercadal and Santo Tomás is the village of San Cristóbal, commonly known as Es Migjorn. Here, tucked away in a side street, is this lovely "insider's" spot for dinner. Except for a simple, small sign on the door, it looks like all the other houses on the block. The decor is tastefully simple, with artwork in a variety of styles shown off to advantage against crisp, white walls. Outdoors there are two patio dining areas where you can sometimes smell the herbs growing in owner José Luis's garden, which provides some of the fruits and vegetables on his menu.

The menu is limited but varied, with many Minorcan specialties such as oliaigua, stuffed eggplant, baked pork chop with potatoes and tomatoes, and a very savory rabbit-and-wild-mushroom stew.

Open: May–Oct, Tues–Sun 8–10:30pm; the rest of the year, Fri–Sun 8–10:30pm.

THINGS TO SEE AND DO

Mercadal, a town of several thousand inhabitants at the foot of Monte Toro, is a picturesque ensemble of white houses with pastel grace notes. Among its claims to local fame are two types of almond confectionery—*carquinyols* (small, hard cookies) and *amargos* (a kind of macaroon). The place to get some is **Pastelería Villalonga**

Ca's Sucrer, Plaça Constitución 11, Mercadal (tel. 37-51-75), open Tuesday through Saturday from 9:30am to 1:30pm and 5 to 8:30pm, with extended hours in winter on Sunday from 11am to 2pm.

Just down the street from this pastelería is a shop called **Es Ventall** (tel. 37-55-27), with a limited but interesting selection of decorative items, towels, clothing, accessories, fans, designer T-shirts, and costume jewelry. Owner Biel Mercadal and his wife design many of these things themselves and scout the island for the work of local artisans. Open in summer Monday through Saturday from 10am to 2pm and 6 to 10:30pm; in winter, Monday through Friday from 5 to 8:30pm and on Saturday from 9am to 2pm.

From Es Mercadal, you can take a road 4 kilometers (2.5 miles) up to **Monte Toro,** the island's tallest mountain (357m, 1,170 ft.), crowned with a sanctuary that is a place of pilgrimage for Minorcans. The winding road leads to a panoramic view of the island's rolling, green countryside dotted with *fincas,* trim fields, and stands of trees. From this vantage point you can also clearly see the contrast between the flatter southern part of the island and the lumpier northern region. The hilltop sanctuary includes a small, simple church with an ornate gilded altar displaying the image (reportedly found nearby in 1290) of the Virgin Mare de Déu d'el Toro, the island's patron saint. In 1936 the church was destroyed, but the statue was saved from the flames and a new church built. The church is open daily all year from early morning to sunset; admission is free. In the courtyard of the sanctuary is a bronze monument to those Minorcans who left for North America in the 18th century, while the island was still a British colony, and founded the town of Saint Augustine in Florida. The large statue of Christ commemorates the Civil War dead. There is a snack bar with a pleasant terrace here.

About halfway along the road from Alaior to Playa Son Bou there is a turnoff to the left to **Torre d'en Gaumes,** the largest prehistoric village on Minorca. Uncovered here during excavations in 1974 was a beautiful bronze Egyptian statue of Imhotep, architect of the world's first pyramid and god of medicine, dating from 650 B.C. Most notable here now are the enclosure of the taula, the hypostilic chamber, the central talayot, and the system for collecting rainwater by means of open channels and hollows cut out of the rock.

Playa Son Bou is a stunning beach defaced by two outsize hotels. Though still enchanting, the mile-long, narrow, sandy beach and clear, turquoise waters are now often crowded, even in the off-season. In July and August they're best avoided. At the eastern end of the beach just beyond the two monster hotels are the ruins of a Paleo-Christian basilica most probably dating from the 5th or 6th century. Visible in the cliffs beyond are some cave dwellings, some of which appear quite prosperous, with painted facades and shades to keep out the noonday sun.

To the east in Cala Porter is a most unique nightspot. Embedded in a series of caves within a sheer cliff face rising from the sea, **La Cova d'en Xoroi** (tel. 37-72-36) is a conglomeration of bars, terraces, intimate nooks and crannies, and a disco floor. For sheer drama the setting can't be beat. As you walk down the entrance stairway, all magnificently unfolds before you. Then you come to the dance floor overlooking the sea at the cliff's edge—no window, just a railing. Prehistoric vessels were found inside these caves, which, according to legend, were once the refuge of a Moor called Xoroi who had abducted a local maid and made his home here with her and their family. So unusual is this place that by day it's a tourist sight. From May to October you can visit it daily from 11am to 1:30pm and 4 to 9pm; admission is 250 ptas. ($2) and includes a refreshment. In summer, it's also open nightly from 10:30pm to 5 or 6am for drinks and dancing. Cover charge is 1,500 ptas. ($12.50), including one drink. Don't miss it!

---

4. Fornells and the Northern Coast

The road leading north from Mercadal to Fornells runs through some of the island's finest scenery. On the northern coast, the tiny town of Fornells snuggles around a bay filled with boats and windsurfers and lined with restaurants and a few chic shops. Built up around four defense edifications—the Talaia de la Mola (now destroyed), the Tower of Fornells at the harbor mouth, the fortress of the Island of Las Sargantanas (the Lizards) situated in the middle of the harbor, and the now-ruined Castle of San Jorge or San Antonio—Fornells today is a flourishing fishing village noted for its upscale restaurants that feature savory lobster calderetas.

ACCOMMODATIONS

There are no mass-tourism hotels in Fornells, only a few small places to stay.

- **Hostal S'Algaret,** Plaça S'Algaret 7, 07748 Fornells, Minorca (tel. 971/37-65-52). 23 rms. A/C TEL

The large, comfortable rooms all have terraces.

RATES (INCLUDING IVA): 4,700 ptas. ($39.25) double; a little over half that price when used as a single. Closed Nov–Mar.

- **Hostal Iris,** Calle Major 17, 07748 Fornells, Minorca (tel. 971/37-63-92). 17 rms. A/C MINIBAR TEL

Just a few doors away from the Hostal S'Algaret, the rooms here are spacious and inviting. Facilities include a pool, solarium, snackbar, lounge, and guest dining rooms.

RATES: 3,400–6,250 ptas. ($28.25–$52) single; 5,000–8,900 ptas. ($41.75–$74.25) double.

DINING

Fornells is noted for its fine seafood restaurants specializing in the Minorcan calderetas. King Juan Carlos has been known to sail in here when he wants to savor some, and in peak summer season people phone up their favorite Fornells restaurant days in advance with their orders.

• **Es Pla,** along the water (tel. 37-66-55). *Prices:* Entrées 1,200–6,500 ptas. ($10–$54.25); three-course daily menu 2,200 ptas. ($18.25).

This is the king's choice in Fornells. Large and informally elegant, Es Pla is an upper-crust restaurant where you can eat indoors or out. There is also a long, stainless-steel bar for sipping pre-meal apéritifs. The daily fish specials and caldereta de langosta are the main attractions.

Open: Daily 1–3:30pm and 7:30–10:30pm. *Reservations:* Imperative. SEAFOOD/MINORCAN

• **Es Cranc,** Escoles 29 (tel. 37-64-42). *Prices:* Entrées 950–6,000 ptas. ($8–$50).

The consensus among Minorcans is that Es Cranc serves the best caldereta. Located several blocks from the harbor near the church, this first-class eatery in a rustic, homey setting would have to be good to thrive at a remove from the prime waterfront action.

Besides the selection of calderetas, the house specialties include paella and arroz caldoso, the local, juicier version of paella. The top-of-the-line calderetas and arroces here feature the spider crab (cranca), from which the restaurant takes its name, or the langosta (spiny lobster). Another dozen and a half seafood dishes and a dozen meat dishes complete the offering.

Open: Nov and Mar–mid-Apr, daily 1:30–3:30pm; mid-Apr–Oct, daily 1:30–4pm and 8pm–whenever. *Closed:* Dec–Feb. SEAFOOD/MINORCAN

• **S'Ancora,** Avenida del Poeta 8, in the port (tel. 37-66-20). *Prices:* Entrées 1,500–8,500 ptas. ($12.50–$70.75).

One of the priciest Fornells restaurants, S'Ancora is large and friendly, with both indoor and outdoor dining. As with most of the other restaurants in the area, the specialty here is—you guessed it—caldereta. The rest of the fish and seafood dishes have a decided Spanish accent. There are also a dozen or so meat and fowl dishes.

Open: Daily 1–4pm and 7:30–11pm. SEAFOOD/SPANISH

• **Can Miquel,** Paseo Marítimo s/n (no street number) (tel. 37-66-23). *Prices:* Meals begin at 2,000 ptas. ($16.75); three-course daily menu 1,200 ptas. ($10).

A bit more moderate in its prices and more modest in its checkered-tablecloth decor, Can Miquel still offers similar Fornells fare. The lobster calderetas are priced by weight and you can choose your own lobster if you like. One unusual feature of the menu is that it distinguishes between fresh-fish and frozen-fish dishes, the latter being cheaper of course.

Open: Mar–Oct, Tues–Sat 1–3:30pm and 8–10:30pm, Sun 1–3:30pm. *Closed:* Nov–Feb. SEAFOOD

• **S'Algaret Restaurant,** Plaça S'Algaret 7 (tel. 37-65-52). *Prices:* Tapas under 300 ptas. ($2.50) per plate; meals begin at 2,000 ptas. ($16.75).

Adjacent to the hostal of the same name mentioned (see "Accomodations," above), S'Algaret is popular with the locals and one of the few economical alternatives in Fornells. Downstairs you can nibble on tapas, sandwiches, and a varied selection of tortillas (Spanish omelets). Upstairs the dining is more formal, and the lobster caldereta costs 5,500 pesetas ($45.75).

Open: Summer, daily 7:30am–1am; winter, daily 9am–10pm; meals served daily 1–4:30pm and 8:30–10:30pm.

THINGS TO SEE AND DO

West of Fornells is **Platja Binimel.la,** a beautiful beach (unofficially nudist) easily accessible by car. Its long, curving, sandy cove is peacefully set against undulating hills. A lone snackbar is the sole concession to civilization.

By far the most splendid panorama on the island is that seen from the promontory at **Cap de Cavalleria,** the northernmost tip of the island, marked by a lighthouse. Getting there, however, is not easy. At a bend in the road to Platja Binimel.la is a closed gate leading to a dirt road. Simply open it and continue on. Since many of the roads leading to the island's undeveloped beaches are similarly closed by gates, the prevailing custom is simply to open them, proceed on through, and close the gates behind you. As you follow the long dirt road (negotiable in a regular car or on motorbike) out to Cap de Cavelleria, you'll come across several more sets of gates and travel through beautiful countryside somewhat reminiscent of the Scottish Highlands, with cultivated fields and scattered, grand fincas. Shortly before the lighthouse there is a "parking area" down to the left. Now brace yourself for the staggeringly beautiful vistas, the visual symphony of dramatic cliffs and jewel-blue water.

SPANISH/CATALAN VOCABULARY

BASIC PHRASES

English	Spanish	Catalan
Pardon	Perdón	Perdó
Excuse me	Perdone usted	Perdoni
Please	Por favor	Si us plau or Per favor
Thank you	Gracias	Gràcies
Thank you very much	Muchas gracias	Moltes gràcies
Good morning	Buenos días	Bon dia
Good afternoon	Buenas tardes	Bona tarda
Good night	Buenas noches	Bona nit
See you tomorrow	Hasta mañana	Fins demà
Good-bye	Adiós or Hasta la vista	Adéu or A reveure
Yes	Sí	Sí
No	No	No
I don't understand	No entiendo	No ho entenc
Do you speak? . . .	¿Habla usted? . . .	Parla? . . .
Catalan	catalán	català
Spanish	español	espanyol
English	inglés	anglès
My name is . . .	Me llamo . . .	Em dic . . .
What is your name?	¿Cómo se llama?	Com es dieu?
How are you?	¿Cómo está usted?	Com està?

English	Spanish	Catalan
I'm fine	Estoy bien	Estic bé
Very well	Muy bién	Molt bé
Not so good	No muy bien	Estic malament
Good weather	Buen tiempo	Bon temps
Bad weather	Mal tiempo	Mal temps
Do you have? . . .	¿Tiene algo? . . .	En té de? . . .
a cheaper one	más barato	més bon preu
a larger one	más grande	més gran
a smaller one	más pequeño	més petit
another color	de otro color	un altre color
What do you want?	¿Qué quiere usted?	Que vols?
I am looking for . . .	Busco . . .	Cerco . . .
I need . . .	Necesito . . .	Necessito . . .
I would like . . .	Quisiera . . .	Voldria . . .
A little	Un poco	Una mica
A lot	Mucho	Força
Too much/too many	Demasiado	Massa
How much?	¿Cuánto?	Quant?
Where is? . . .	¿Dónde está? . . .	On és? . . .
How do I get to? . . .	¿Para ir a? . . .	Per anar a? . . .
On the left	A la izquierda	A l'esquerra
On the right	A la derecha	A la dreta
What time do you serve? . . .	¿A qué hora se sirve? . . .	A quina hora es pot? . . .
breakfast	el desayuno	esmorzar
lunch	la comida	dinar
dinner	la cena	sopar
Do you have a vacant room?	¿Tiene alguna habitación libre?	Té alguna habitació lliure?

COMMON WORDS

English	Spanish	Catalan
miss	señorita	senyoreta
mister/sir	señor	senyor
missus/lady	señora	senyora
morning	mañana	matí
midday/noon	mediodía	migdia
evening	tarde	tarda
night	noche	nit
yesterday	ayer	ahir
today	hoy	avui
tomorrow	mañana	demà
day	día	dia
week	semana	setmana
bakery	panadería	forn or fleca
bank	banco	banc
bookshop	librería	llibreria
exchange (money)	cambio	canvi
haircut	cortar el cabello	tallar els cabells
hairdresser	peluquero	perruquer
pastry shop	pastelería	pastisseria
pharmacy	farmacia	farmàcia
bad	mal	malament
cheap	barato	barat
expensive	caro	car
open	abierto	obert
closed	cerrado	tancat
large	grande	gran
small	pequeño	petit
right (correct)	correcto	correcte
hot	calor or caliente	calor or calenta
cold (temperature)	frío	fred
weather	tiempo	temps
early	temprano	aviat
late	tarde	tard
near	cerca	prop
far	lejos	lluny
more	más	més
tall	alto	alt
to call/telephone	llamar	trucar
to dye	teñir	tenyir

English	Spanish	Catalan
to pay	pagar	pagar
to eat	comer	menjar
to drink	beber	beure
to order	pedir	demanar
bill/check	cuenta	compte
price	precio	preu
money	dinero	diners
traveler's check	cheque de viajes	xec de viatge
blouse	blusa	brusa
pants	pantalones	pantalons
shirt	camisa	camisa
shoes	zapatos	sabates
to try on	probar	emprovar *or* provar
book	libro	llibre
guidebook	guía	guia
newspaper	periódico	periòdic *or* diari
magazine	revista	reviste
map	mapa	mapa
post office	oficina de correos	oficina de correus
postcard	tarjeta postal	targeta postal
stamp	sello	segell
border	frontera	frontera
driver's license	carnet de conducir	carnet de conducir
Customs	aduana	duana
Customs duties	derechos de aduana	drets de duana
passport	pasaporte	passaport
ambulance	ambulancia	ambulància
bandage	vendaje	embenat
cold (illness)	resfriado	refredat
cough	tos	tos
dentist	dentista	dentista
diarrhea	diarrea	diarrea
dizziness	mareo	mareig
doctor	médico	doctor
fever	fiebre	febre
headache	dolor de cabeza	mal de cap
hospital	hospital	hospital
indigestion	indigestión	indigestió
sick	enfermo	malalt
toothache	dolor de muelas	mal de queixal

English	Spanish	Catalan
bathroom	baño	bany
bed	cama	llit
hot water	agua caliente	aigua calenta
room	habitación	habitació
sink	lavabo	lavabo
downstairs	abajo	a baxi *or* sota
upstairs	arriba	a dalt *or* dalt

Days of the Week

Monday	lunes	dilluns
Tuesday	martes	dimarts
Wednesday	miércoles	dimecres
Thursday	jueves	dijous
Friday	viernes	divendres
Saturday	sábado	dissabte
Sunday	domingo	diumenge

Numbers

one	uno	u *or* un
two	dos	dos *or* dues
three	tres	tres
four	cuatro	quatre
five	cinco	cinc
six	seis	sis
seven	siete	set
eight	ocho	vuit
nine	nueve	nou
ten	diez	deu
eleven	once	onze
twelve	doce	dotze
thirteen	trece	tretze
fourteen	catorce	catorze
fifteen	quince	quinze
sixteen	dieciséis	setze
seventeen	diecisiete	disset
eighteen	dieciocho	divuit
nineteen	diecinueve	dinou
twenty	veinte	vint
thirty	treinta	trenta
forty	cuarenta	quaranta
fifty	cincuenta	cinquanta
sixty	sesenta	seixanta
seventy	setenta	setanta
eighty	ochenta	vuitanta
ninety	noventa	noranta
one hundred	cien/ciento	cent
one thousand	mil	mil

half	medio	mig *or* mitjà
third	tercio	terç
quarter	cuarto	quart
fifth	quinto	cinqué

MENU TRANSLATIONS

English	**Spanish**	**Catalan**
fruit	fruta	fruita
apple	manzana	poma
banana	plátano	banana
grapes	uvas	raïm
melon	melón	meló
orange	naranja	taronja
peach	melocotón	préssec
pear	pera	pera
strawberries	fresas	maduixes
vegetables	verdura	verdura
asparagus	espárragos	espàrrecs
beans	judías	mongetes
carrots	zanahorias	pastanagues
mushrooms	setas	bolets
olives	aceitunas	olives
onions	cebollas	cebes
peas	guisantes	pèsols
potatoes	patatas	patates
rice	arroz	arròs
beef	carne de buey *or* carne de vaca	carn de bou
chop	chuleta	xuleta
escalope	escalopa	escalopa
game	caza	caça
lamb (roast)	cordero (asado)	xai (rostit)
liver	hígado	fetge
pork (roast)	cerdo (asado)	porc (rostit)
rabbit (roast)	conejo (asado)	conill (rostit)
snails	caracoles	cargols
veal (roast)	ternera (asada)	vedella (rostità)
clams	almejas	cloïses
codfish	bacalao	bacallà
eel	anguila	anguila
lobster	langosta	llagosta
oysters	ostras	ostres
prawns (shrimp)	gambas	gambes

English	Spanish	Catalan
salmon	salmón	salmó
shellfish	marisco	marisc
sole	lenguado	llenguado
trout	trucha	truita (de riu)
tuna (tunny)	atún	tonyina
turbot	rodaballo	rèmol
dessert	postre	postres
cakes/pastries	pastelería	pastisseria
ice cream	helado	gelat
beer	cerveza	cervesa
coffee	café	café
milk	leche	llet
mineral water	agua mineral	aigua mineral
tea	té	te
water	agua	aigua
wine	vino	vi
breakfast	desayuno	esmorzar or desdejuni
lunch	comida or almuerzo	dinar
dinner	cena	sopar
bread	pan	pa
butter	mantequilla	mantega
cheese	queso	formatge
garlic	ajo	all
salt	sal	sal
sugar	azúcar	sucre
bottle	botella	ampolla
glass	vaso	got
fork	tenedor	forquilla
knife	cuchillo	ganivet
spoon	cuchara	cullera
hors d'oeuvres	entremeses	entremesos
pasta	pasta	pasta
soup	sopa	sopa
salad	ensalada	amanida
menu	carta	carta
tip	propina	propina
waiter	camarero	cambrer

CONVERSION CHARTS

CLOTHING SIZES

WOMEN'S DRESSES, COATS, AND SKIRTS

American	3–4	5–6	7–8	9–10	11	12	13	14	15	16	18
Continental	36	38	38	40	40	42	42	44	44	46	48
British	8	10	11	12	13	14	15	16	17	18	20

WOMEN'S BLOUSES AND SWEATERS

American	10	12	14	16	18	20
Continental	38	40	42	44	46	48
British	32	34	36	38	40	42

WOMEN'S SHOES

American	5	6	7	8	9	10
Continental	36	37	38	39	40	41
British	3½	4½	5½	6½	7½	8½

MEN'S SUITS

American	34	36	38	40	42	44	46	48
Continental	44	46	48	50	52	54	56	58
British	34	36	38	40	42	44	46	48

MEN'S SHIRTS

American	14½	15	15½	16	16½	17	17½	18
Continental	37	38	39	41	42	43	44	45
British	14½	15	15½	16	16½	17	17½	18

MEN'S SHOES

American	7	8	9	10	11	12	13
Continental	39½	41	42	43	44½	46	47
British	6	7	8	9	10	11	12

CHILDREN'S CLOTHING

American	3	4	5	6	6X
Continental	98	104	110	116	122
British	18	20	22	24	26

CHILDREN'S SHOES

American	8	9	10	11	12	13	1	2	3
Continental	24	25	27	28	29	30	32	33	34
British	7	8	9	10	11	12	13	1	2

WEIGHTS AND MEASURES

Europeans use the metric system of weighing and measuring, and if you are prepared for it, you can avoid confusion.

LENGTH

1 millimeter = 0.04 inches (*or* less than ¹⁄₁₆ inch)
1 centimeter = 0.39 inches (*or* just under ½ inch)
1 meter = 1.09 yards (*or* about 39 inches)
1 kilometer = 0.62 mile (*or* about ⅔ mile)

To convert kilometers to miles, take the number of kilometers and multiply by .62 (for example, 25km × .62 = 15.5 miles).

To convert miles to kilometers, take the number of miles and multiply by 1.61 (for example, 50 miles × 1.61 = 80.5 km).

CAPACITY

1 liter = 33.92 ounces
= 1.06 quarts
= 0.26 gallons

To convert liters to gallons, take the number of liters and multiply by .26 (for example, 50 l × .26 = 13 gal).

To convert gallons to liters, take the number of gallons and multiply by 3.79 (for example, 10 gal × 3.79 = 37.9 l).

WEIGHT

1 gram = 0.04 ounce (*or* about a paperclip's weight)
1 kilogram = 2.2 pounds

To convert kilograms to pounds, take the number of kilos and multiply by 2.2 (for example, 75kg × 2.2 = 165 lbs).

To convert pounds to kilograms, take the number of pounds and multiply by .45 (for example, 90 lb × .45 = 40.5kg).

AREA

1 hectare (100m²) = 2.47 acres

To convert hectares to acres, take the number of hectares and multiply by 2.47 (for example, 20ha × 2.47 = 49.4 acres).

To convert acres to hectares, take the number of acres and multiply by .41 (for example, 40 acres × .41 = 16.4 ha).

TEMPERATURE

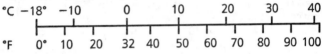

To convert degrees C to degrees F, multiply degrees C by 9, divide by 5, then add 32.

To convert degrees F to degrees C, subtract 32 from degrees F, then multiply by 5, and divide by 9

INDEX

GENERAL INFORMATION

Note: Geographical place names beginning with common words such as "Platja" (beach), "Cala" (cove), or "Plaça" (plaza) have been listed in this index under the next significant word (e.g., "*Platja* de Mitjorn" can be found under "Mitjorn, *Platja de*").

SIGHTS AND ATTRACTIONS

Barcelona

M a j o r c a

I b i z a

Minorca

ACCOMMODATIONS

Barcelona

Majorca

Key to Abbreviations: A = Apartment accommodations; B = Budget; E = Expensive; M = Moderate; VE = Very Expensive

I b i z a

M i n o r c a

RESTAURANTS

B a r c e l o n a

Key to Abbreviations: *B* = Budget; *E* = Expensive; *M* = Moderate; *VE* = Very Expensive

Majorca

I b i z a

M i n o r c a

NOW, SAVE MONEY ON ALL YOUR TRAVELS!
Join Frommer's™ Dollarwise® Travel Club

Saving money while traveling is never a simple matter, which is why the **Dollarwise Travel Club** was formed 31 years ago. Developed in response to requests from Frommer Travel Guide readers, the Club provides cost-cutting travel strategies, up-to-date travel information, and a sense of community for value-conscious travelers from all over the world.

In keeping with the money-saving concept, the annual membership fee is low —$18 (U.S. residents) or $20 (residents of Canada, Mexico, and other countries)— and is immediately exceeded by the value of your benefits, which include:

1. Any TWO books listed on the following pages.
2. Plus any ONE Frommer City Guide.
3. A subscription to our quarterly newspaper, *The Dollarwise Traveler.*
4. A membership card that entitles you to purchase through the Club all Frommer publications for 33% to 50% off their retail price.

The eight-page *Dollarwise Traveler* tells you about the latest developments in good-value travel worldwide and includes the following columns: **Hospitality Exchange** (for those offering and seeking hospitality in cities all over the world); **Share-a-Trip** (for those looking for travel companions to share costs); and **Readers Ask . . . Readers Reply** (for those with travel questions that other members can answer).

Aside from the Frommer Guides, the Serious Shopper Guides, and the Gault Millau Guides, you can also choose from our Special Editions. These include such titles as **California with Kids** (a compendium of the best of California's accommodations, restaurants, and sightseeing attractions appropriate for those traveling with toddlers through teens); **Candy Apple: New York with Kids** (a spirited guide to the Big Apple by a savvy New York grandmother that's perfect for both visitors and residents); **Caribbean Hideaways** (the 100 most romantic places to stay in the Islands, all rated on ambience, food, sport opportunities, and price); **Honeymoon Destinations** (a guide to planning and choosing just the right destination from hundreds of possibilities in the U.S., Mexico, and the Caribbean); **Marilyn Wood's Wonderful Weekends** (a selection of the best mini-vacations within a 200-mile radius of New York City, including descriptions of country inns and other accommodations, restaurants, picnic spots, sights, and activities); and **Paris Rendez-Vous** (a delightful guide to the best places to meet in Paris whether for power breakfasts or dancing till dawn).

To join this Club, simply send the appropriate membership fee with your name and address to: Frommer's Dollarwise Travel Club, 15 Columbus Circle, New York, NY 10023. Remember to specify which single city guide and which two other guides you wish to receive in your initial package of member's benefits. Or tear out the next page, check off your choices, and send the page to us with your membership fee.

FROMMER BOOKS
PRENTICE HALL TRAVEL
15 COLUMBUS CIRCLE
NEW YORK, NY 10023
212-373-8125

Date_____

Friends:
Please send me the books checked below:

FROMMER™ GUIDES

(Guides to sightseeing and tourist accommodations and facilities from budget to deluxe, with emphasis on the medium-priced.)

☐ Alaska	$14.95	☐ Germany	$14.95
☐ Australia	$14.95	☐ Italy	$14.95
☐ Austria & Hungary	$14.95	☐ Japan & Hong Kong	$14.95
☐ Belgium, Holland & Luxembourg	$14.95	☐ Mid-Atlantic States	$14.95
☐ Bermuda & The Bahamas	$14.95	☐ New England	$14.95
☐ Brazil	$14.95	☐ New York State	$14.95
☐ Canada	$14.95	☐ Northwest	$14.95
☐ Caribbean	$14.95	☐ Portugal, Madeira & the Azores	$14.95
☐ Cruises (incl. Alaska, Carib, Mex, Hawaii,		☐ Skiing Europe	$14.95
Panama, Canada & US)	$14.95	☐ South Pacific	$14.95
☐ California & Las Vegas	$14.95	☐ Southeast Asia	$14.95
☐ Egypt	$14.95	☐ Southern Atlantic States	$14.95
☐ England & Scotland	$14.95	☐ Southwest	$14.95
☐ Florida	$14.95	☐ Switzerland & Liechtenstein	$14.95
☐ France	$14.95	☐ USA	$15.95

FROMMER $-A-DAY® GUIDES

(In-depth guides to sightseeing and low-cost tourist accommodations and facilities.)

☐ Europe on $40 a Day	$15.95	☐ New York on $60 a Day	$13.95
☐ Australia on $30 a Day	$12.95	☐ New Zealand on $45 a Day	$13.95
☐ Eastern Europe on $25 a Day	$13.95	☐ Scandinavia on $60 a Day	$13.95
☐ England on $50 a Day	$13.95	☐ Scotland & Wales on $40 a Day	$13.95
☐ Greece on $35 a Day	$13.95	☐ South America on $35 a Day	$13.95
☐ Hawaii on $60 a Day	$13.95	☐ Spain & Morocco on $40 a Day	$13.95
☐ India on $25 a Day	$12.95	☐ Turkey on $30 a Day	$13.95
☐ Ireland on $35 a Day	$13.95	☐ Washington, D.C. & Historic Va. on	
☐ Israel on $40 a Day	$13.95	$40 a Day	$13.95
☐ Mexico on $35 a Day	$13.95		

FROMMER TOURING GUIDES

(Color illustrated guides that include walking tours, cultural and historic sites, and other vital travel information.)

☐ Australia	$9.95	☐ Paris	$8.95
☐ Egypt	$8.95	☐ Scotland	$9.95
☐ Florence	$8.95	☐ Thailand	$9.95
☐ London	$8.95	☐ Venice	$8.95

TURN PAGE FOR ADDITONAL BOOKS AND ORDER FORM.

0190

FROMMER CITY GUIDES

(Pocket-size guides to sightseeing and tourist accommodations and facilities in all price ranges.)

☐ Amsterdam/Holland	$7.95	☐ Minneapolis/St. Paul	$7.95
☐ Athens	$7.95	☐ Montréal/Québec City	$7.95
☐ Atlantic City/Cape May	$7.95	☐ New Orleans	$7.95
☐ Barcelona*	$7.95	☐ New York	$7.95
☐ Belgium	$7.95	☐ Orlando/Disney World/EPCOT	$7.95
☐ Boston	$7.95	☐ Paris	$7.95
☐ Cancún/Cozumel/Yucatán	$7.95	☐ Philadelphia	$7.95
☐ Chicago	$7.95	☐ Rio	$7.95
☐ Denver/Boulder*	$7.95	☐ Rome	$7.95
☐ Dublin/Ireland	$7.95	☐ San Francisco	$7.95
☐ Hawaii	$7.95	☐ Santa Fe/Taos/Albuquerque	$7.95
☐ Hong Kong*	$7.95	☐ Seattle/Portland*	$7.95
☐ Las Vegas	$7.95	☐ Sydney	$7.95
☐ Lisbon/Madrid/Costa del Sol	$7.95	☐ Tokyo*	$7.95
☐ London	$7.95	☐ Vancouver/Victoria*	$7.95
☐ Los Angeles	$7.95	☐ Washington, D.C.	$7.95
☐ Mexico City/Acapulco	$7.95	*Available June 1990	

SPECIAL EDITIONS

☐ A Shopper's Guide to the Caribbean	$12.95	☐ Manhattan's Outdoor Sculpture	$15.95
☐ Beat the High Cost of Travel	$6.95	☐ Motorist's Phrase Book (Fr/Ger/Sp)	$4.95
☐ Bed & Breakfast—N. America	$11.95	☐ Paris Rendez-Vous	$10.95
☐ California with Kids	$14.95	☐ Swap and Go (Home Exchanging)	$10.95
☐ Caribbean Hideaways	$14.95	☐ The Candy Apple (NY with Kids)	$12.95
☐ Honeymoon Destinations (US, Mex & Carib)	$12.95	☐ Travel Diary and Record Book	$5.95

☐ Where to Stay USA (Lodging from $3 to $30 a night) $10.95
☐ Marilyn Wood's Wonderful Weekends (Conn, Del, Mass, NH, NJ, NY, Pa, RI, VT) $11.95
☐ The New World of Travel (Annual sourcebook by Arthur Frommer for savvy travelers) $16.95

SERIOUS SHOPPER'S GUIDES

(Illustrated guides listing hundreds of stores, conveniently organized alphabetically by category.)

☐ Italy	$15.95	☐ Los Angeles	$14.95
☐ London	$15.95	☐ Paris	$15.95

GAULT MILLAU

(The only guides that distinguish the truly superlative from the merely overrated.)

☐ The Best of Chicago	$15.95	☐ The Best of Los Angeles	$14.95
☐ The Best of France	$16.95	☐ The Best of New England	$15.95
☐ The Best of Hong Kong	$16.95	☐ The Best of New York	$14.95
☐ The Best of Italy	$16.95	☐ The Best of Paris	$16.95
☐ The Best of London	$16.95	☐ The Best of San Francisco	$14.95

☐ The Best of Washington, D.C. $14.95

ORDER NOW!

In U.S. include $2 shipping UPS for 1st book; $1 ea. add'l book. Outside U.S. $3 and $1, respectively.
Allow four to six weeks for delivery in U.S., longer outside U.S.
Enclosed is my check or money order for $_____

NAME_____

ADDRESS_____

CITY_____ STATE_____ ZIP_____

0190